BRODY'S GHOST

BRODY'S GHOST ™

BOOK 6

STORY AND ART BY
MARK CRILLEY

DARK HORSE BOOKS

President and Publisher - Mike Richardson
Digital Production - Christina McKenzie
Designer - Rick DeLucco
Editor - Brendan Wright

Special thanks to Dave Land

Published by Dark Horse Books
A division of Dark Horse Comics, Inc.
10956 SE Main Street
Milwaukie, Oregon 97222

DarkHorse.com

To find a comic shop in your area call the Comic Shop Locator Service toll-free at (888) 266-4226
International Licensing: (503) 905-2377

First edition: April 2015
ISBN 978-1-61655-461-3

BRODY'S GHOST BOOK 6

10 9 8 7 6 5 4 3 2 1

Printed in the United States of America

THIS BOOK IS
DEDICATED TO MY WIFE, MIKI,
AND TO OUR CHILDREN,
MATTHEW AND MIO.

THE STORY SO FAR...

Brody is a young man living in a decaying metropolis a number of decades from now. After being dumped by his girlfriend, Nicole, he allows his life to spiral into a directionless mess. One afternoon he finds himself face to face with the ghost of a teenage girl, Talia, who enlists his help in pursuing a serial killer known as the Penny Murderer. After training with an ancient samurai ghost named Kagemura, Brody acquires great physical strength and, in time, powers of telekinesis and extrasensory perception. Finding the killer grows more urgent when Brody's ESP shows him that his ex-girlfriend Nicole is destined to be the next victim. He then gathers information about the Penny Murderer by sneaking into police headquarters, where he learns that Talia was in fact the Penny Murderer's first victim, and that her determination to go after him is founded entirely on her desire for vengeance.

Brody becomes desperate for a breakthrough clue when he realizes that Nicole will be attacked by the Penny Murderer within twenty-four hours. Though Talia is violently opposed to the idea, Brody travels to her childhood home to meet her mother, in hopes of finding the last remaining clues to her murder. There he finds a photo that suggests the Penny Murderer is connected to an ice cream stand called the Little Lamb, located in an amusement park Talia visited with her mother many years earlier. Brody heads to the park but is arrested on the orders of Nicole's new boyfriend, Landon James. Though Talia is in a position to help Brody evade arrest, she deliberately allows him to be captured by the police. With just hours left before Nicole is to be killed, Landon leaves Brody locked up and about to be tortured.

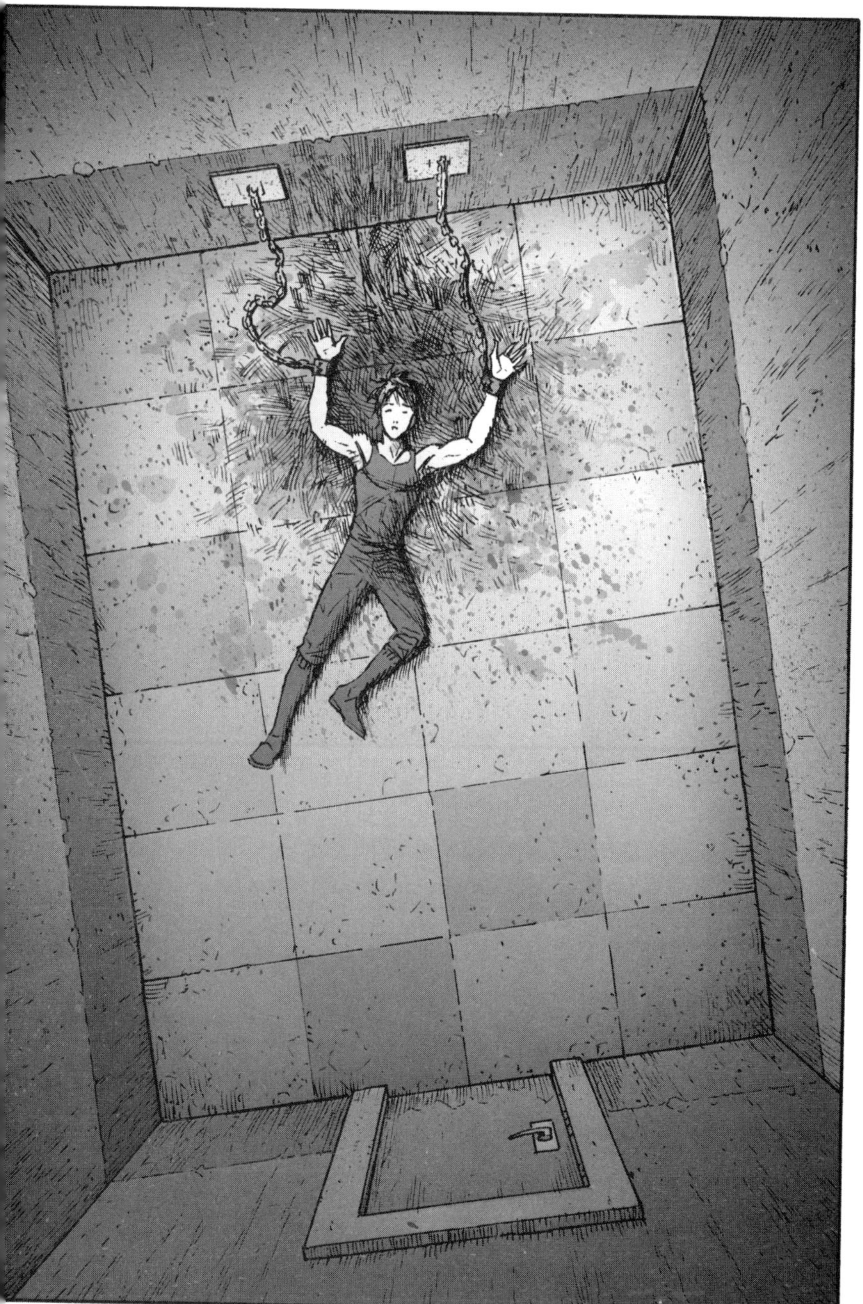

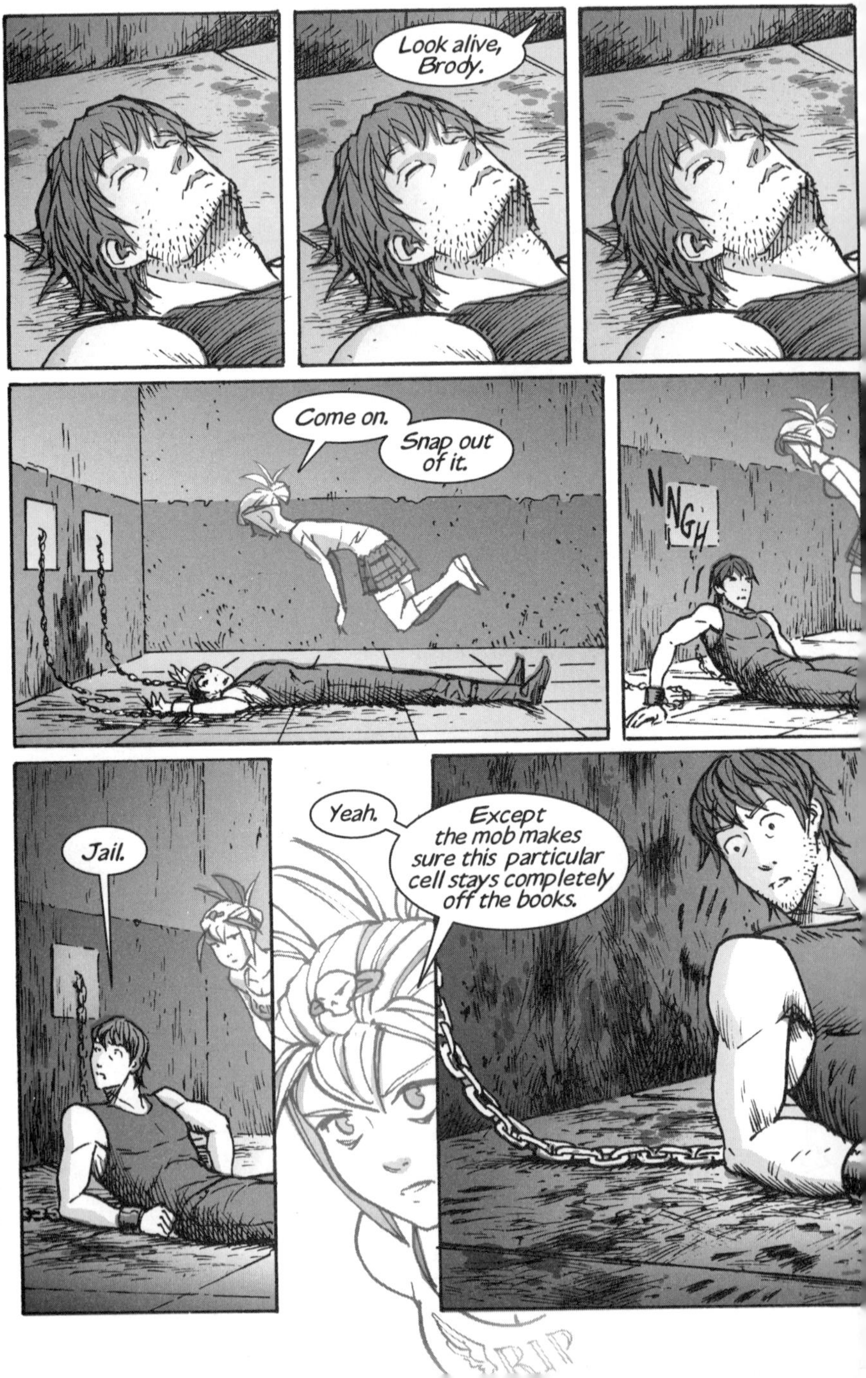
Look alive, Brody.
Come on.
Snap out of it.
NNGH
Jail.
Yeah.
Except the mob makes sure this particular cell stays completely off the books.

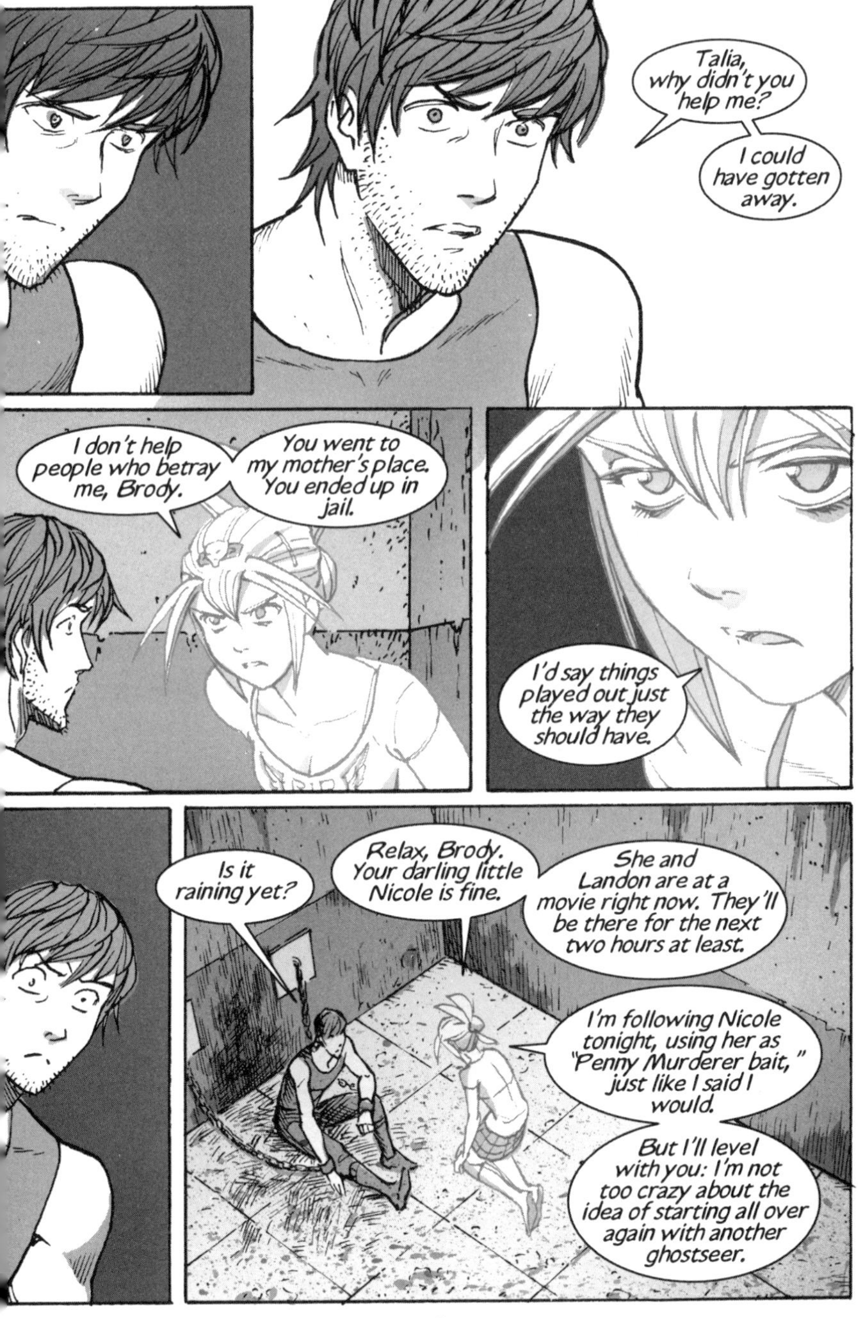
Talia, why didn't you help me?
I could have gotten away.
I don't help people who betray me, Brody.
You went to my mother's place. You ended up in jail.
I'd say things played out just the way they should have.
Is it raining yet?
Relax, Brody. Your darling little Nicole is fine.
She and Landon are at a movie right now. They'll be there for the next two hours at least.
I'm following Nicole tonight, using her as "Penny Murderer bait," just like I said I would.
But I'll level with you: I'm not too crazy about the idea of starting all over again with another ghostseer.

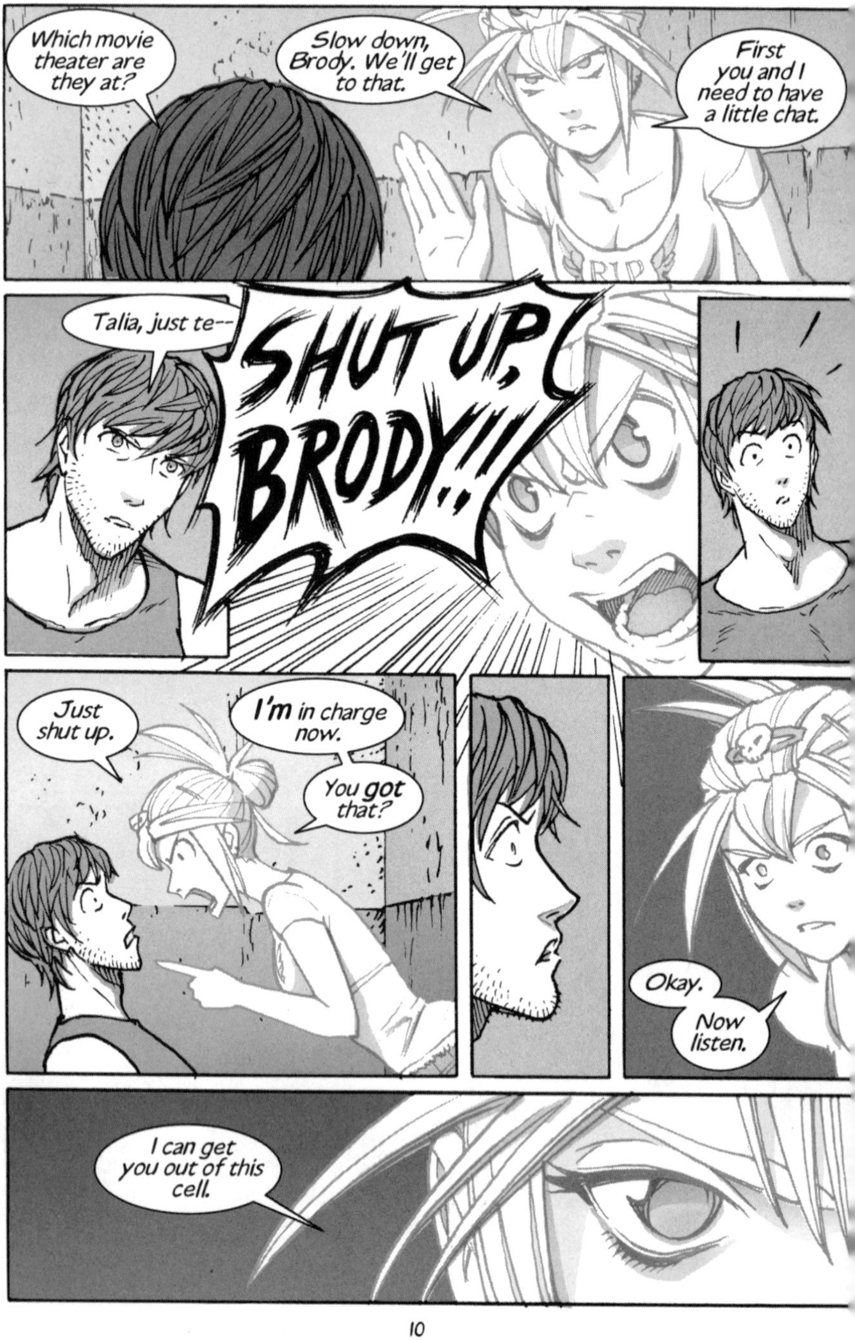
Which movie theater are they at?
Slow down, Brody. We'll get to that.
First you and I need to have a little chat.
Talia, just te--
SHUT UP, BRODY!!
Just shut up.
I'm in charge now.
You got that?
Okay.
Now listen.
I can get you out of this cell.

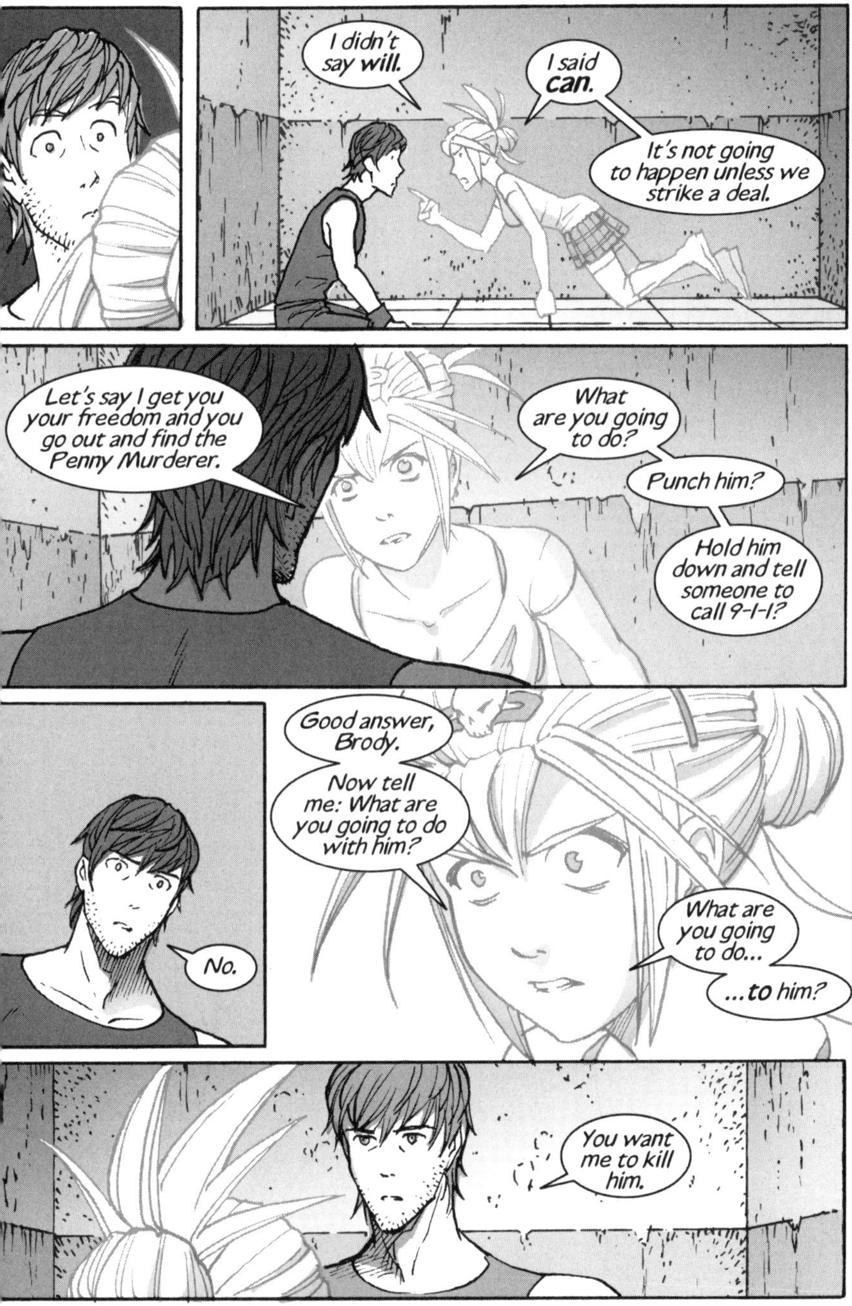
I didn't say **will.**
I said **can.**
It's not going to happen unless we strike a deal.
Let's say I get you your freedom and you go out and find the Penny Murderer.
What are you going to do?
Punch him?
Hold him down and tell someone to call 9-1-1?
Good answer, Brody.
Now tell me: What are you going to do with him?
No.
What are you going to do...
...**to** him?
You want me to kill him.

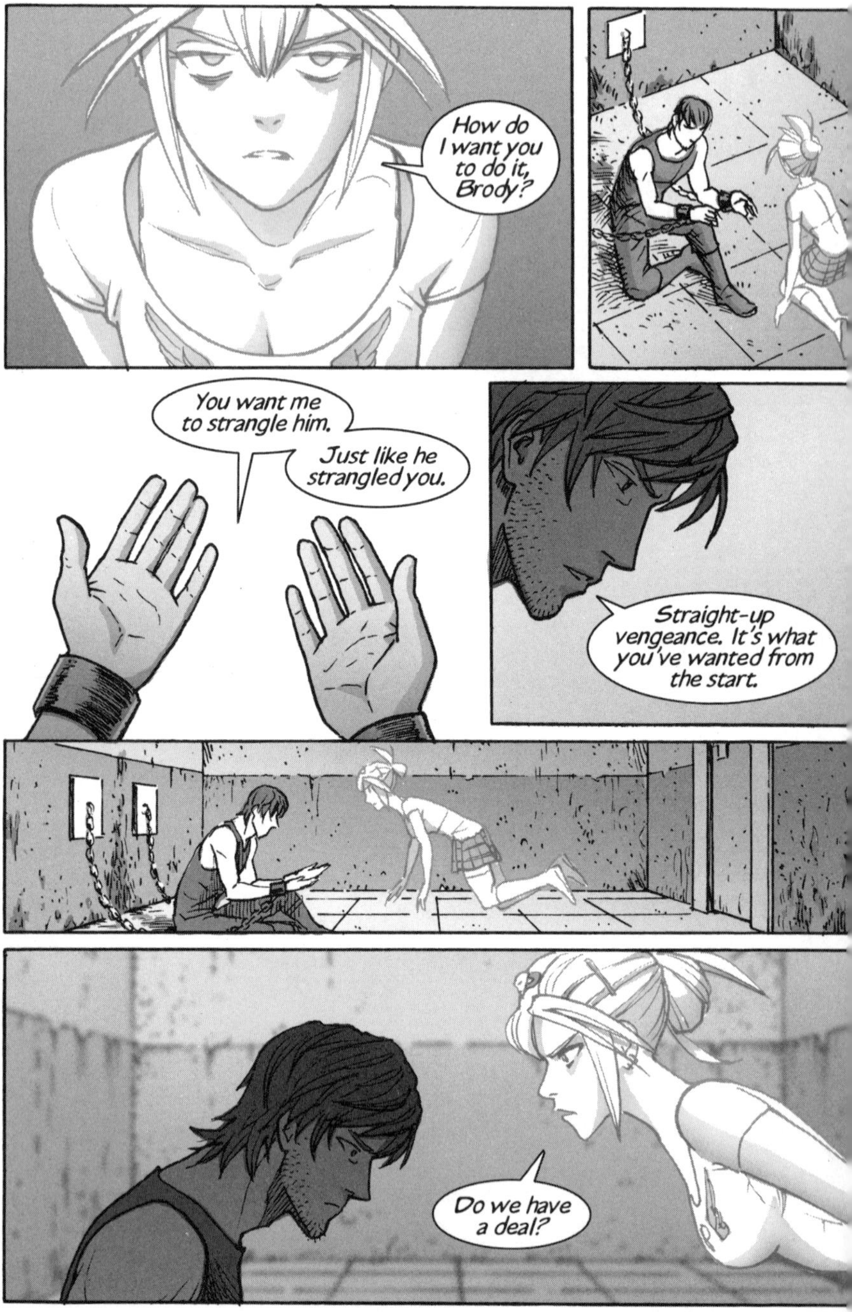
How do I want you to do it, Brody?
You want me to strangle him.
Just like he strangled you.
Straight-up vengeance. It's what you've wanted from the start.
Do we have a deal?

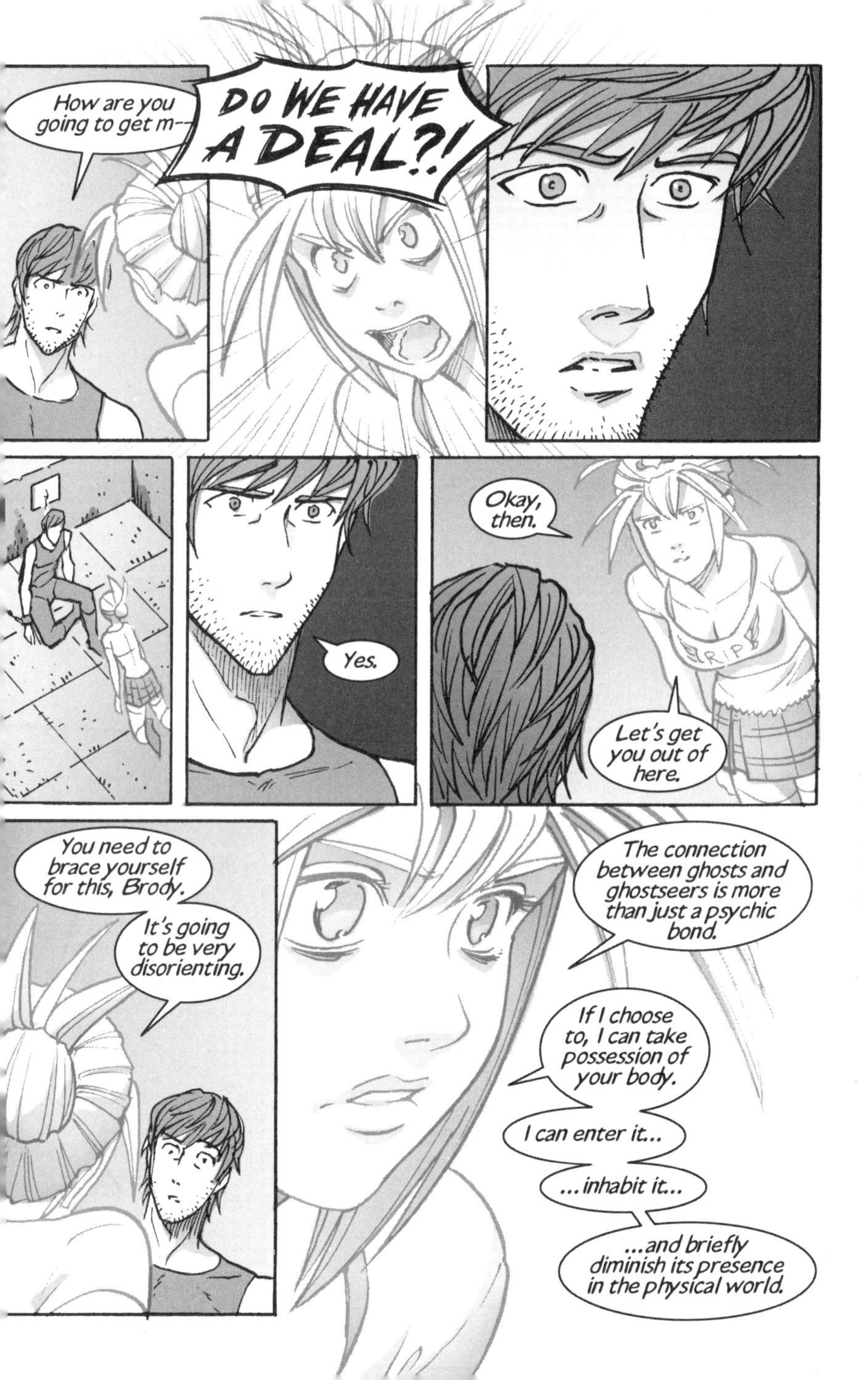
How are you going to get m--
DO WE HAVE A DEAL?!
Yes.
Okay, then.
Let's get you out of here.
You need to brace yourself for this, Brody.
It's going to be very disorienting.
The connection between ghosts and ghostseers is more than just a psychic bond.
If I choose to, I can take possession of your body.
I can enter it...
...inhabit it...
...and briefly diminish its presence in the physical world.

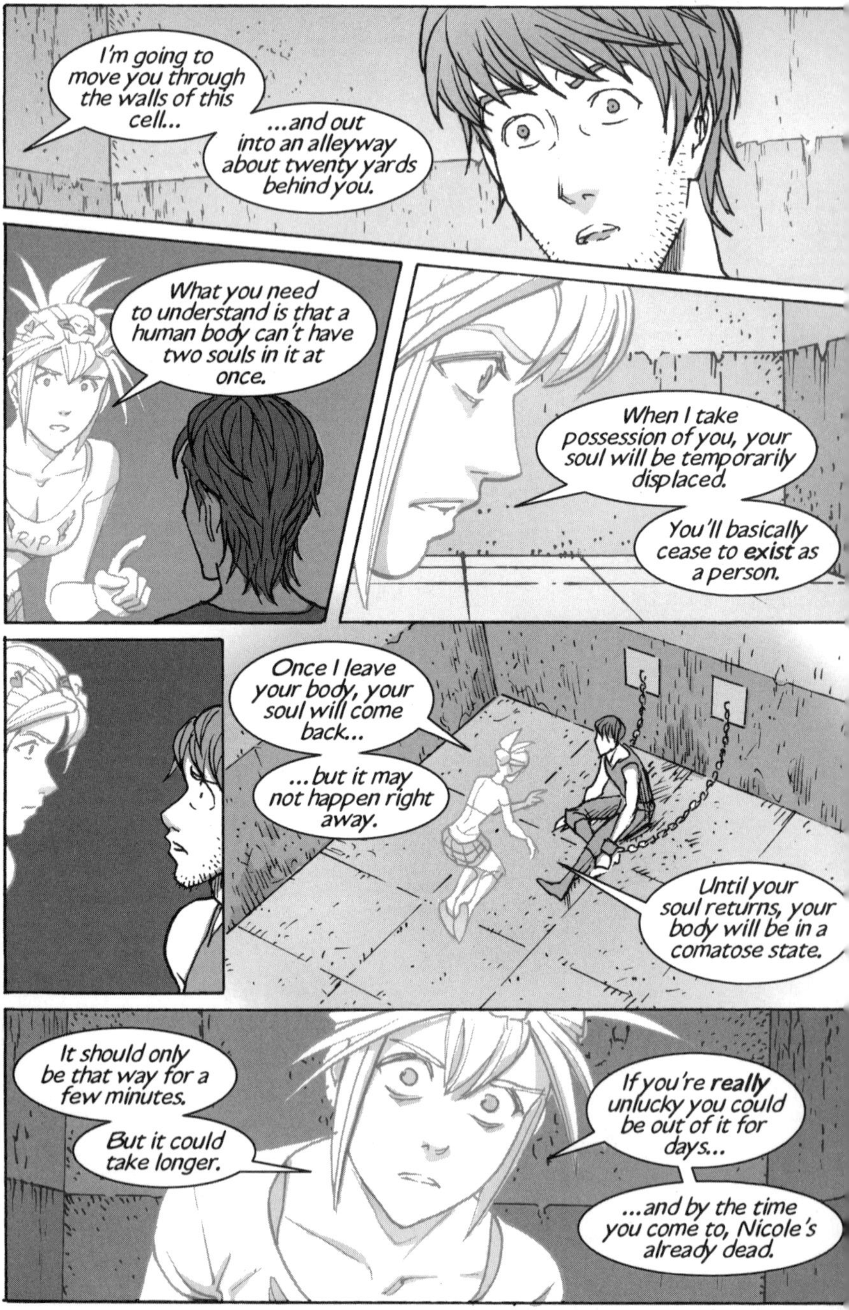
I'm going to move you through the walls of this cell...
...and out into an alleyway about twenty yards behind you.
What you need to understand is that a human body can't have two souls in it at once.
When I take possession of you, your soul will be temporarily displaced.
You'll basically cease to **exist** as a person.
Once I leave your body, your soul will come back...
...but it may not happen right away.
Until your soul returns, your body will be in a comatose state.
It should only be that way for a few minutes.
But it could take longer.
If you're **really** unlucky you could be out of it for days...
...and by the time you come to, Nicole's already dead.
RIP

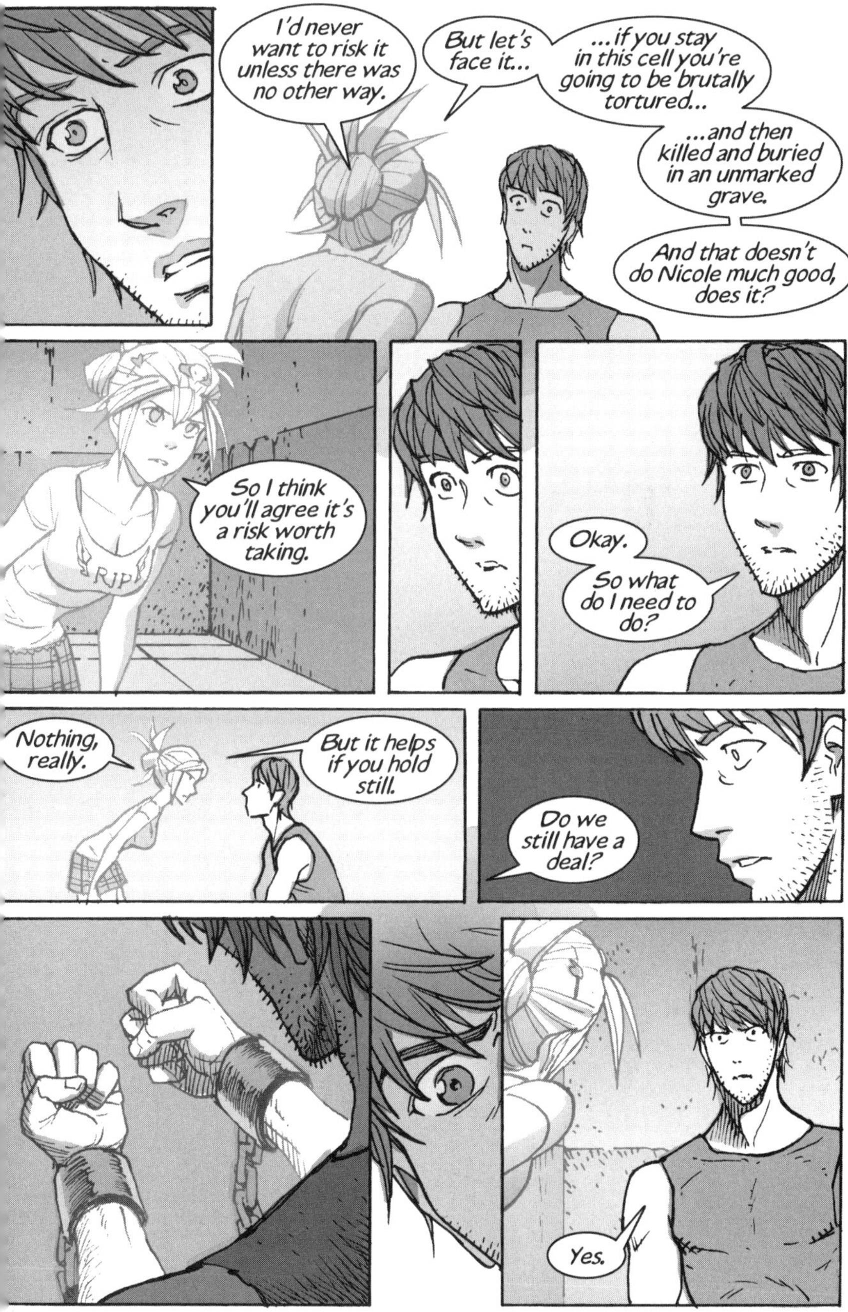
I'd never want to risk it unless there was no other way.
But let's face it...
...if you stay in this cell you're going to be brutally tortured...
...and then killed and buried in an unmarked grave.
And that doesn't do Nicole much good, does it?
So I think you'll agree it's a risk worth taking.
Okay.
So what do I need to do?
Nothing, really.
But it helps if you hold still.
Do we still have a deal?
Yes.

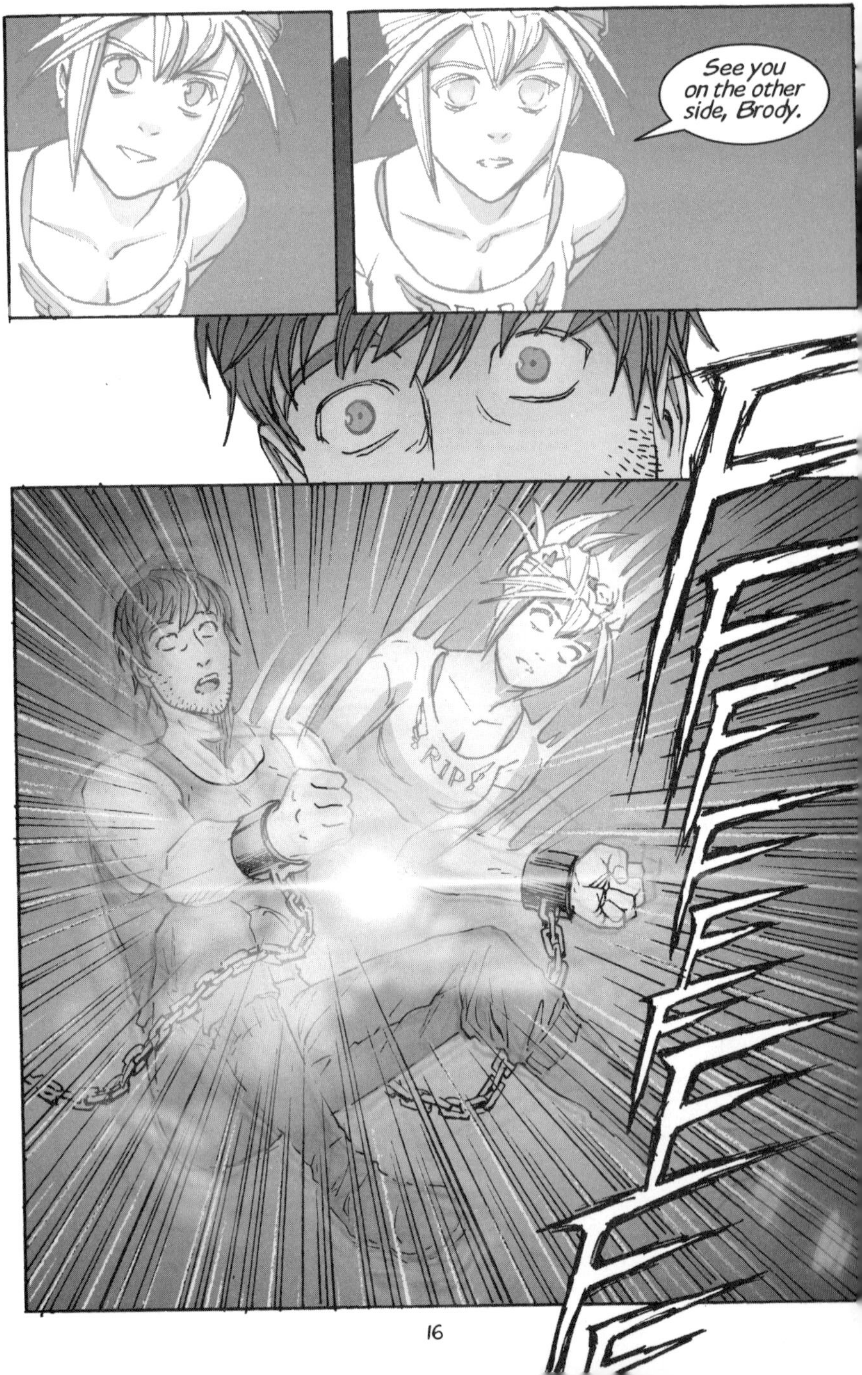
See you on the other side, Brody.
RIP

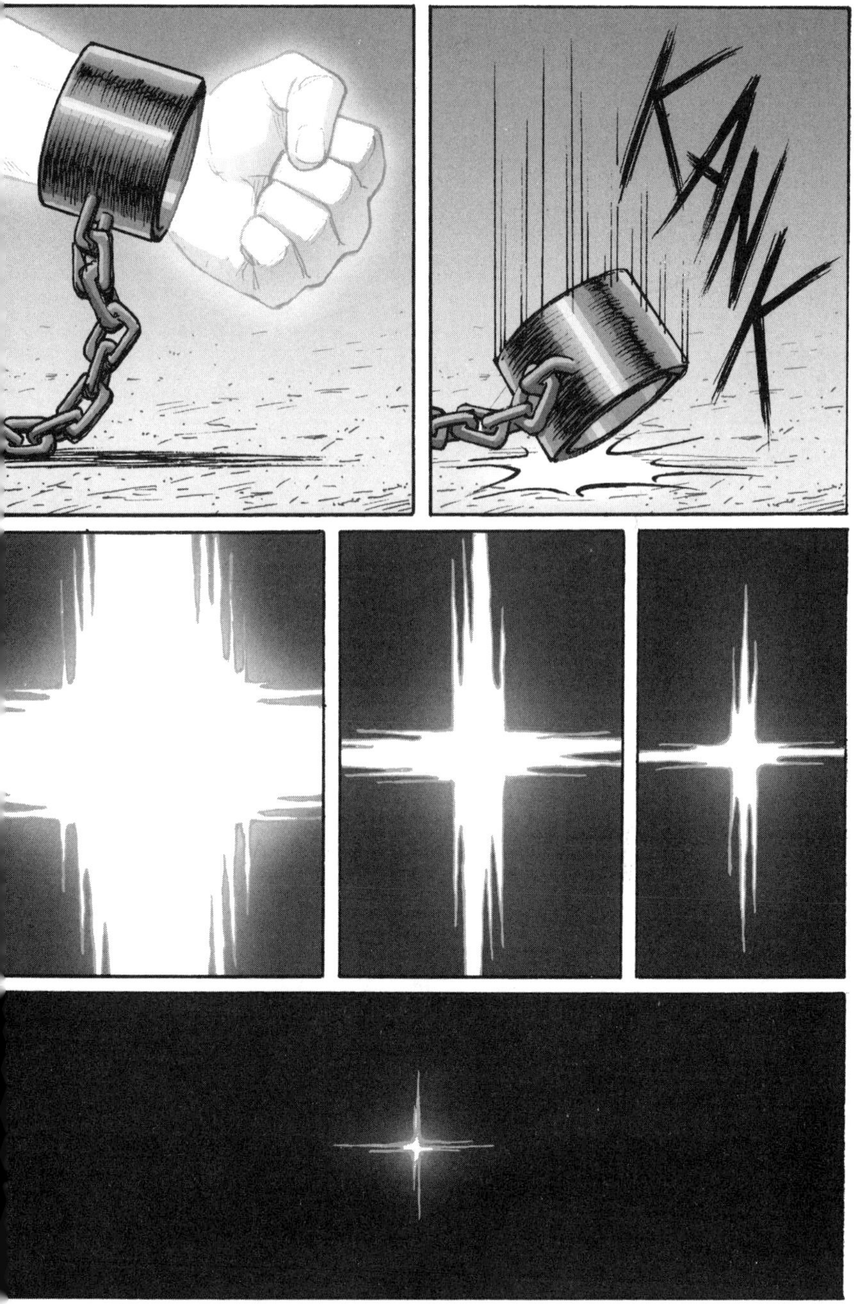
KANK

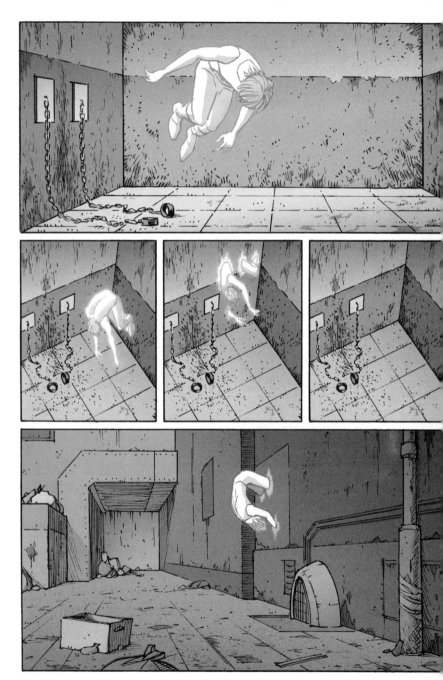

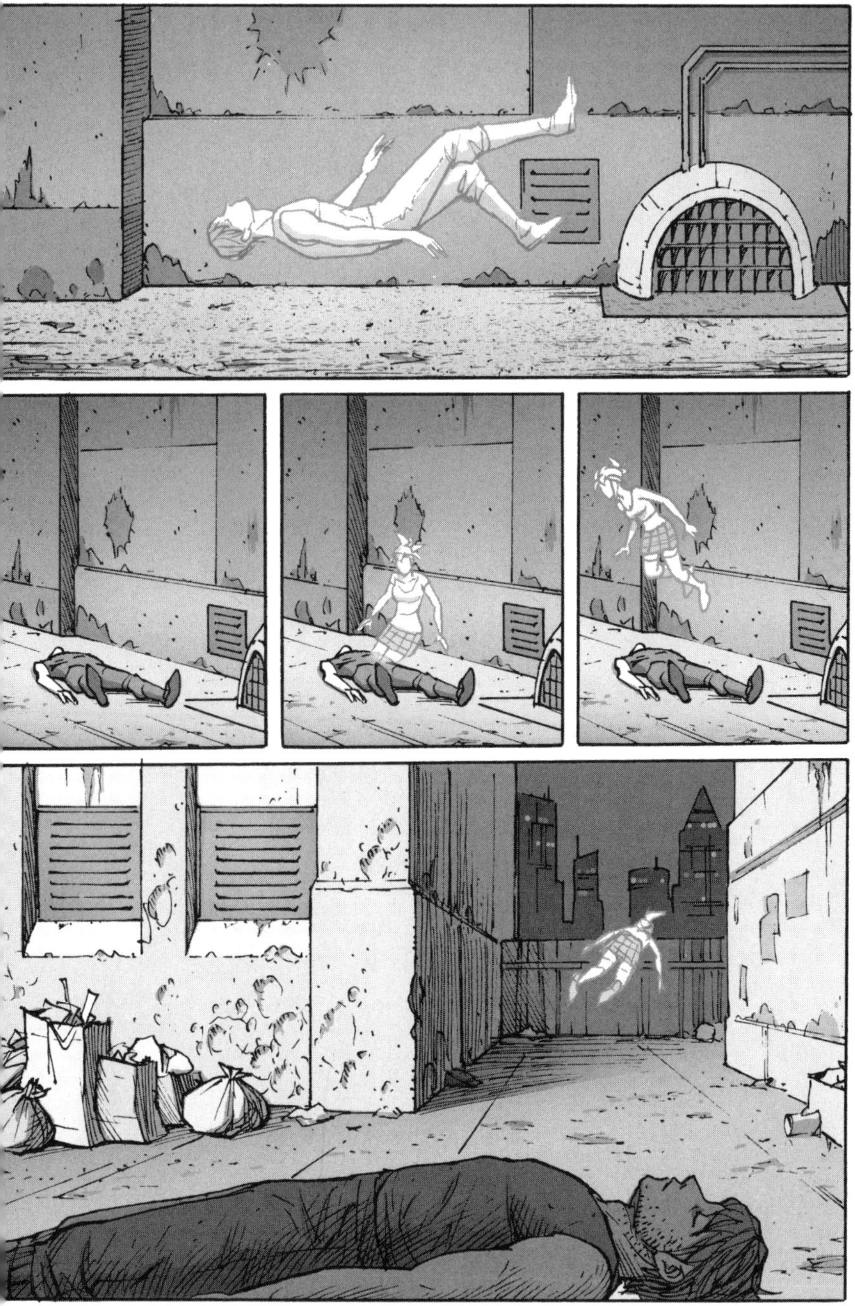

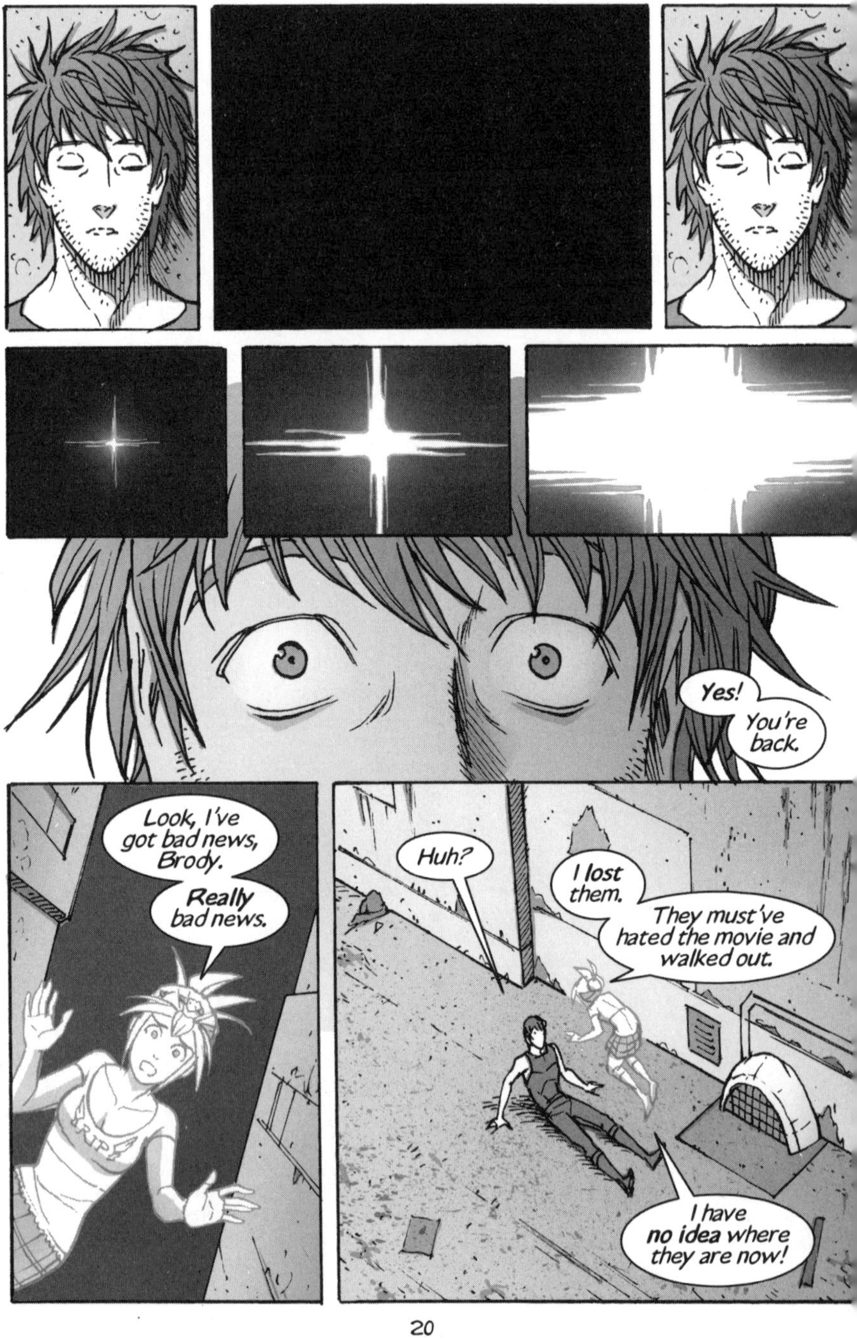
Yes!
You're back.
Look, I've got bad news, Brody.
Really bad news.
Huh?
I lost them.
They must've hated the movie and walked out.
I have no idea where they are now!

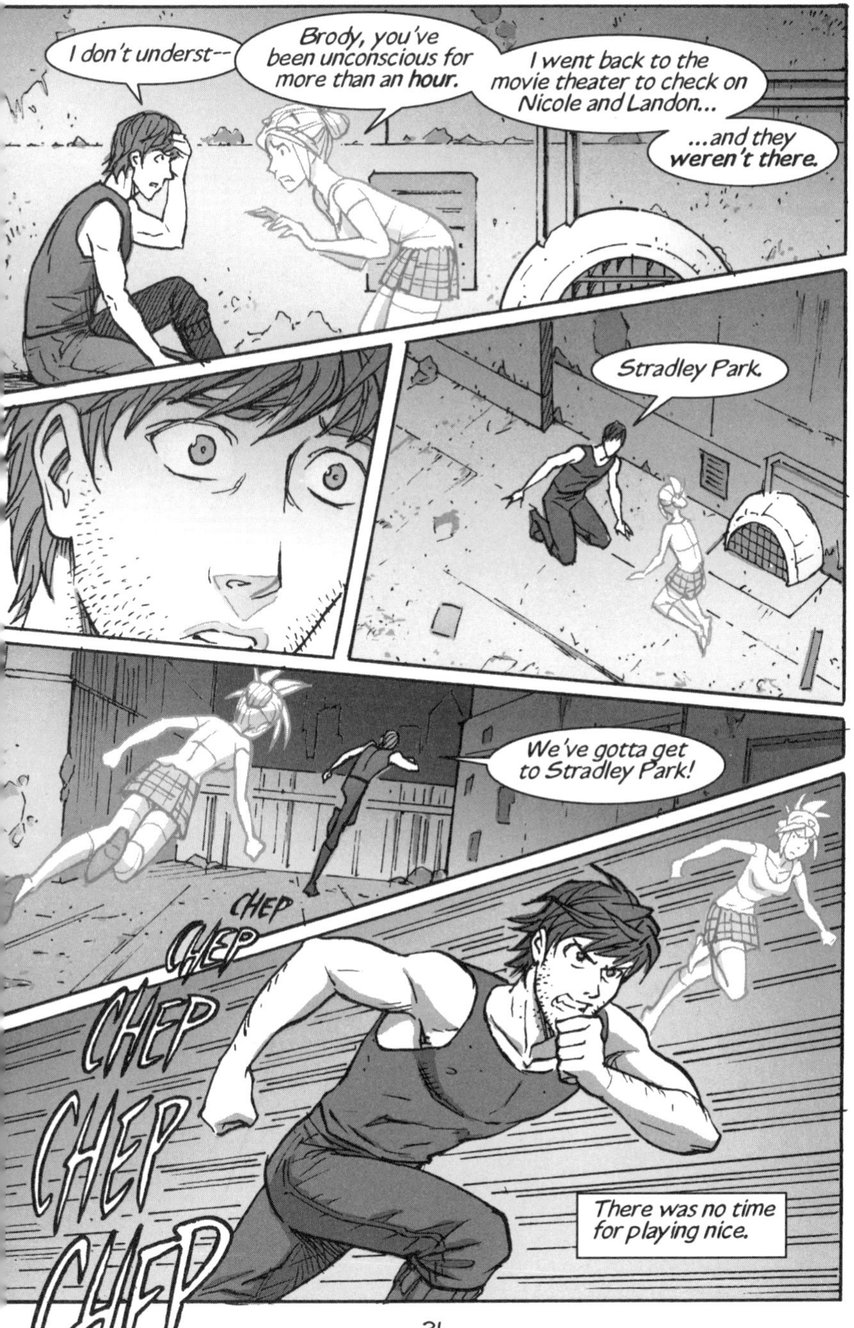
I don't underst--
Brody, you've been unconscious for more than an hour.
I went back to the movie theater to check on Nicole and Landon...
...and they weren't there.
Stradley Park.
We've gotta get to Stradley Park!
CHEP
CHEP
CHEP
CHEP
CHEP
There was no time for playing nice.

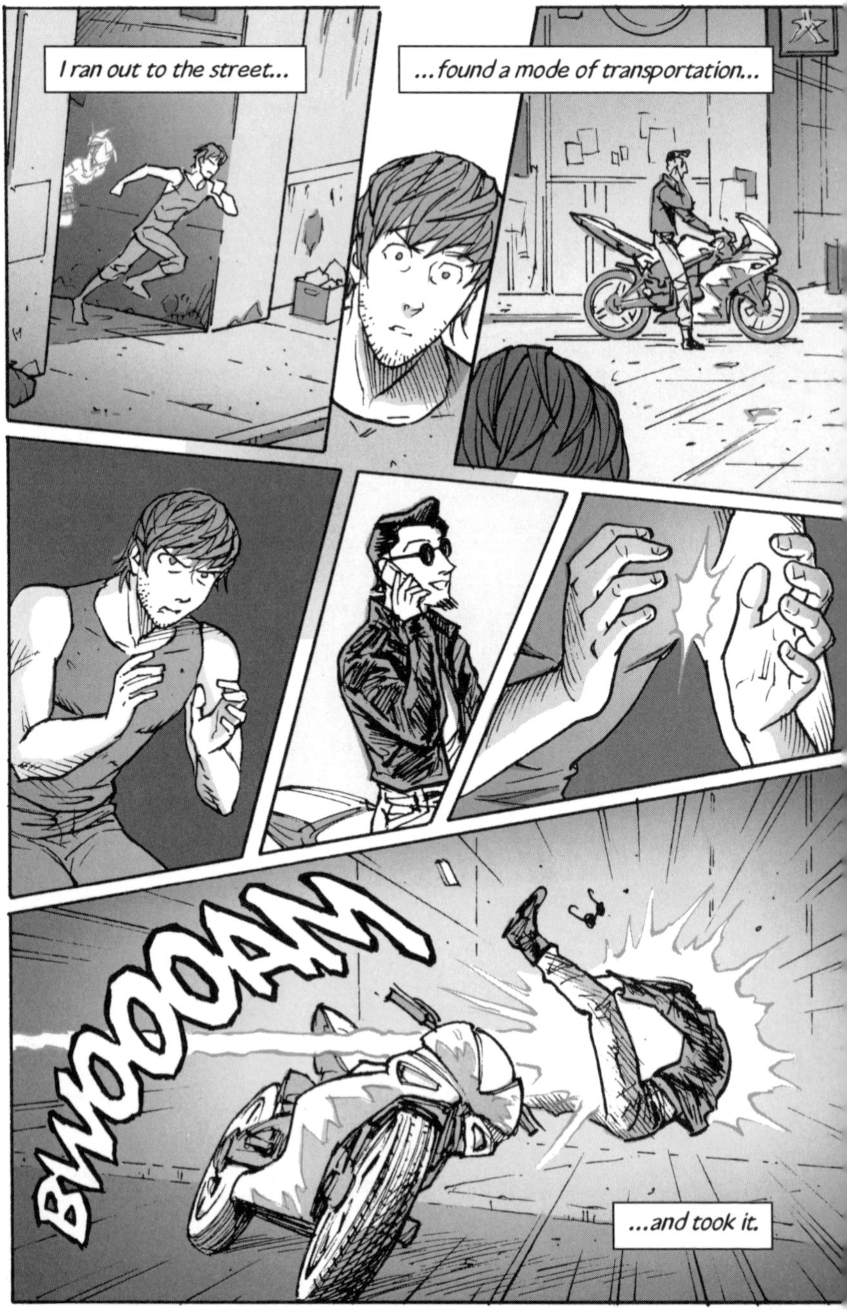
I ran out to the street...
...found a mode of transportation...
BWOOOAM
...and took it.

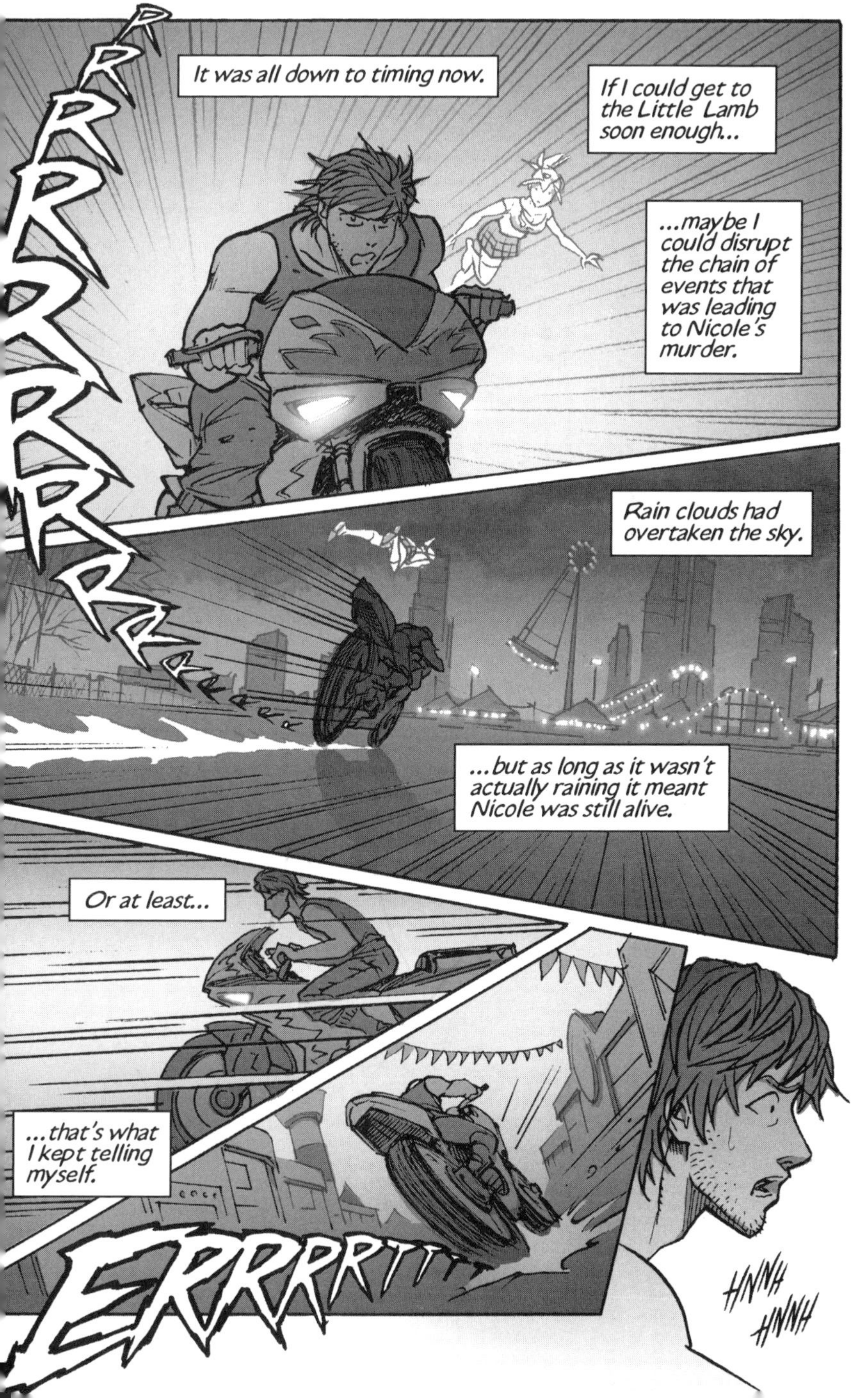
RRRRRRRRRR
It was all down to timing now.
If I could get to the Little Lamb soon enough...
...maybe I could disrupt the chain of events that was leading to Nicole's murder.
Rain clouds had overtaken the sky.
...but as long as it wasn't actually raining it meant Nicole was still alive.
Or at least...
...that's what I kept telling myself.
ERRRRRTTT
HNNH HNNH

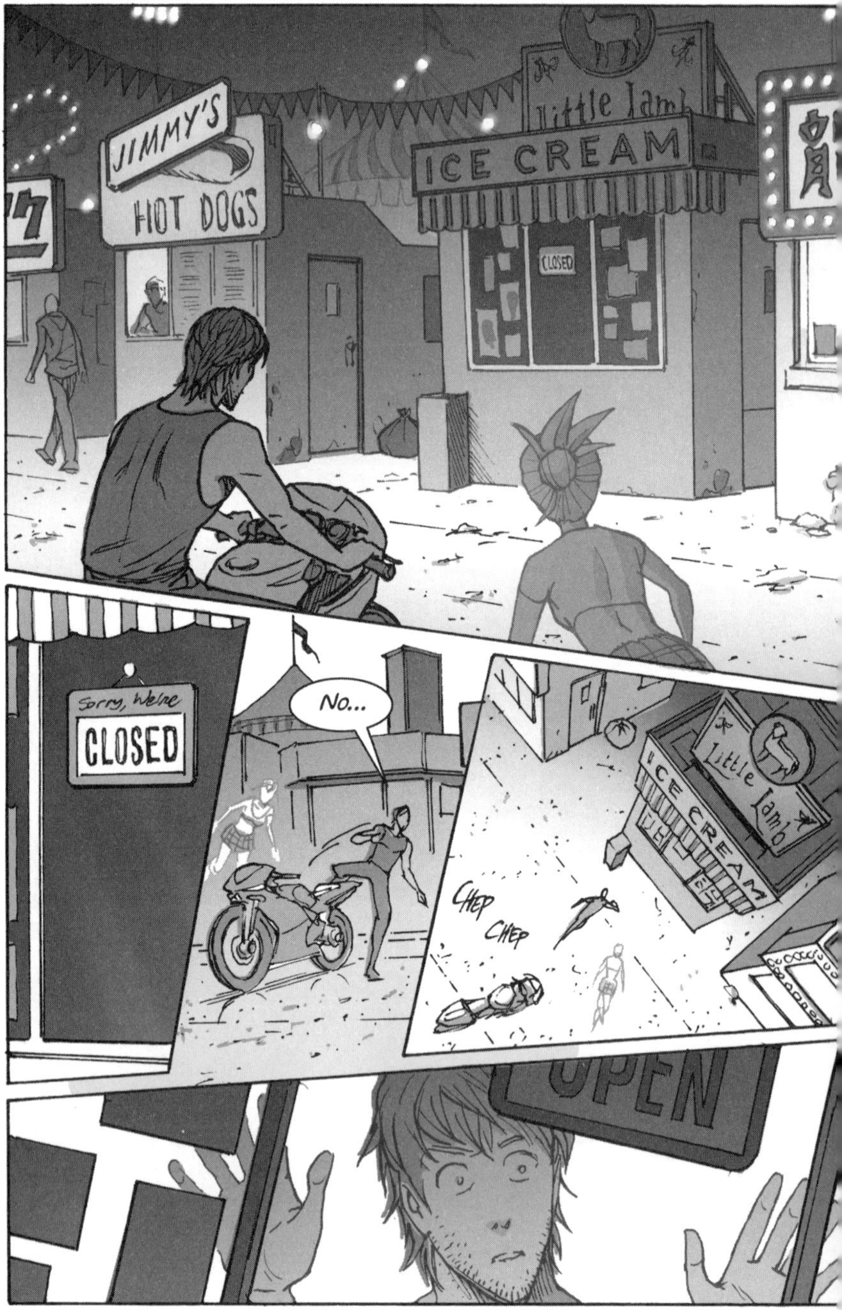
JIMMY'S
HOT DOGS
Little Lamb
ICE CREAM
CLOSED
Sorry, We're
CLOSED
No...
Little Lamb
ICE CREAM
CHEP
CHEP
OPEN

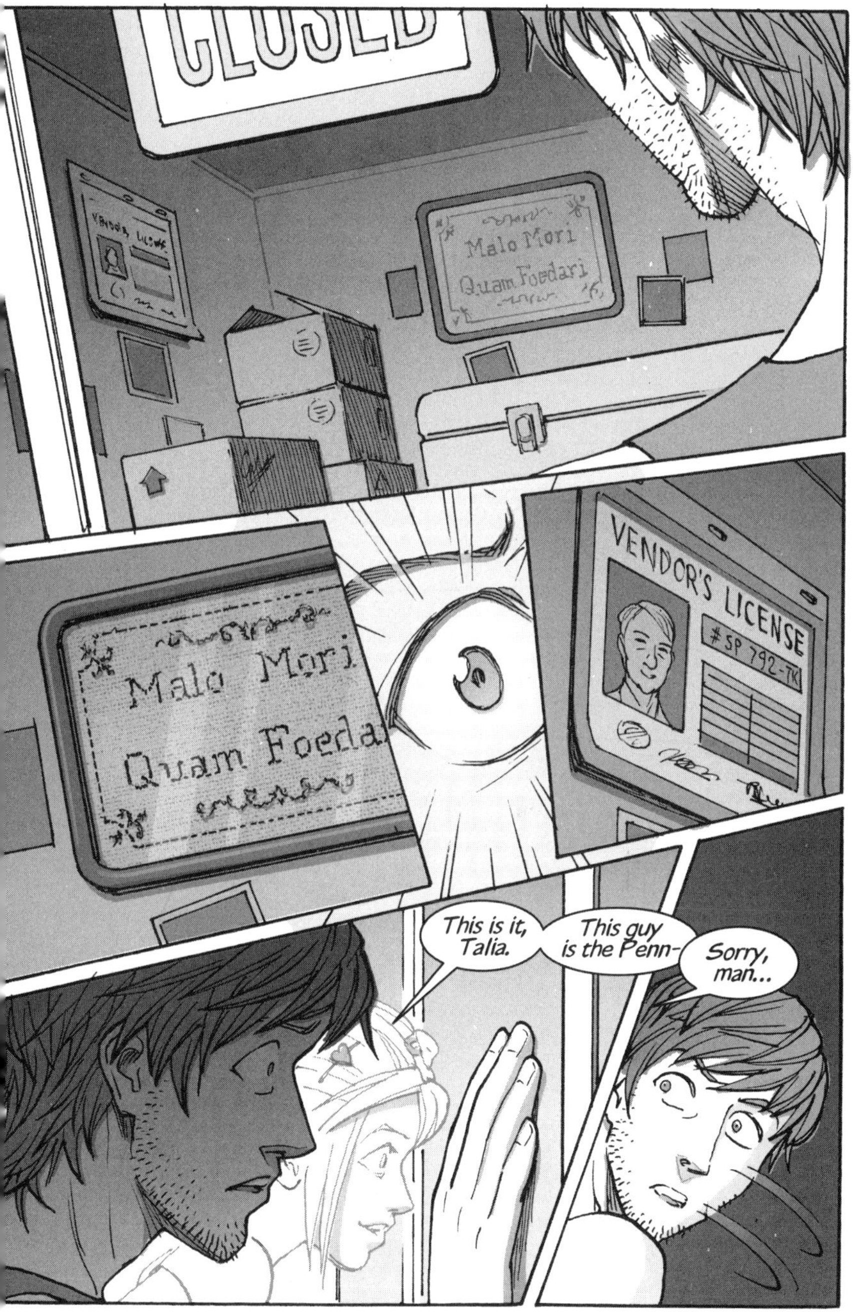
CLOSED
Malo Mori Quam Foedari
Malo Mori Quam Foedari
VENDOR'S LICENSE
#SP 792-7K
This is it, Talia.
This guy is the Penn-
Sorry, man...

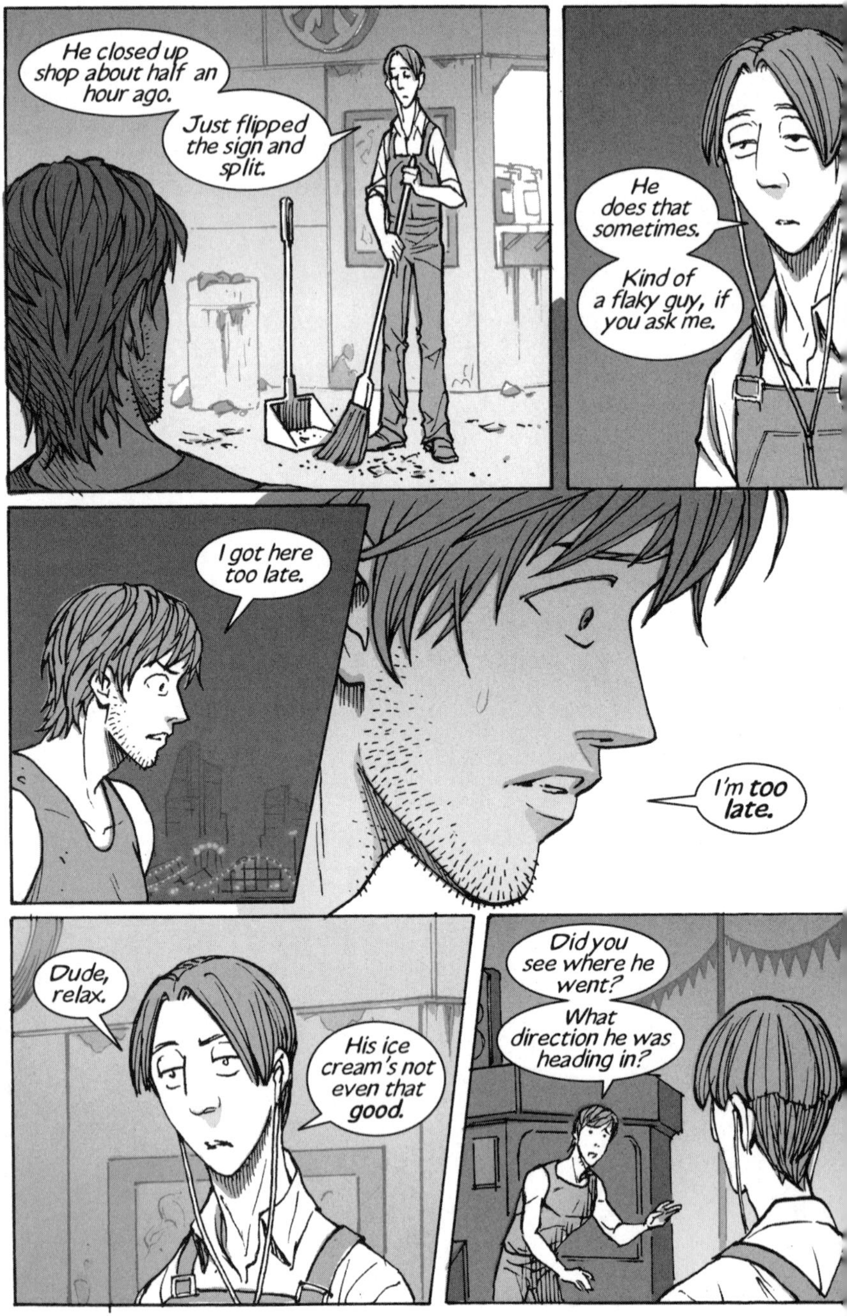
He closed up shop about half an hour ago.
Just flipped the sign and split.
He does that sometimes.
Kind of a flaky guy, if you ask me.
I got here too late.
I'm **too late.**
Dude, relax.
His ice cream's not even that **good.**
Did you see where he went?
What direction he was heading in?

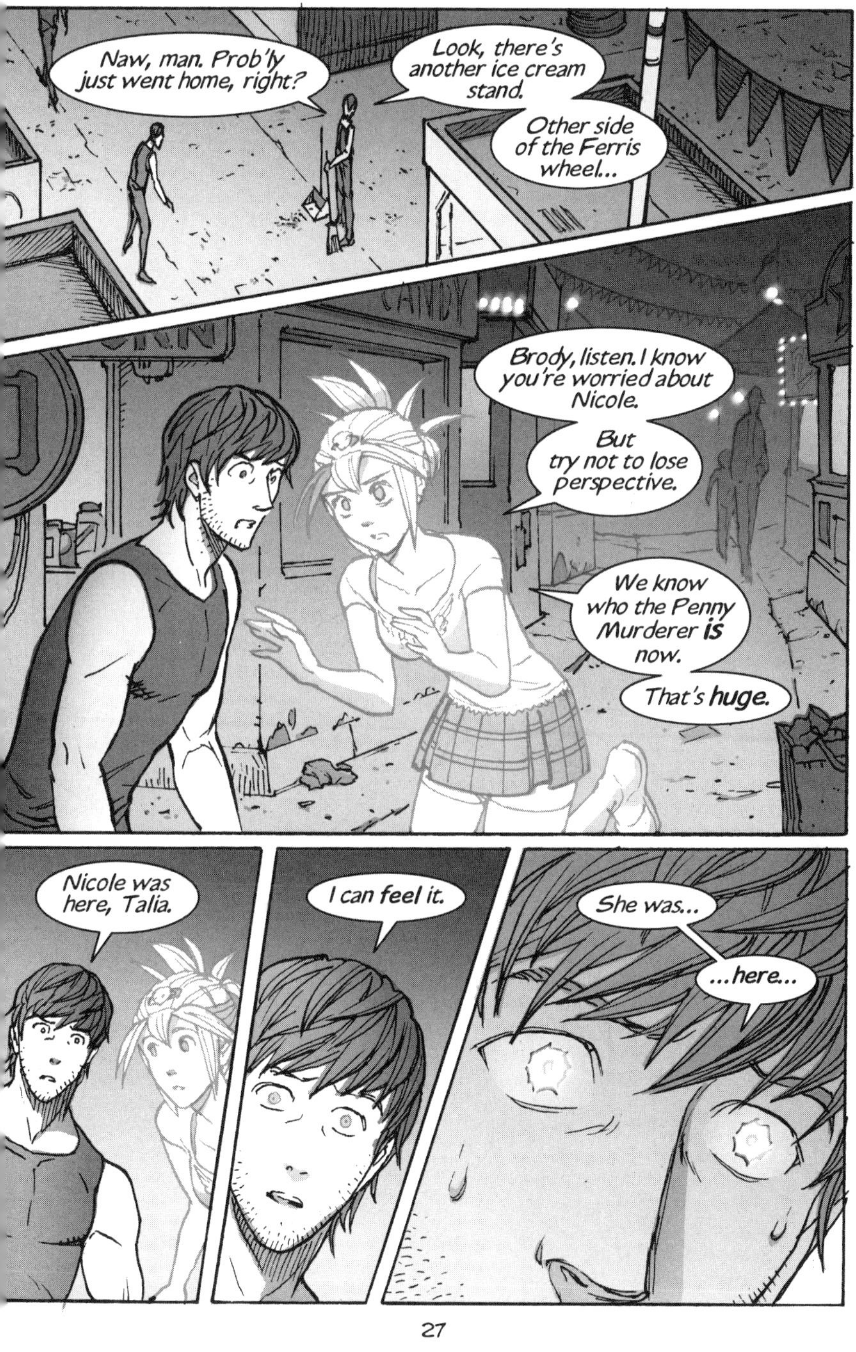
Naw, man. Prob'ly just went home, right?
Look, there's another ice cream stand.
Other side of the Ferris wheel...
Brody, listen. I know you're worried about Nicole.
But try not to lose perspective.
We know who the Penny Murderer **is** now.
That's **huge.**
Nicole was here, Talia.
I can **feel** it.
She was...
...here...

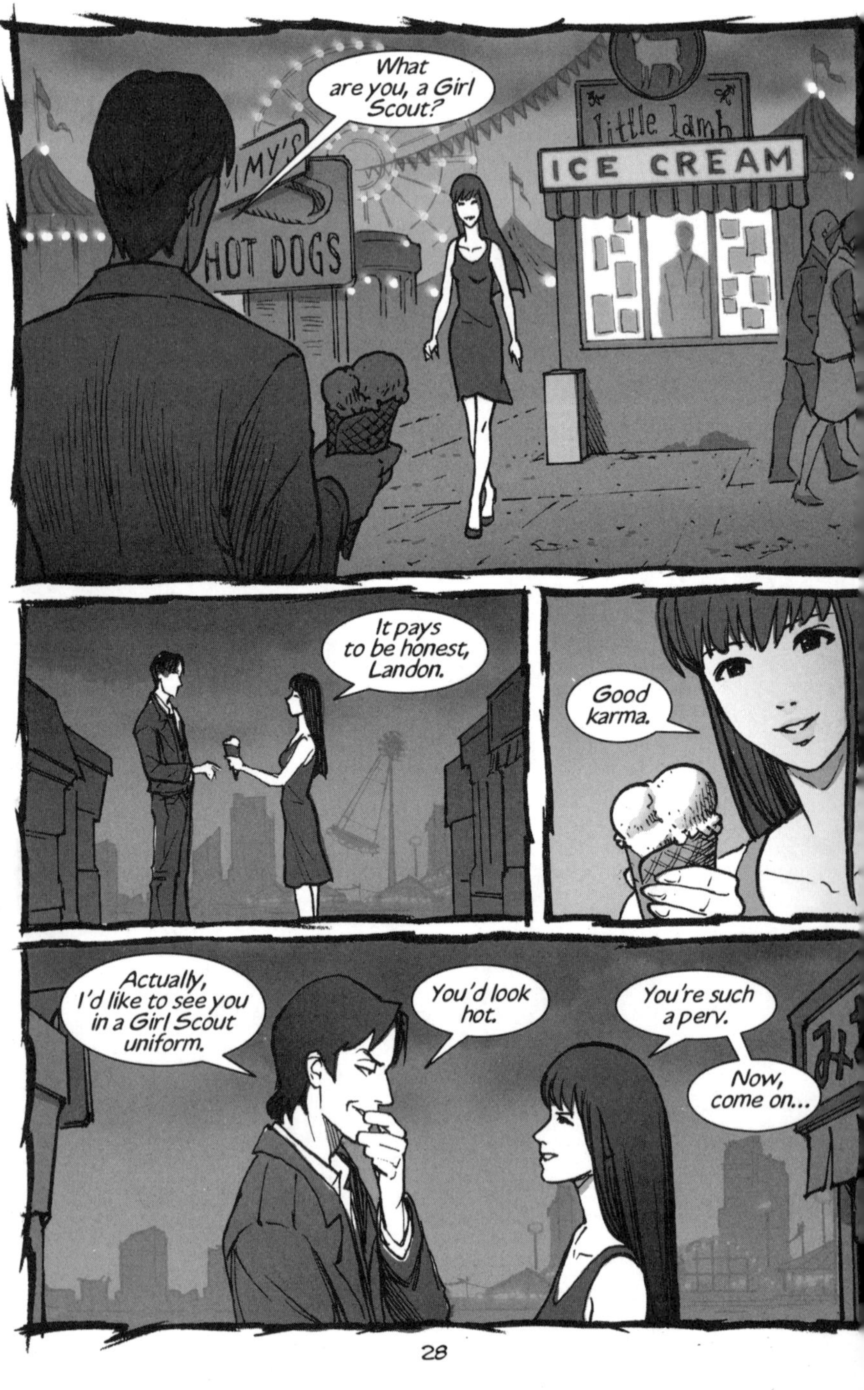
What are you, a Girl Scout?
IMY'S
HOT DOGS
Little Lamb
ICE CREAM
It pays to be honest, Landon.
Good karma.
Actually, I'd like to see you in a Girl Scout uniform.
You'd look hot.
You're such a perv.
Now, come on...

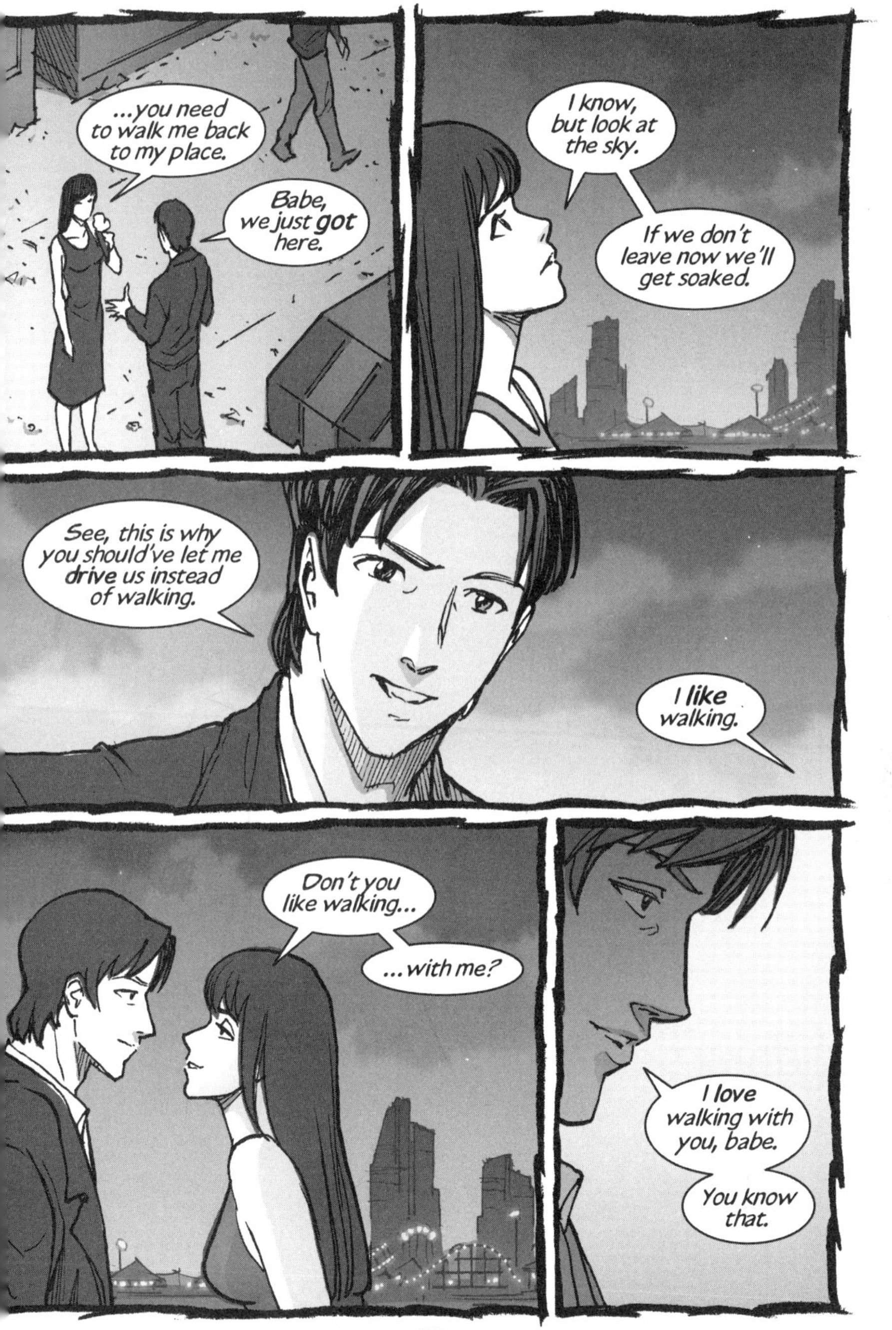
...you need to walk me back to my place.
Babe, we just **got** here.
I know, but look at the sky.
If we don't leave now we'll get soaked.
See, this is why you should've let me **drive** us instead of walking.
I **like** walking.
Don't you like walking...
...with me?
I **love** walking with you, babe.
You know that.

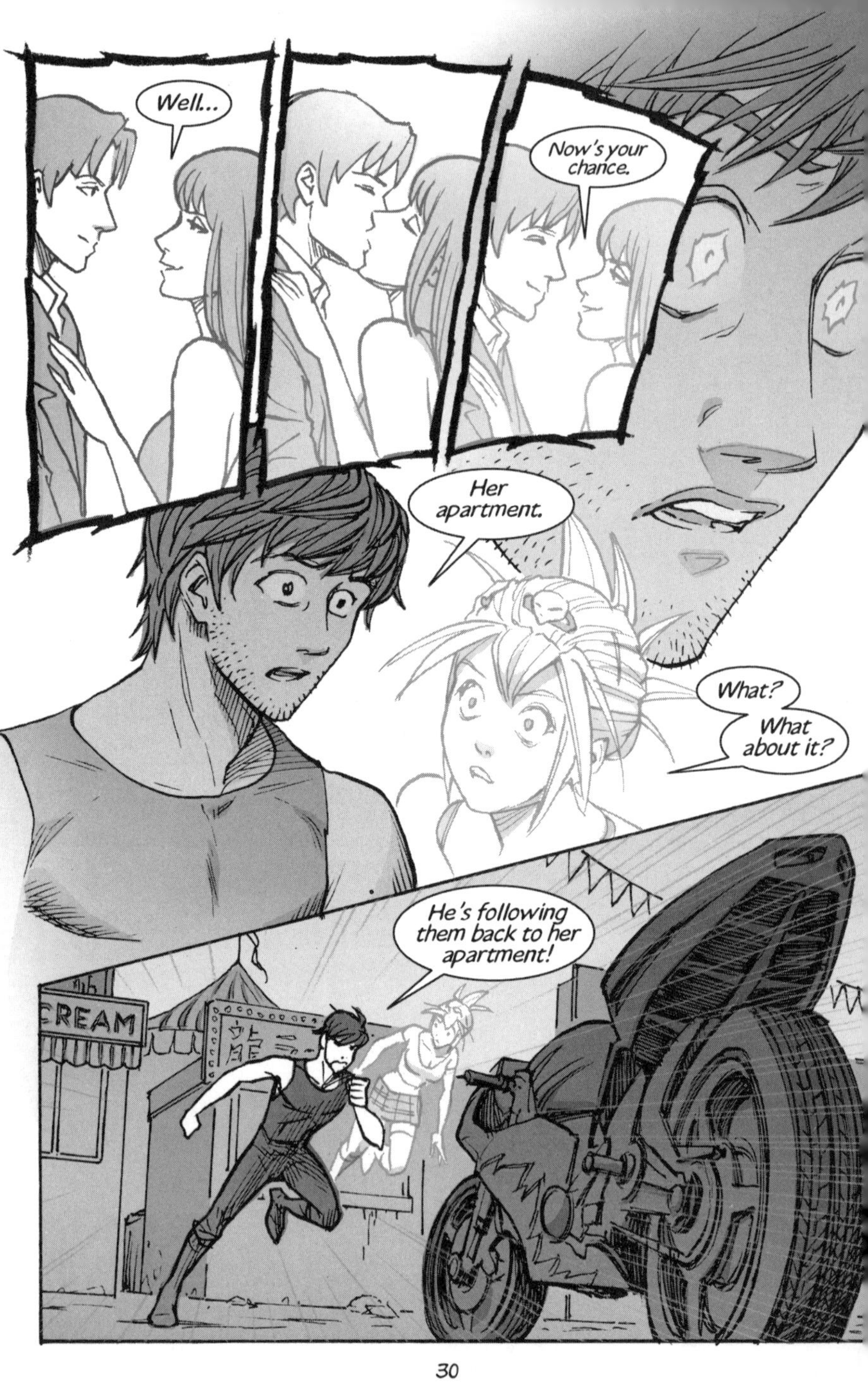
Well...
Now's your chance.
Her apartment.
What? What about it?
He's following them back to her apartment!
CREAM

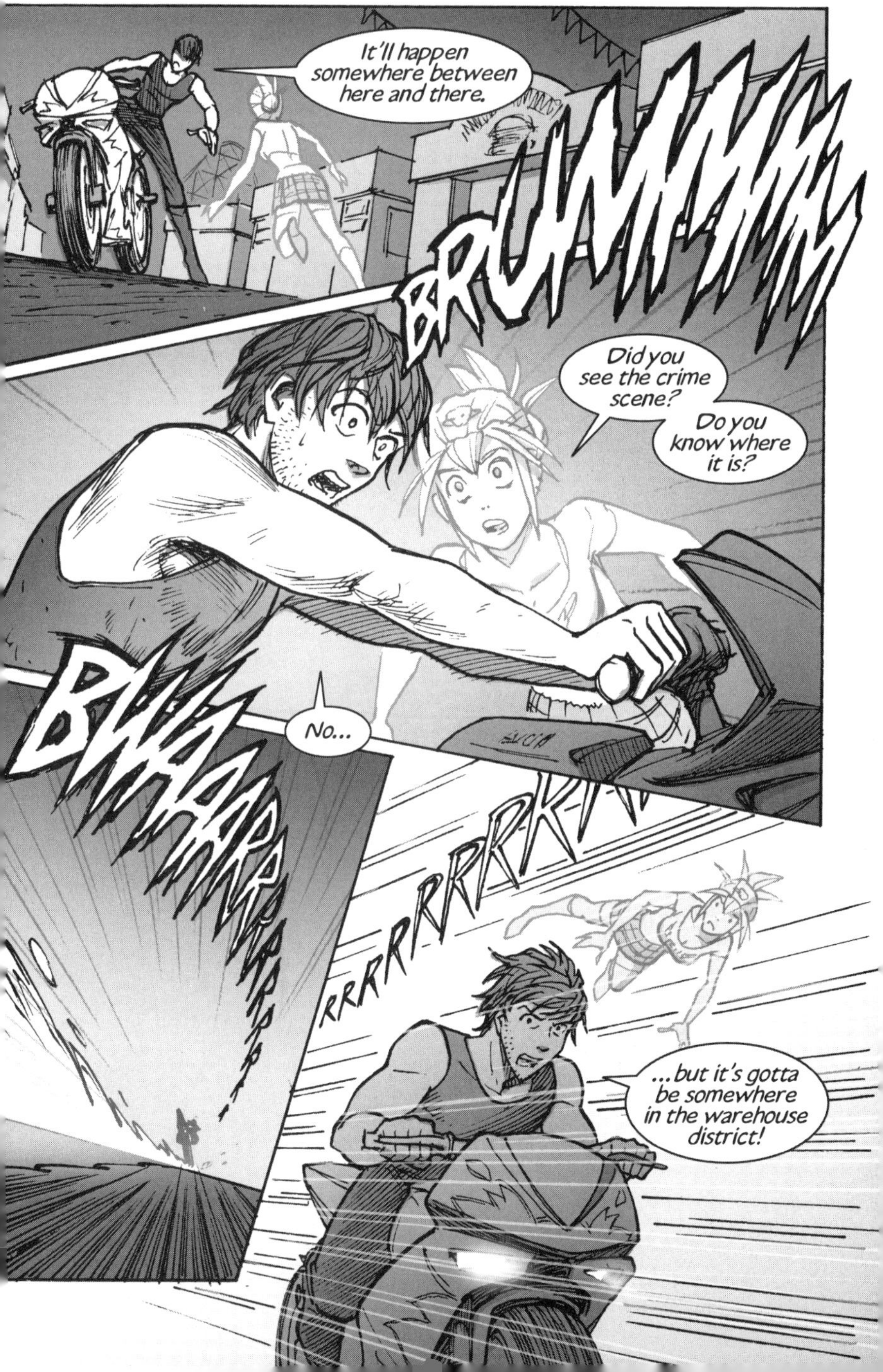
It'll happen somewhere between here and there.
BRUMMMM
Did you see the crime scene?
Do you know where it is?
No...
BWAARRRRRRR
RRRRRRRRRRRRRRRRRRR
...but it's gotta be somewhere in the warehouse district!

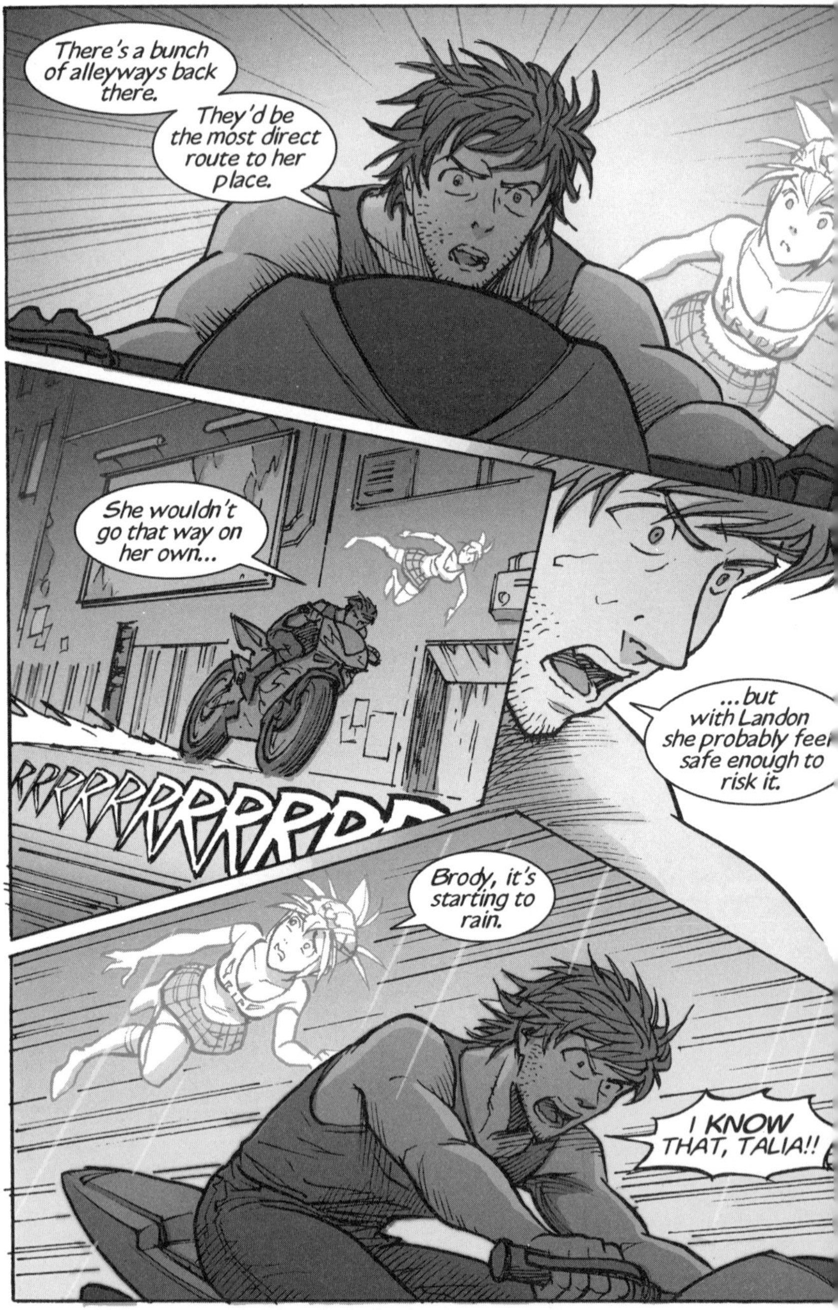
There's a bunch of alleyways back there.
They'd be the most direct route to her place.
She wouldn't go that way on her own...
...but with Landon she probably feel safe enough to risk it.
RRRRRRRRRRRRR
Brody, it's starting to rain.
I KNOW THAT, TALIA!!

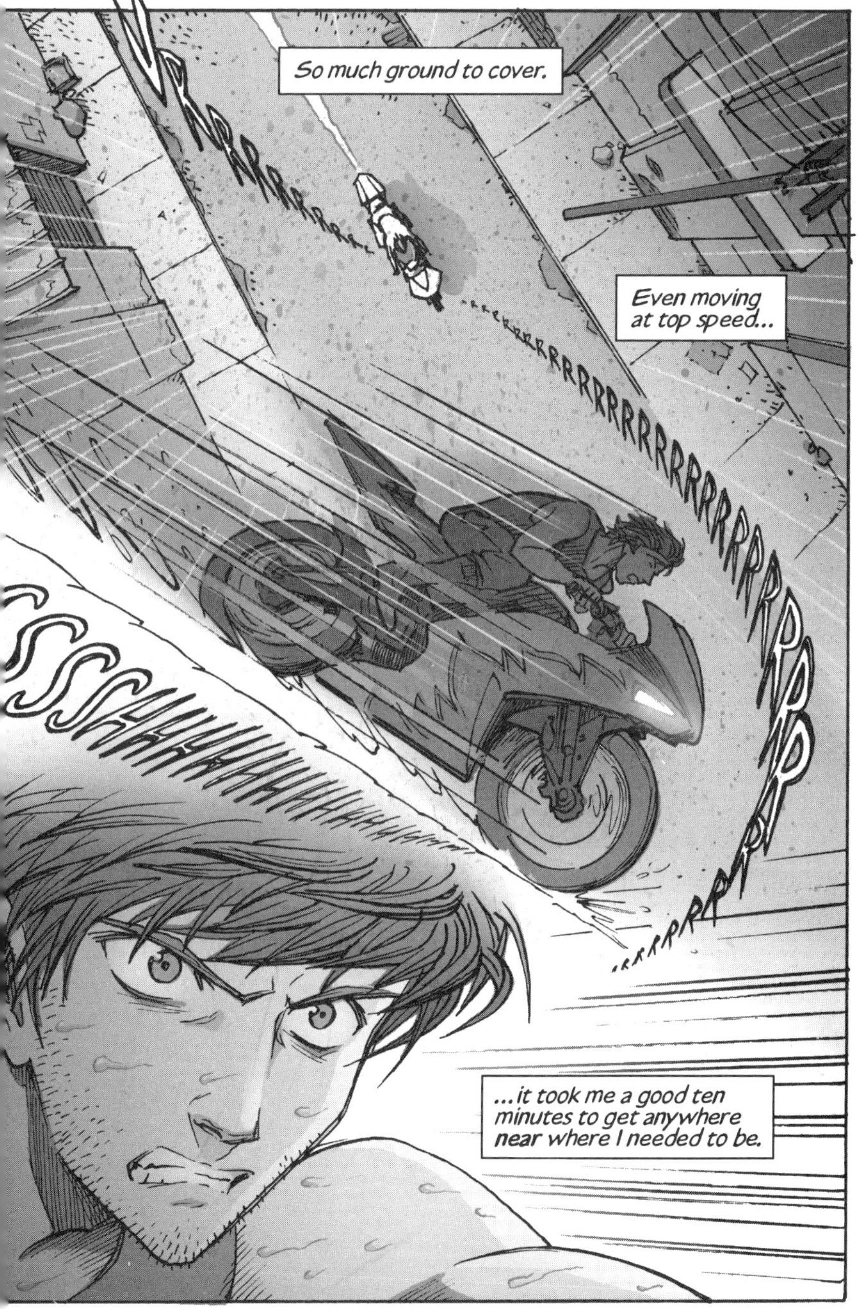
So much ground to cover.
VRRRAARRRRrrrrr
Even moving at top speed...
rrrrrrrRRRRRRRRRRRRRRRRRRRRRRRRRRRRRRRRRRRRRRRRRRRRRrrrr
SSSCHHHHHHHHHHHH
...it took me a good ten minutes to get anywhere **near** where I needed to be.

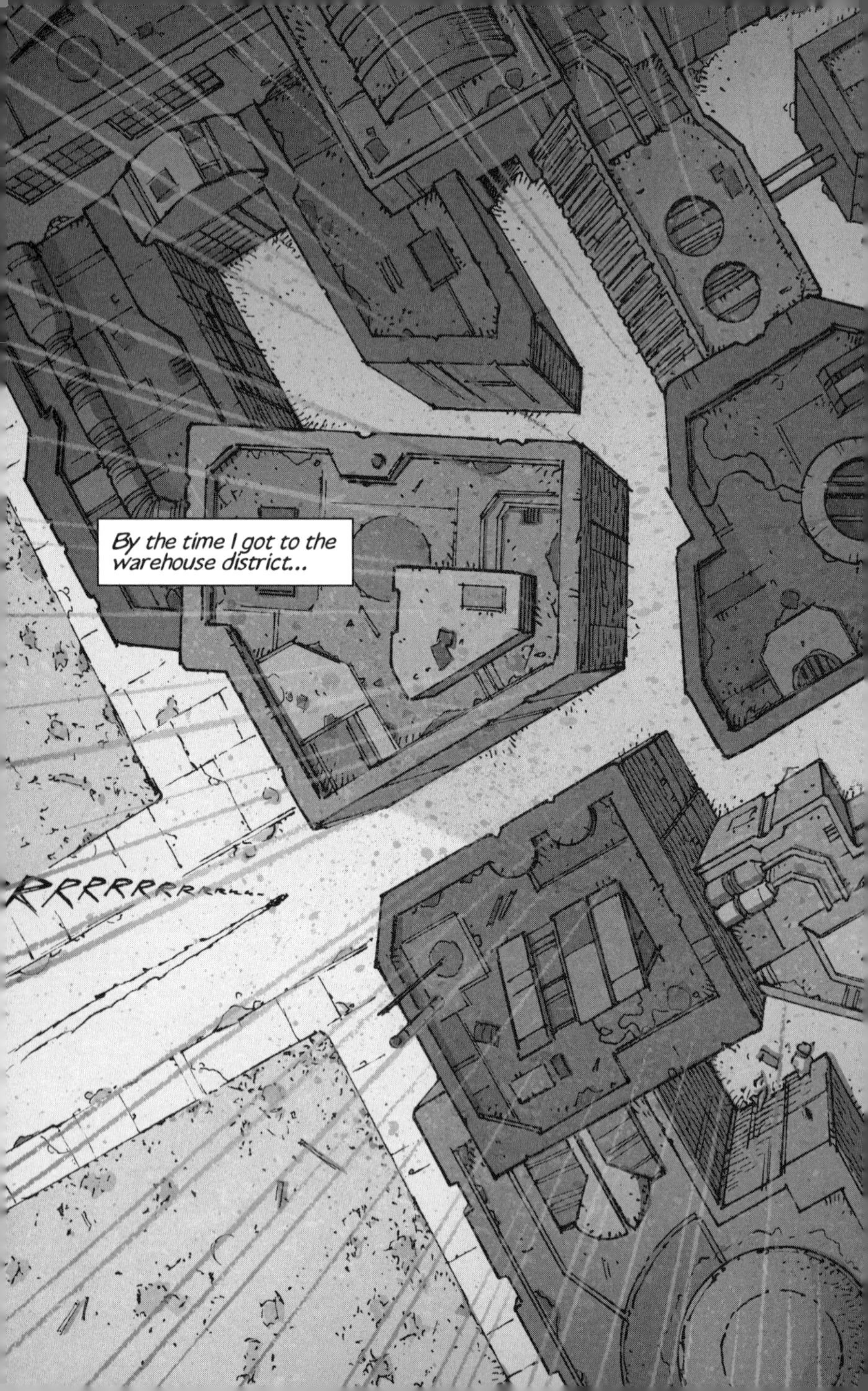
By the time I got to the warehouse district...
RRRRRRRrrr...

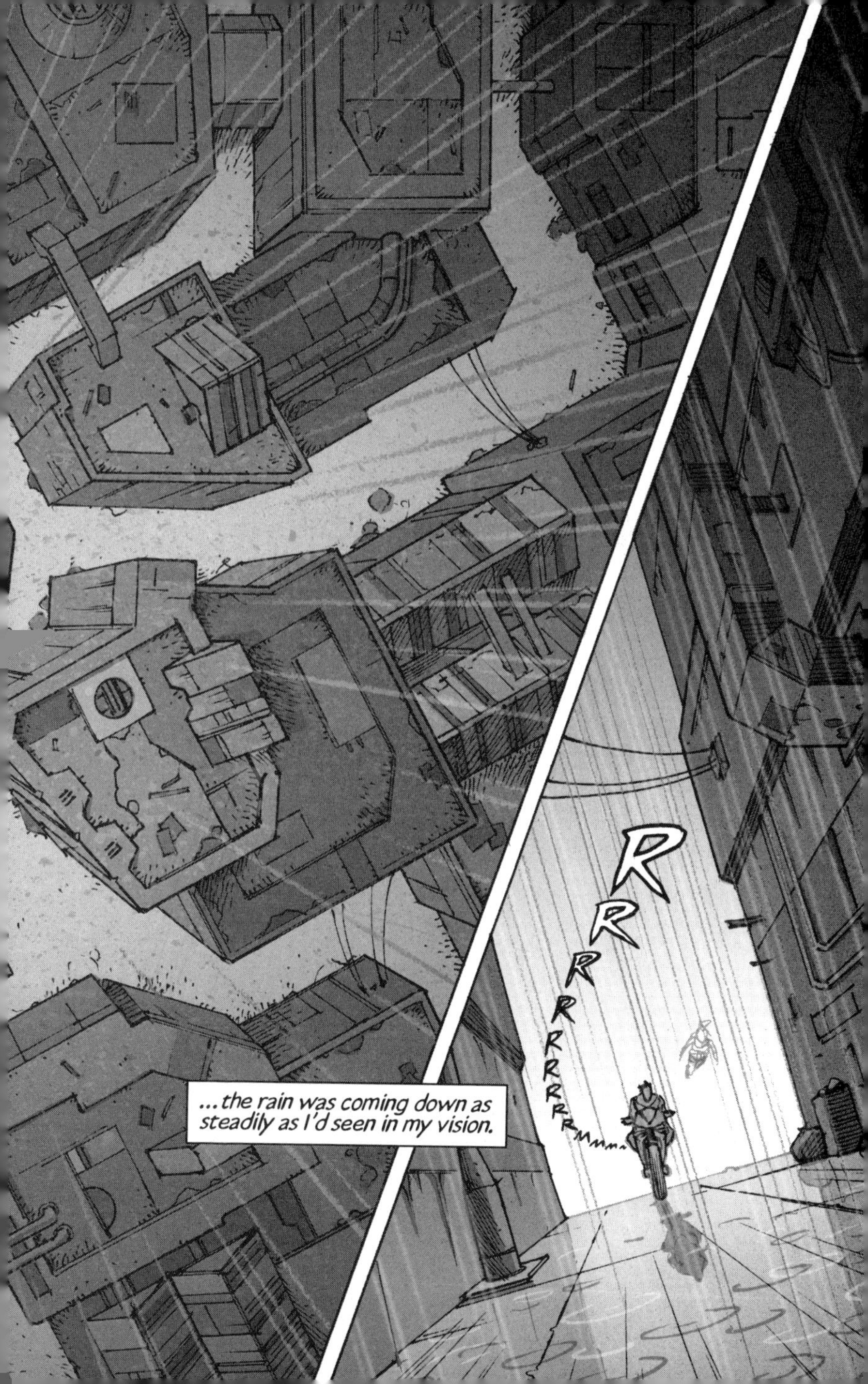
...the rain was coming down as steadily as I'd seen in my vision.
RRRRRRRRRRMMMM...

RRRRRRRMMMMM

VRRT

There were dozens of paths Nicole and Landon could have followed.

But something kicked in once I got back there.

Something was guiding me...

BRRRRRRR

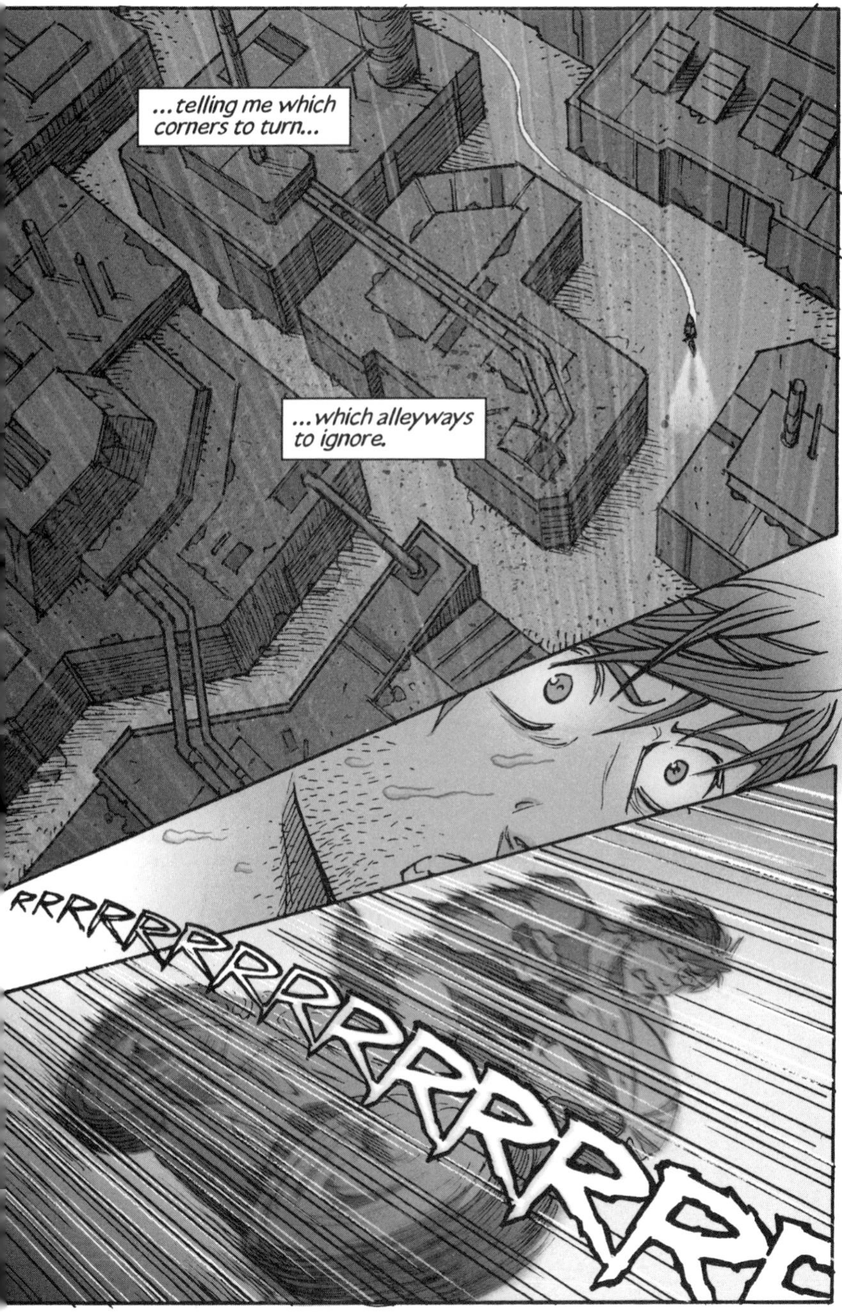
...telling me which corners to turn...
...which alleyways to ignore.
RRRRRRRRRRRRRR

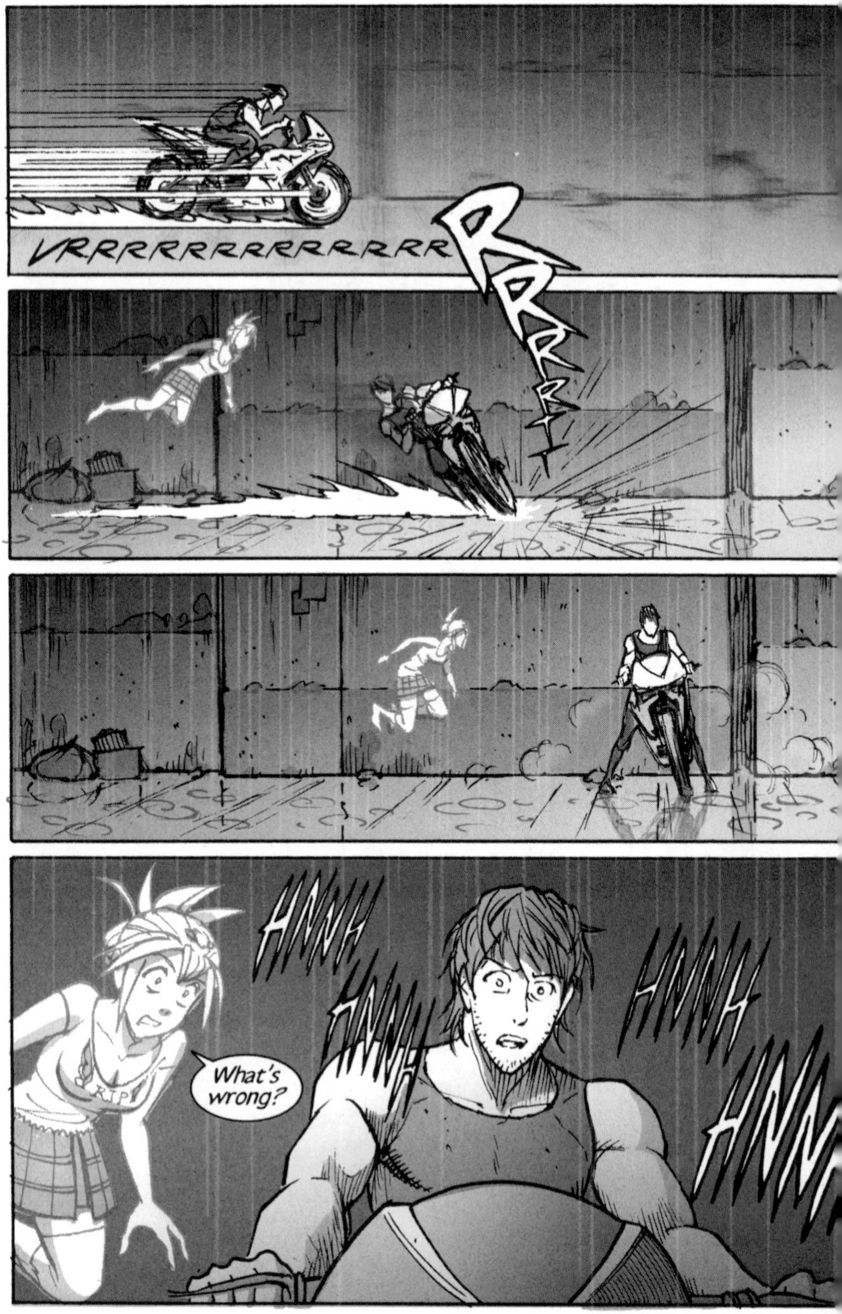
VRRRRRRRRRRRRRRR
RRRRRT
What's wrong?

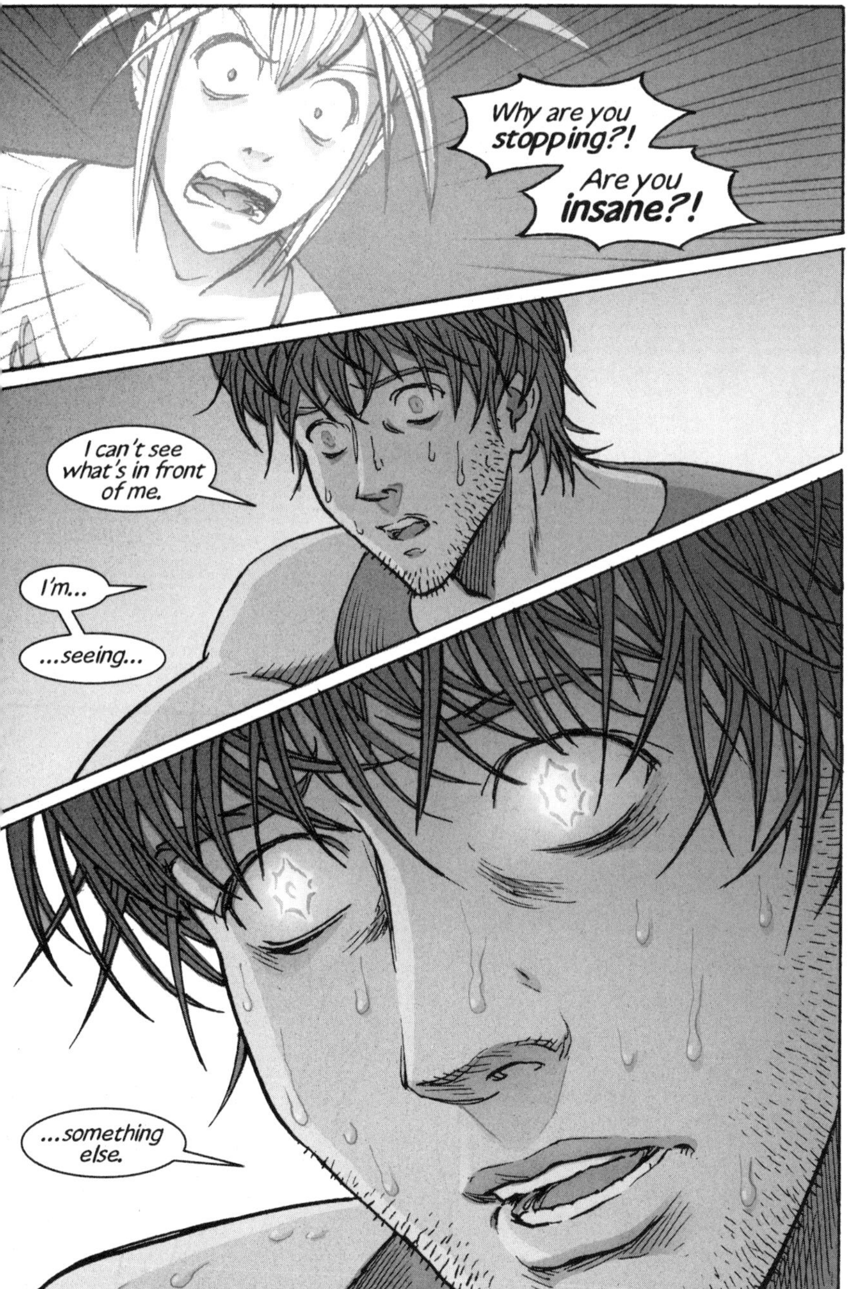
Why are you stopping?!
Are you insane?!
I can't see what's in front of me.
I'm...
...seeing...
...something else.

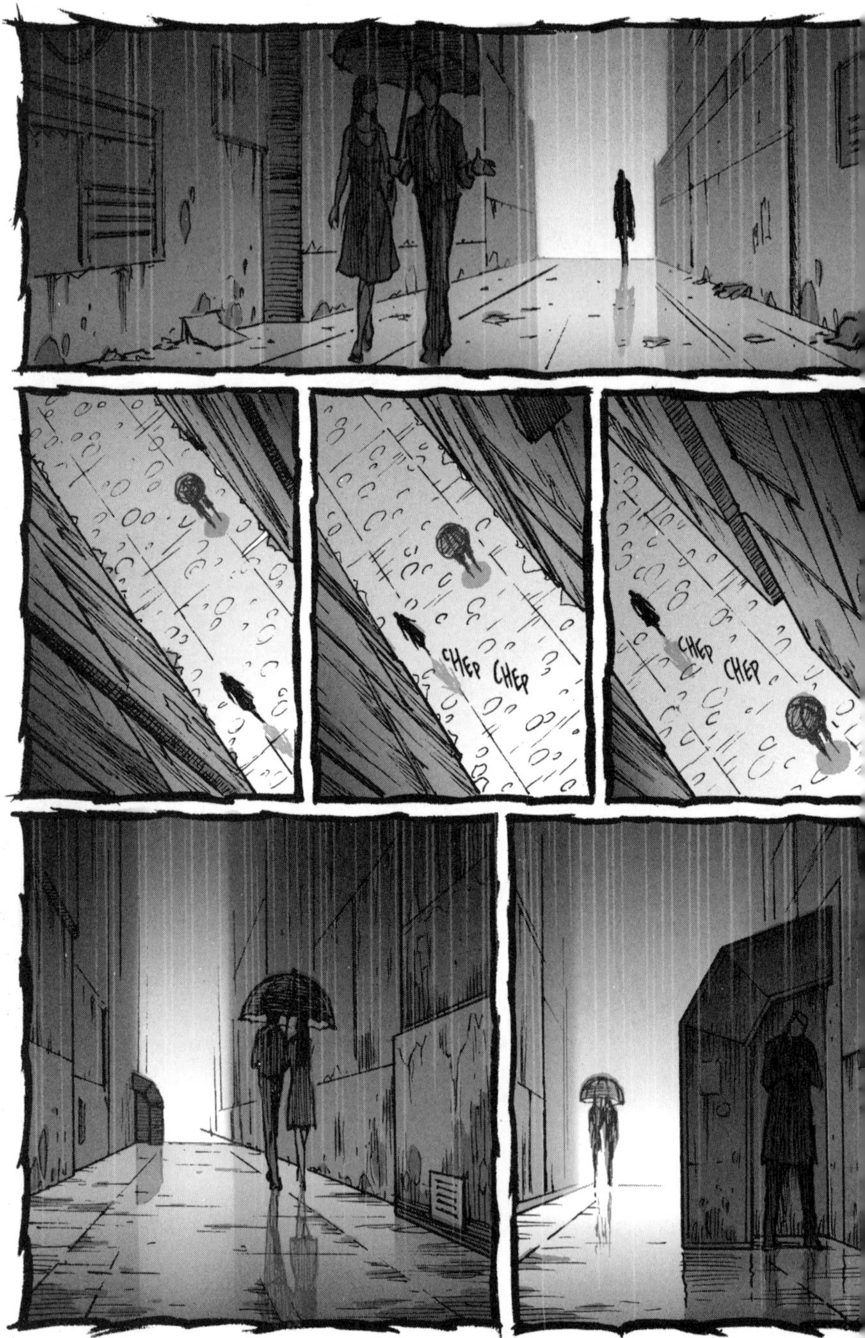
CHEP CHEP
CHEP CHEP

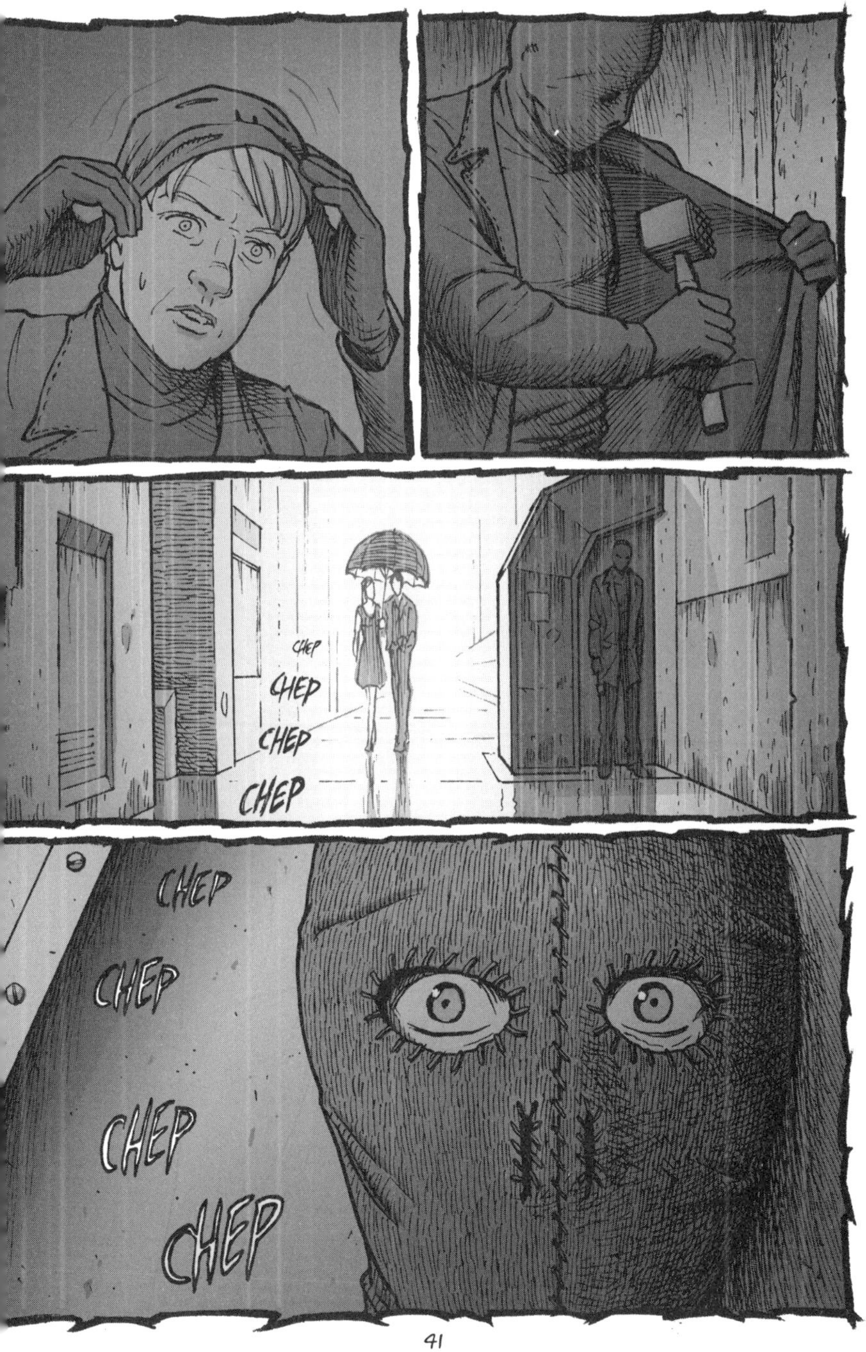
CHEP
CHEP
CHEP
CHEP
CHEP
CHEP
CHEP
CHEP

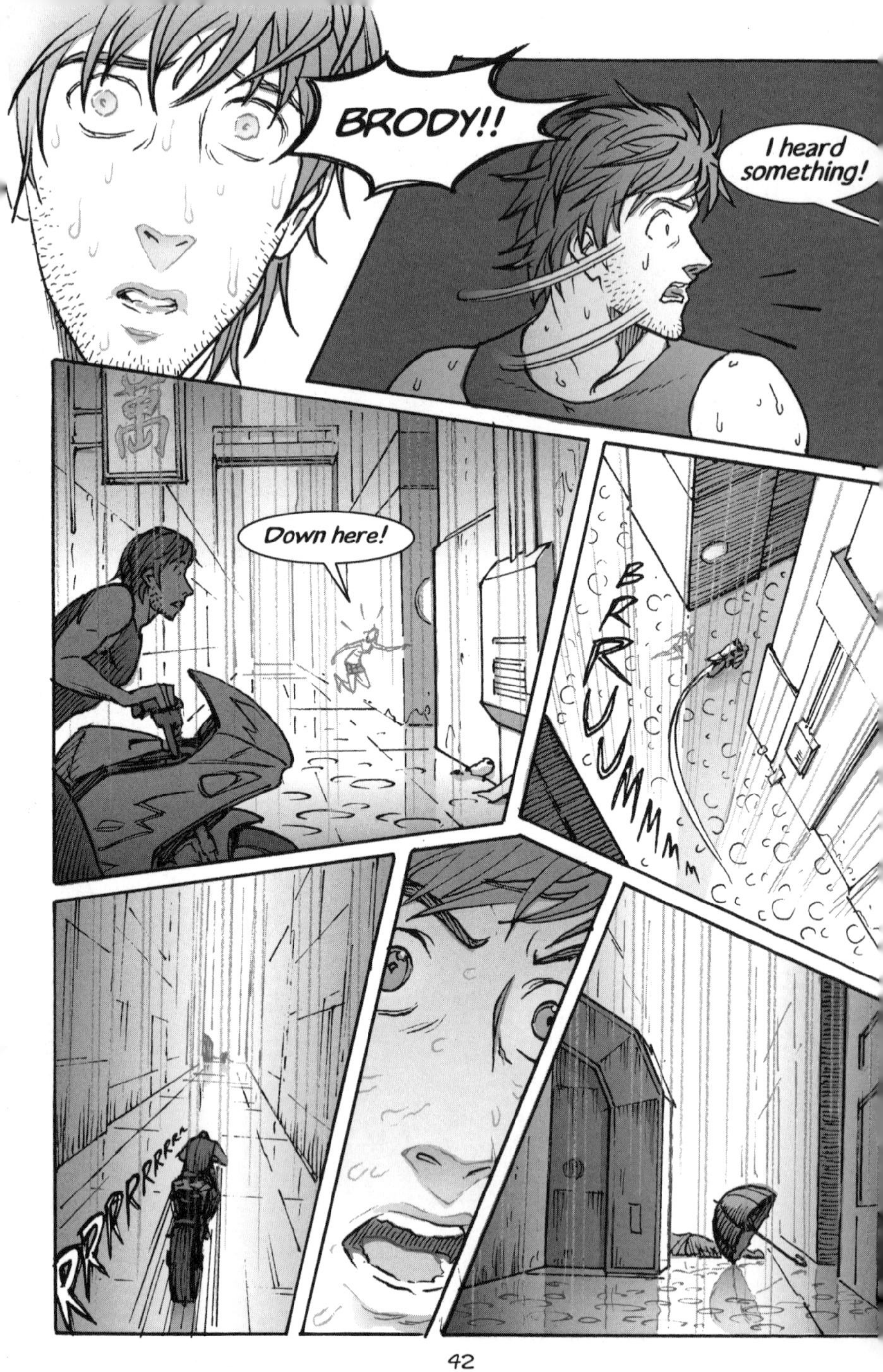
BRODY!!
I heard something!
Down here!
BRRRUMMMMM
RRRRRRRRRR

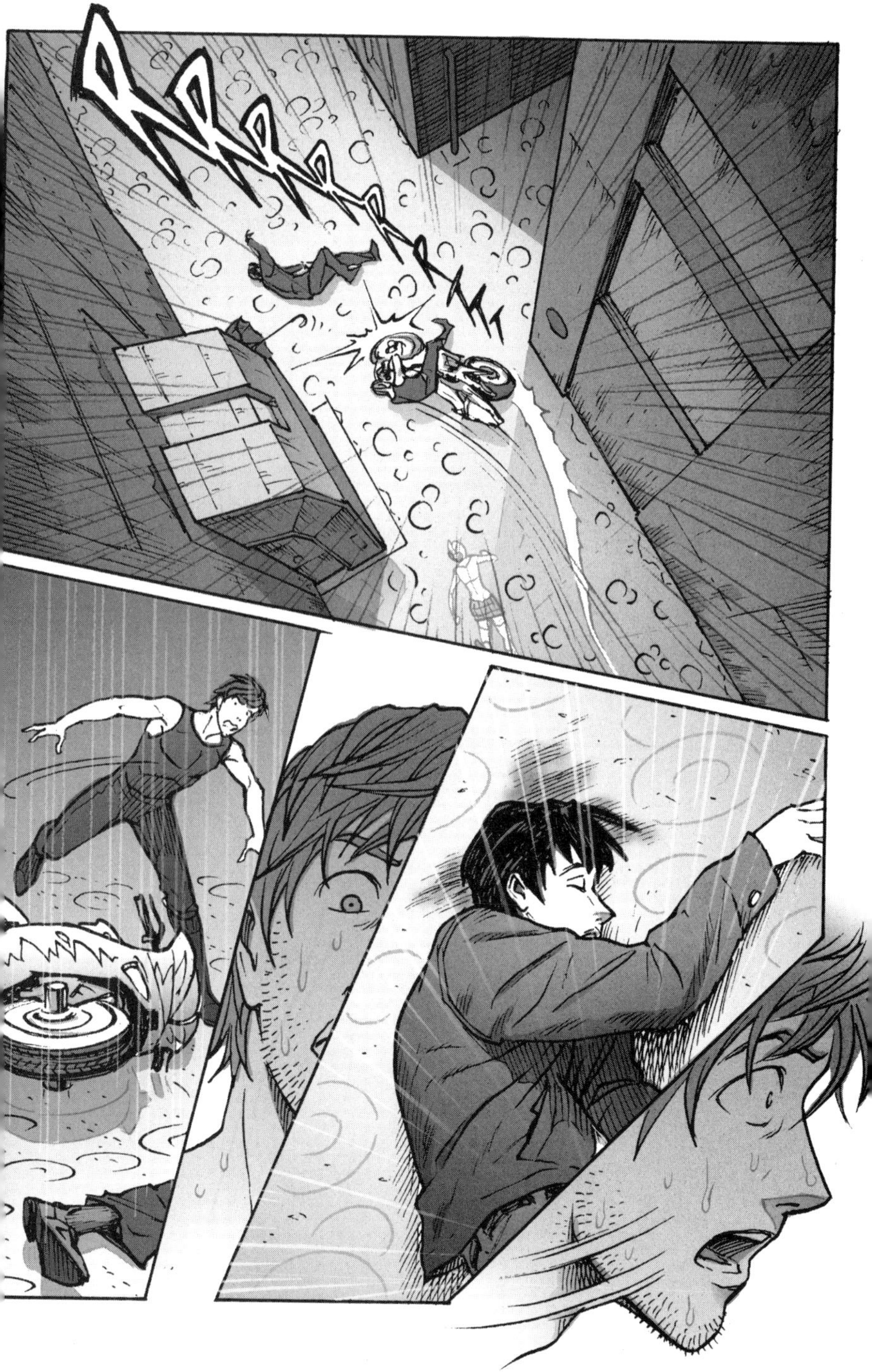
BRRRRRAAT

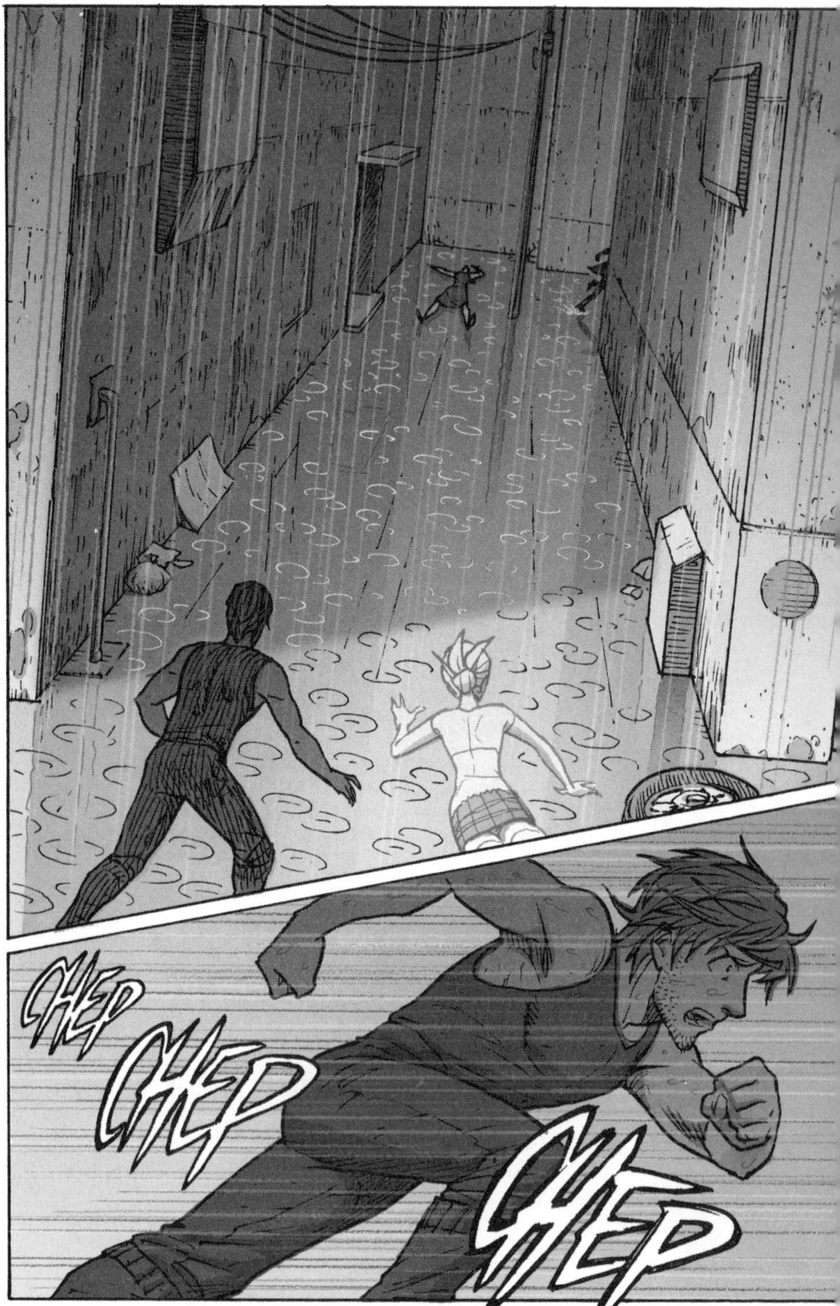
CHEP
CHEP
CHEP

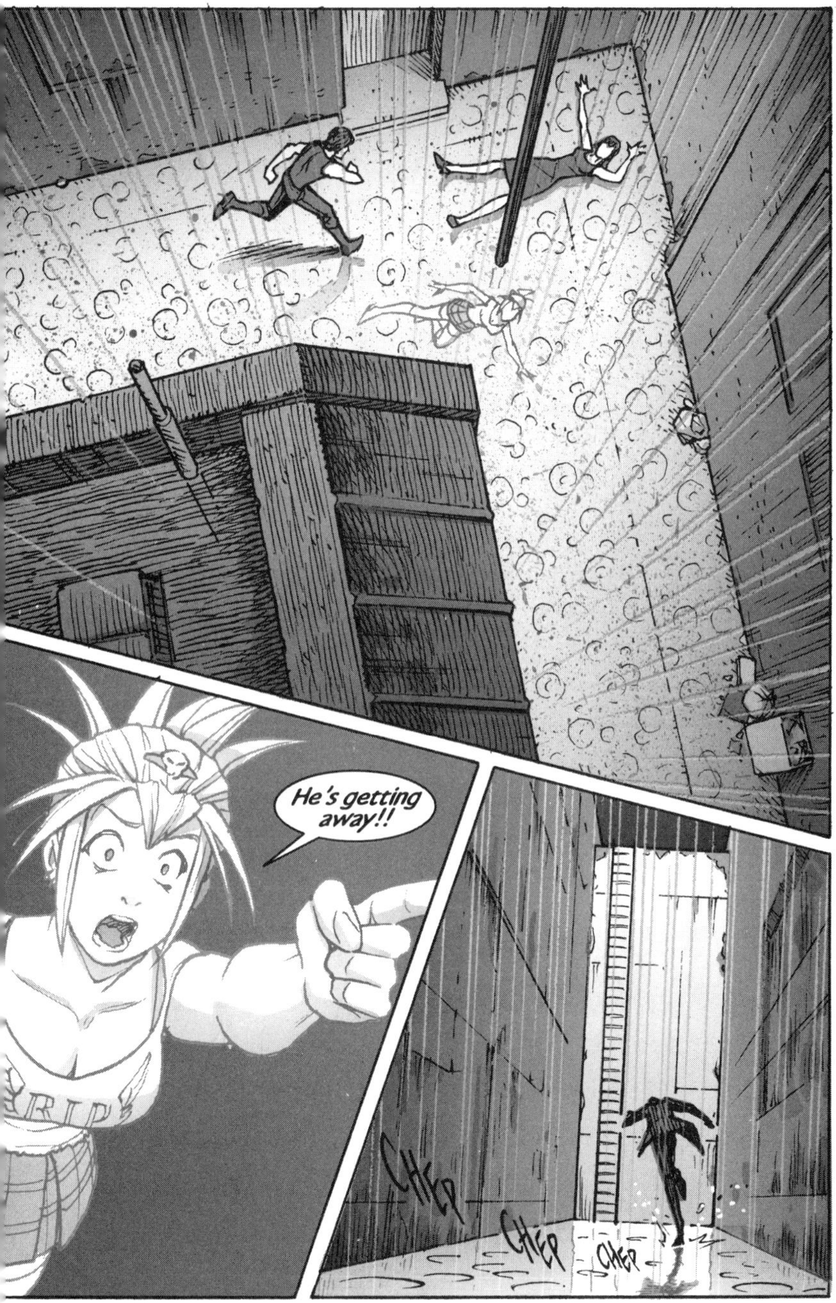
He's getting away!!
CHEP
CHEP
CHEP

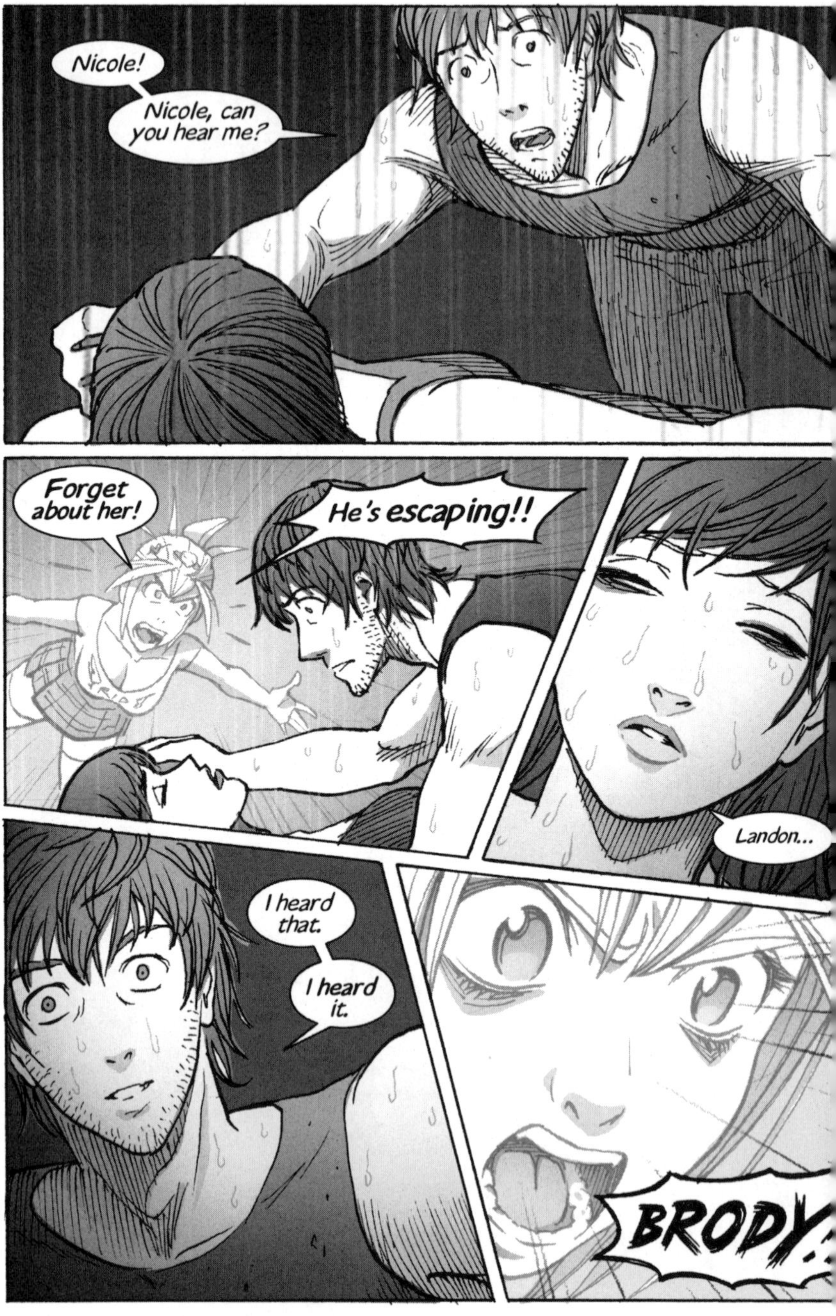
Nicole!
Nicole, can you hear me?
Forget about her!
He's escaping!!
Landon...
I heard that.
I heard it.
BRODY!

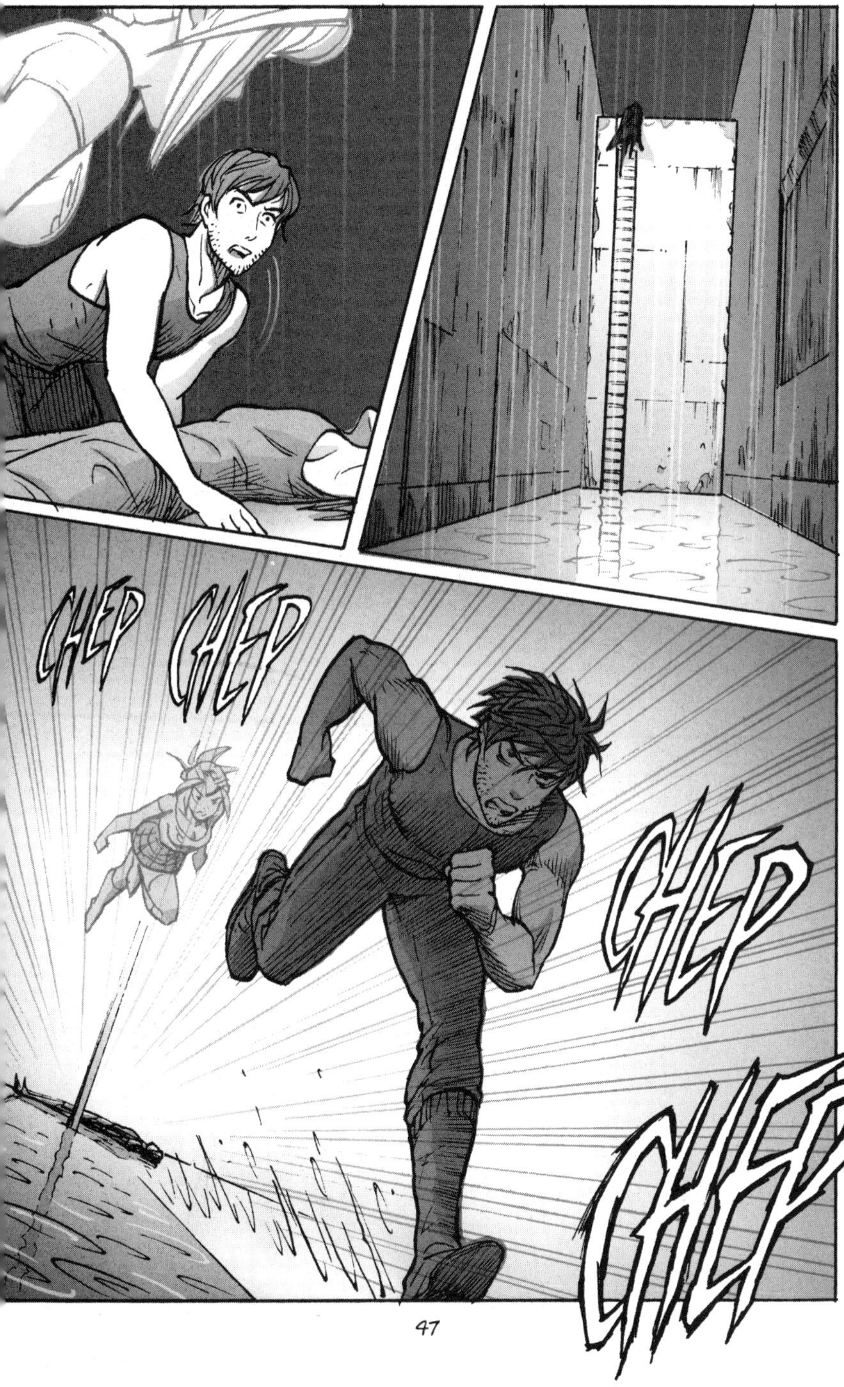
CHEP CHEP
CHEP
CHEP

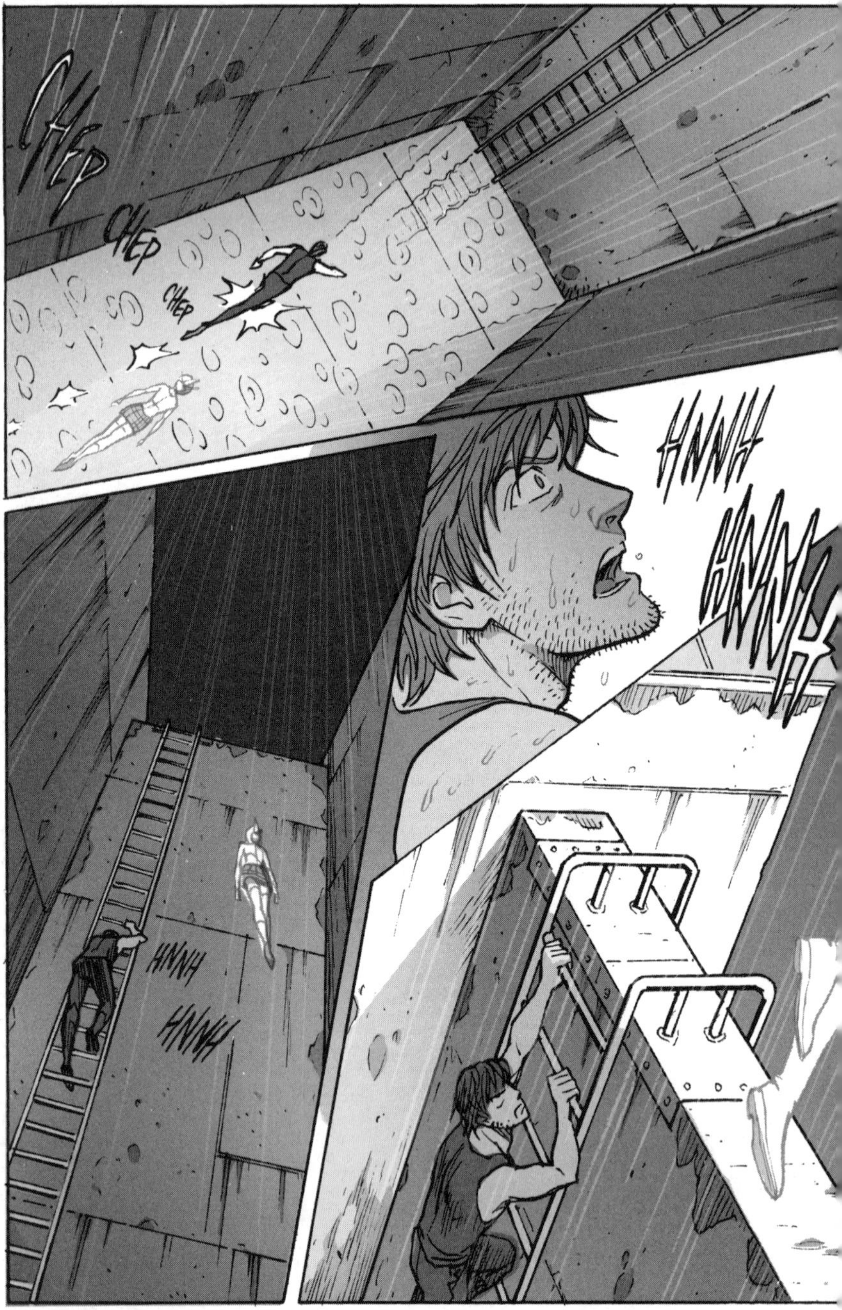
CHEP
CHEP
CHEP
HNH
HNH
HNH
HNH

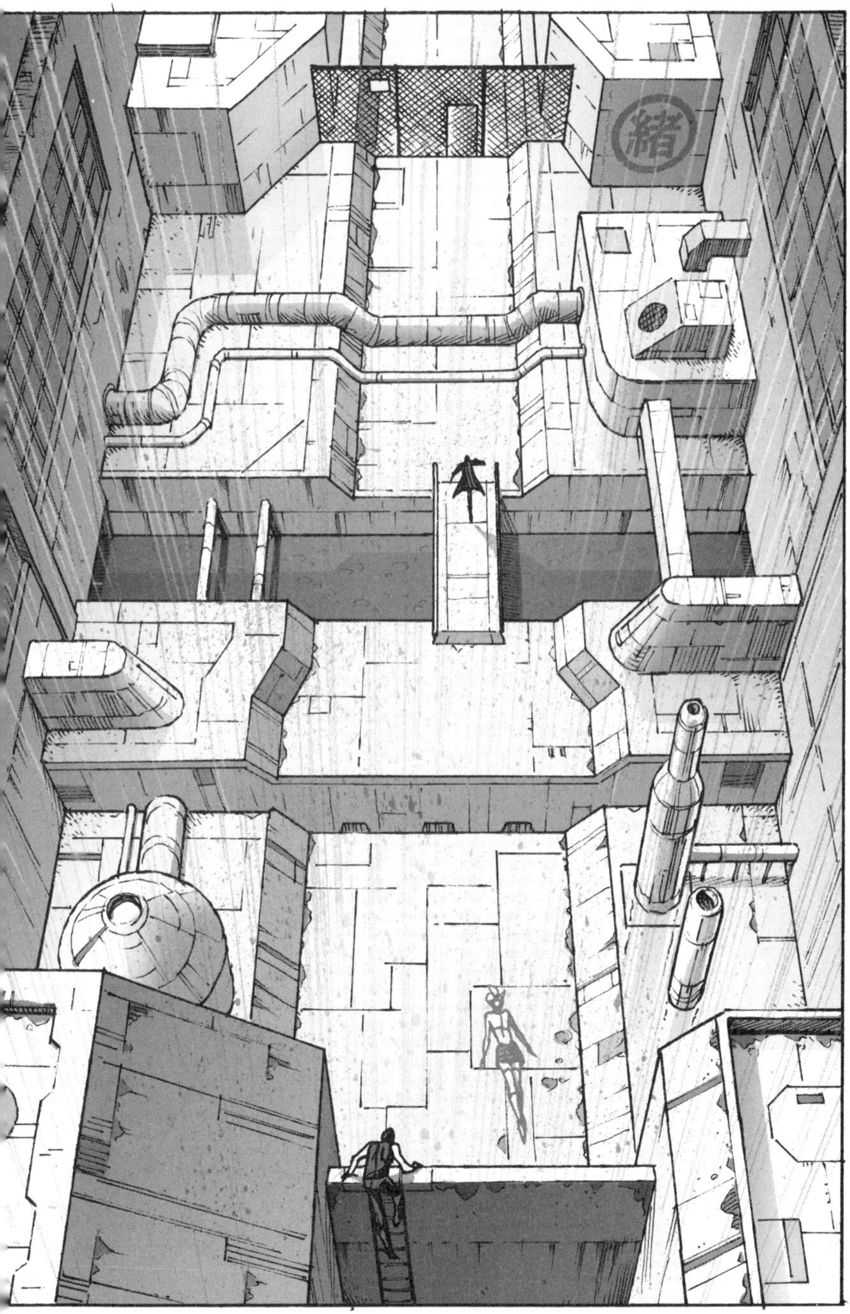

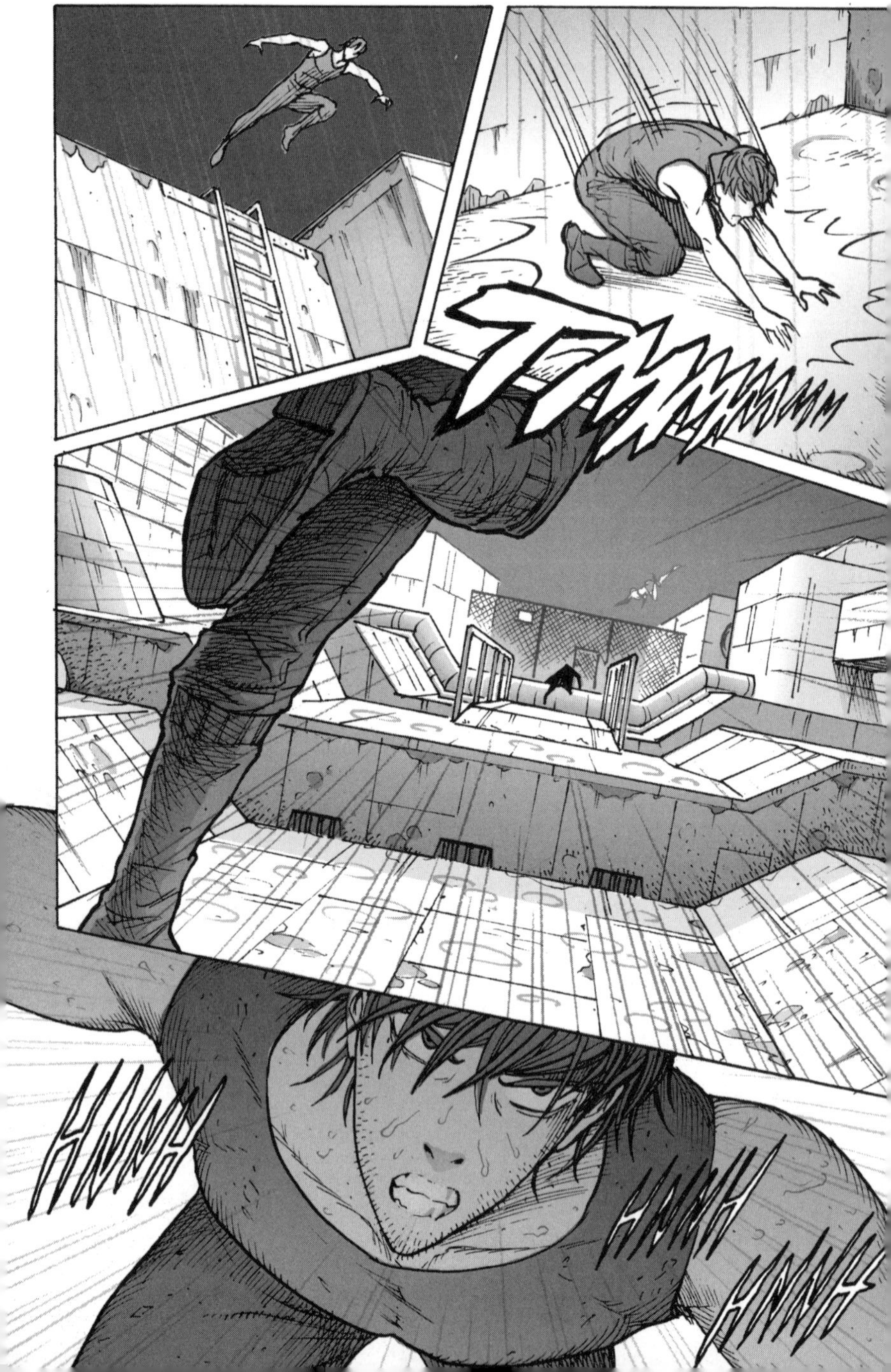
HNNH
HNNH
HNNH

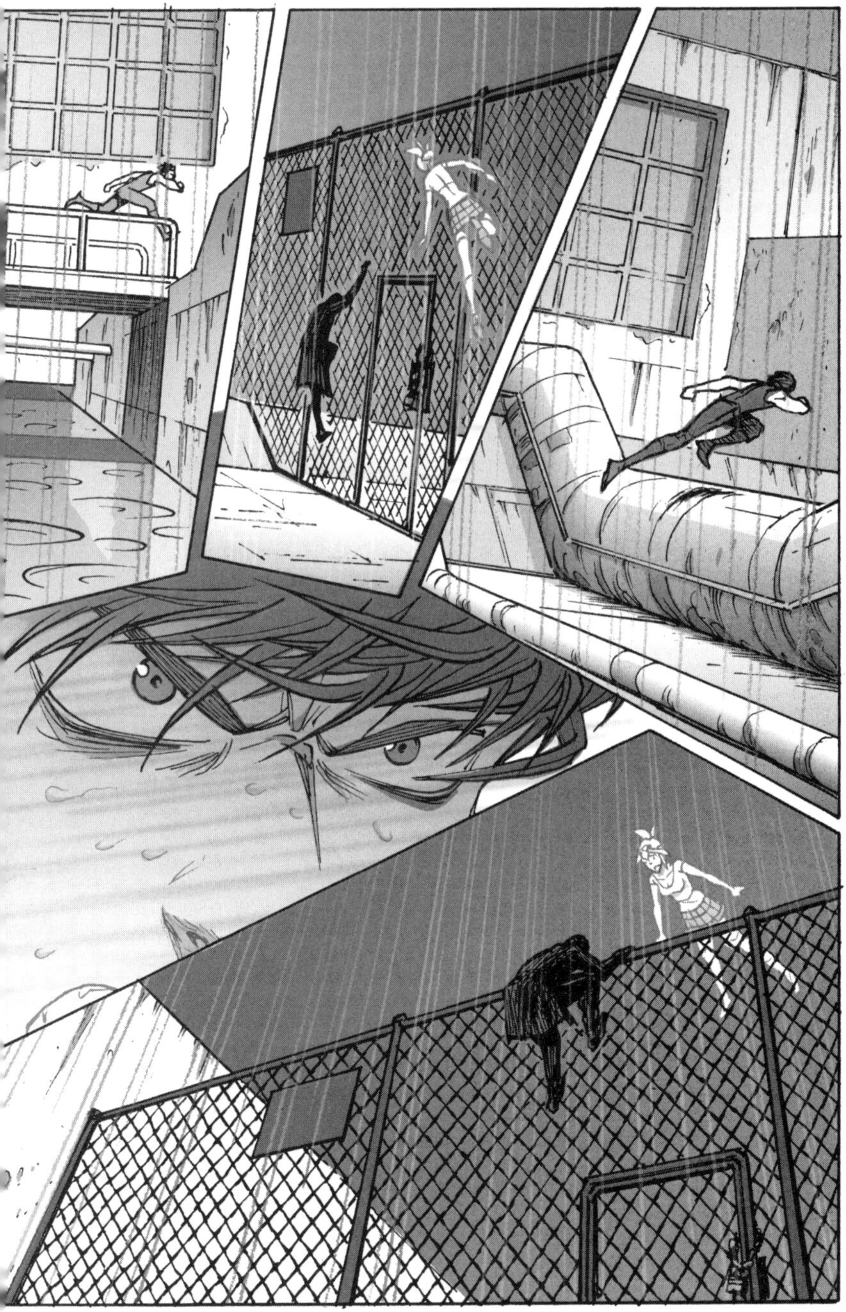

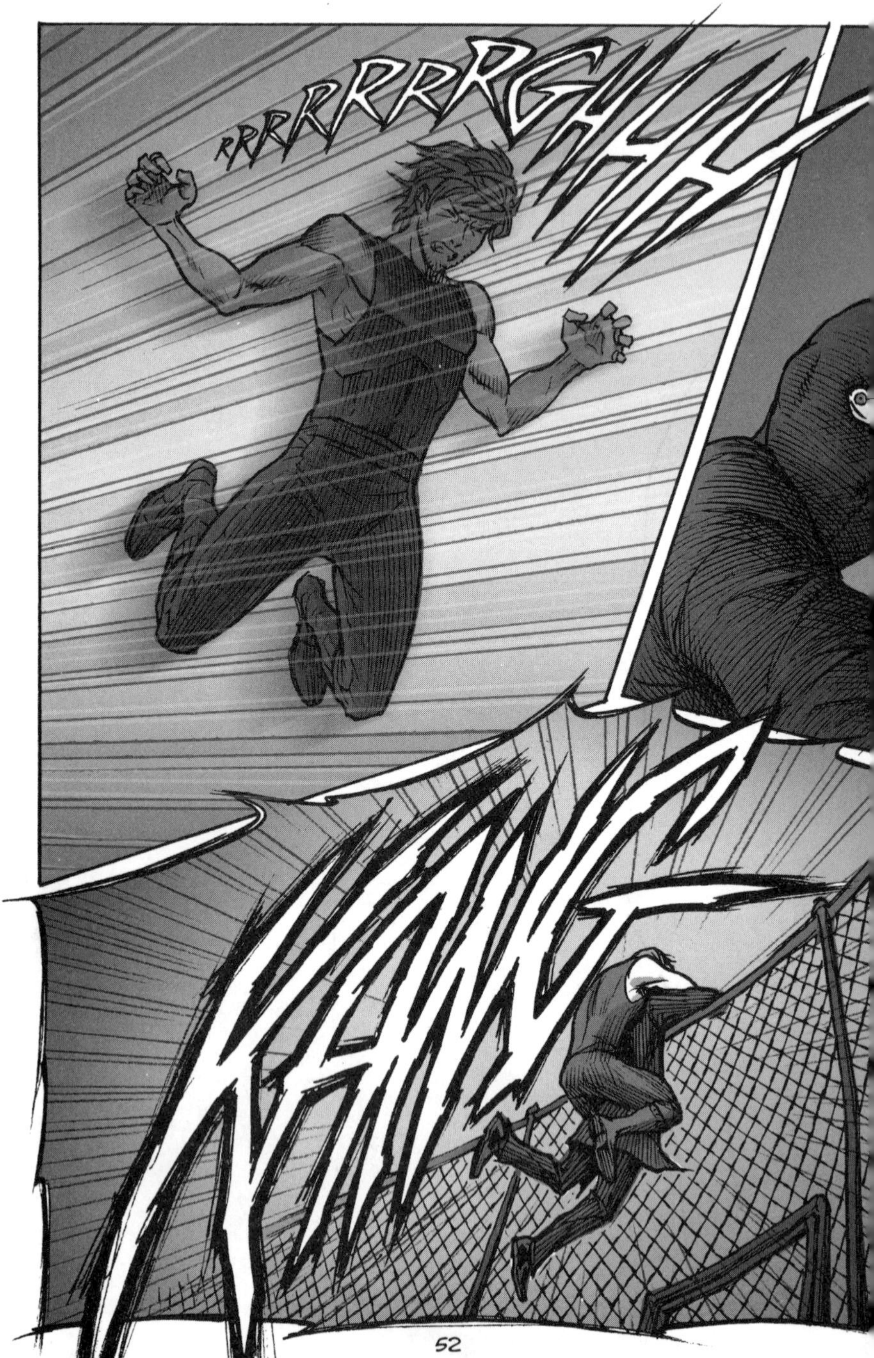

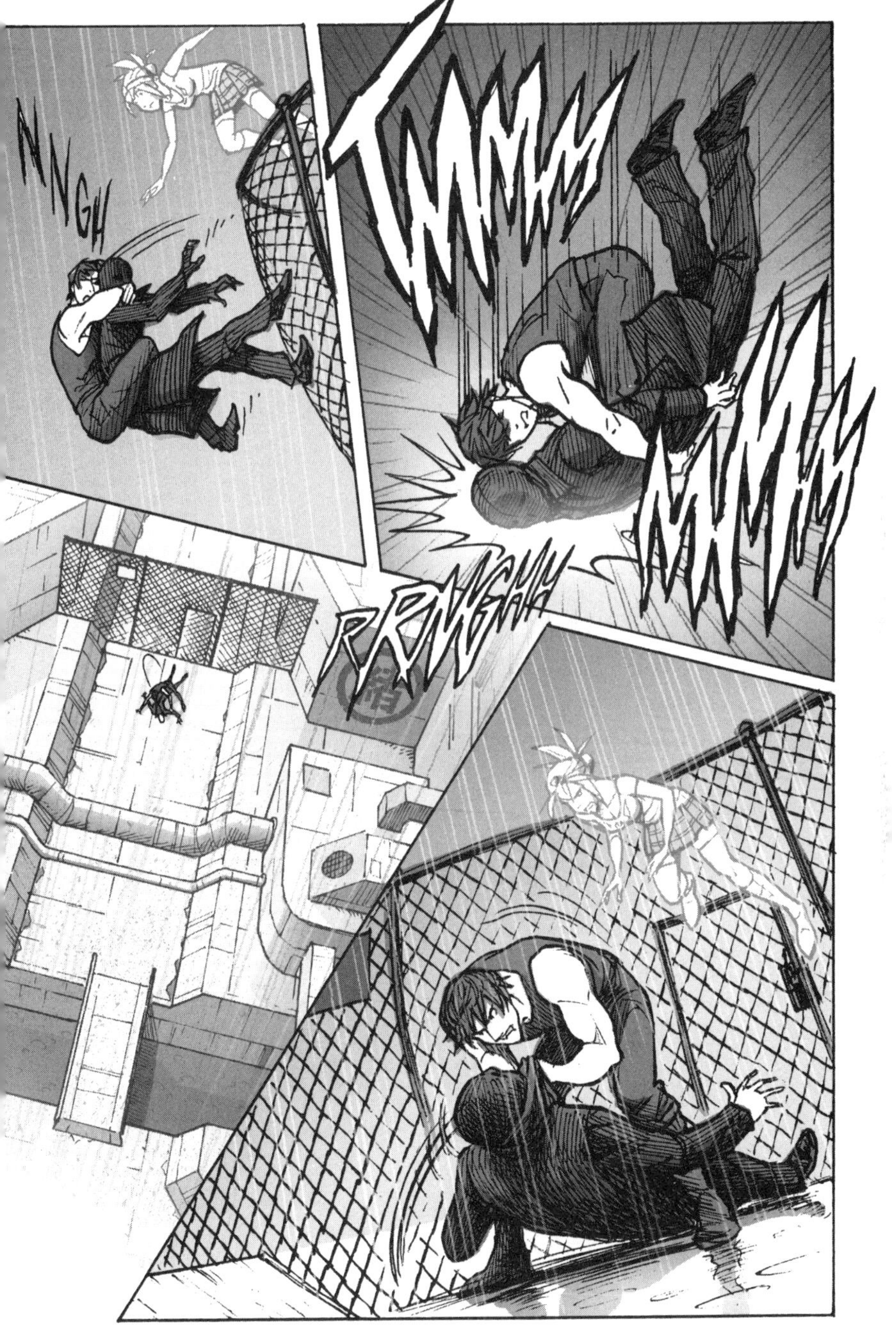
NNGH
TAMM
RRMSHH
MMM

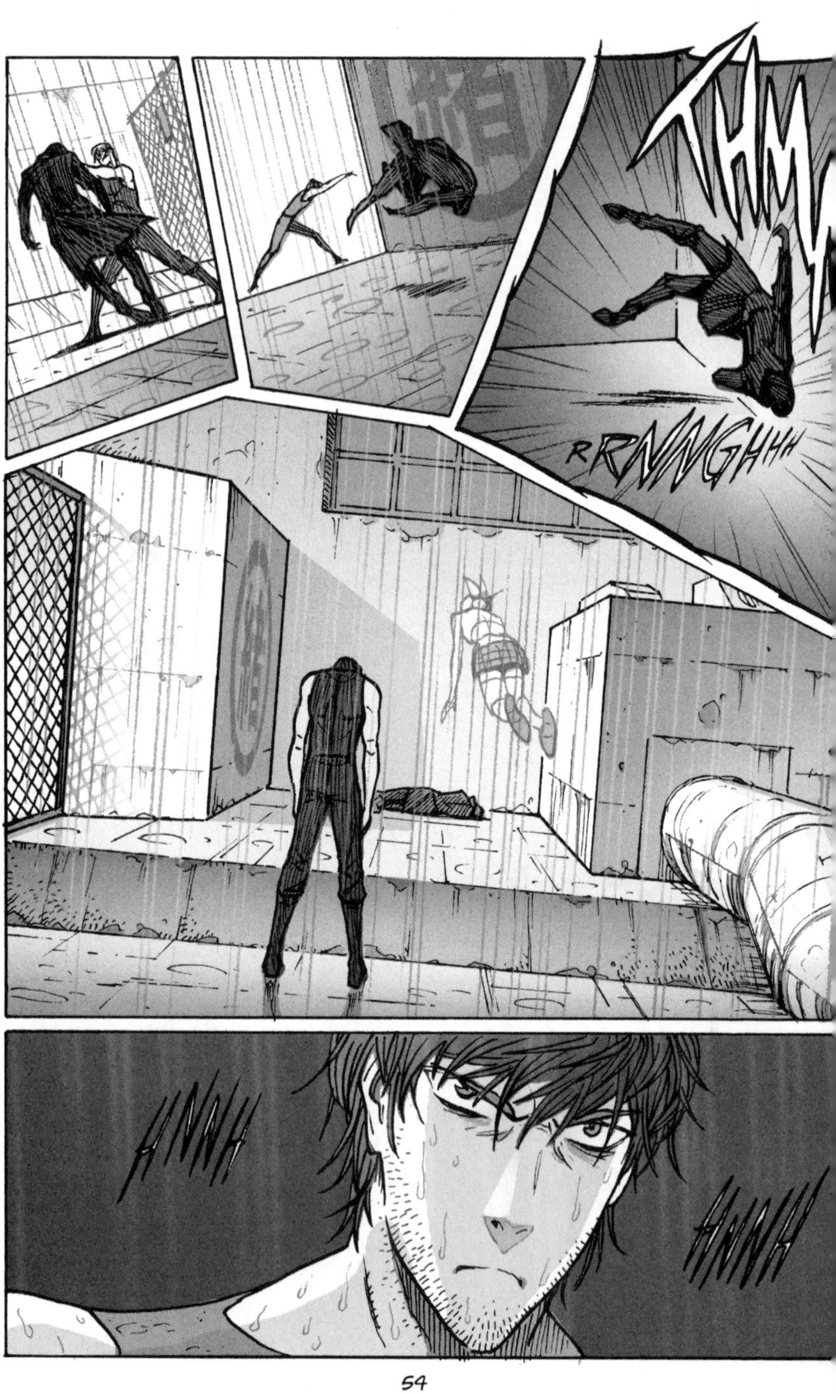
THAM
RRNNGHHH
HNNH
HNNH

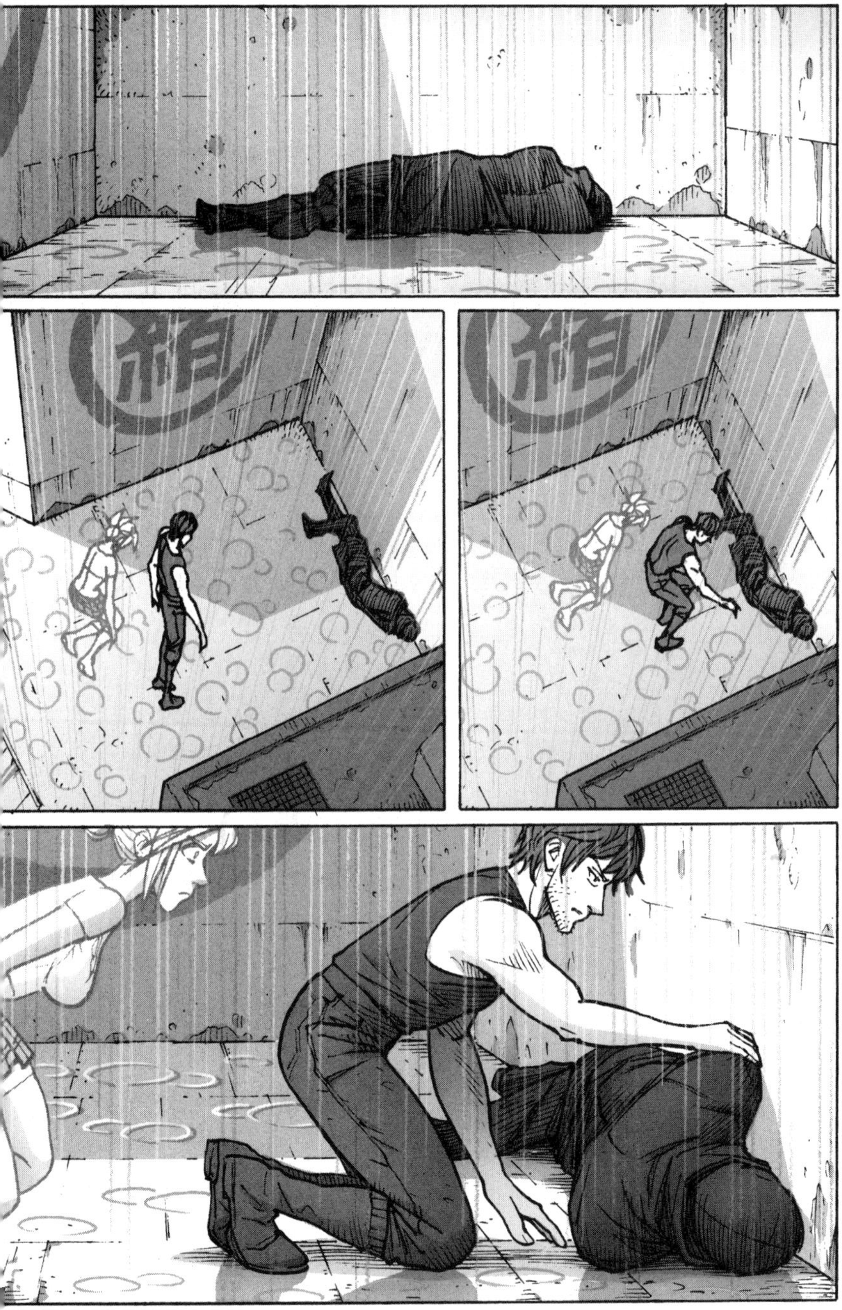

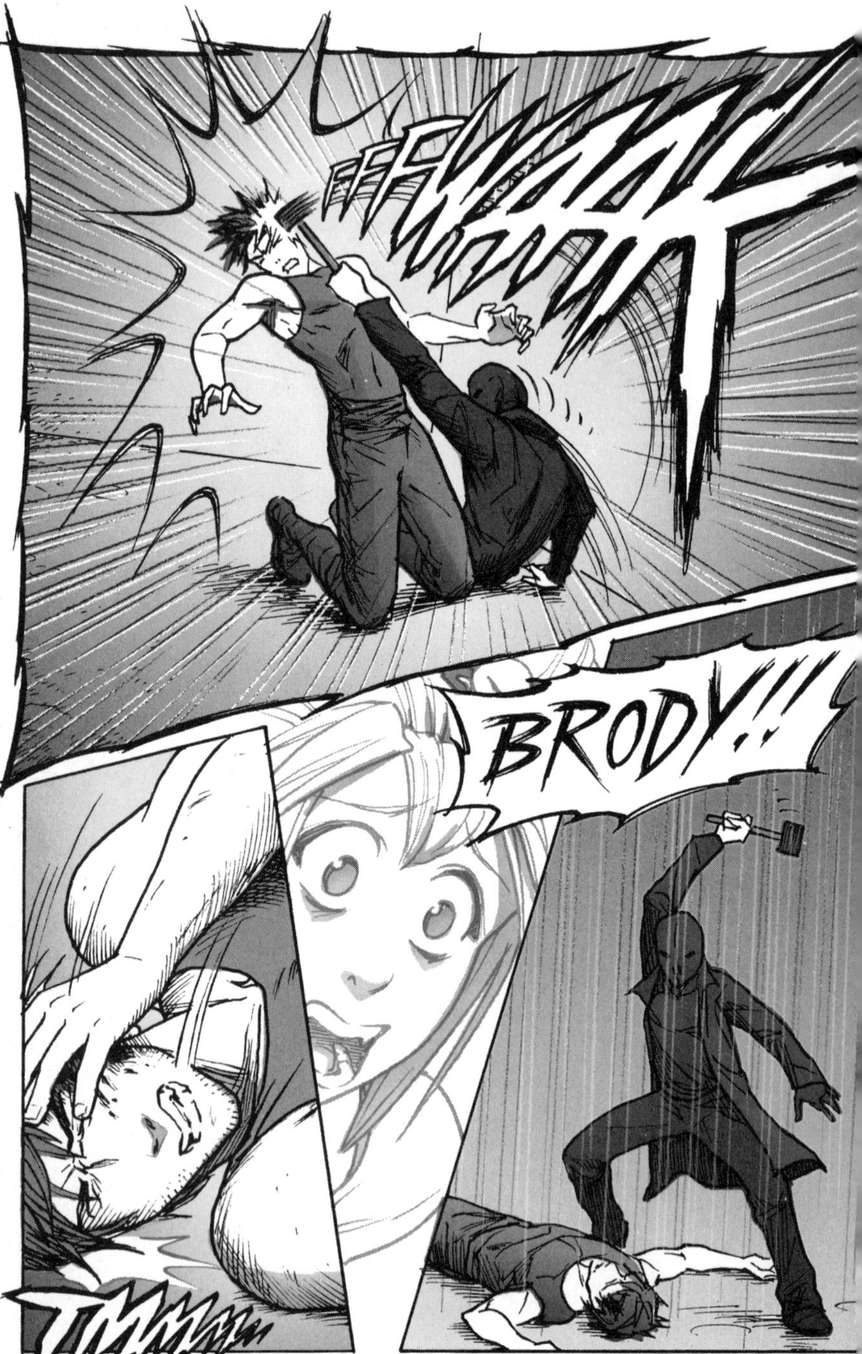
BRODY!!

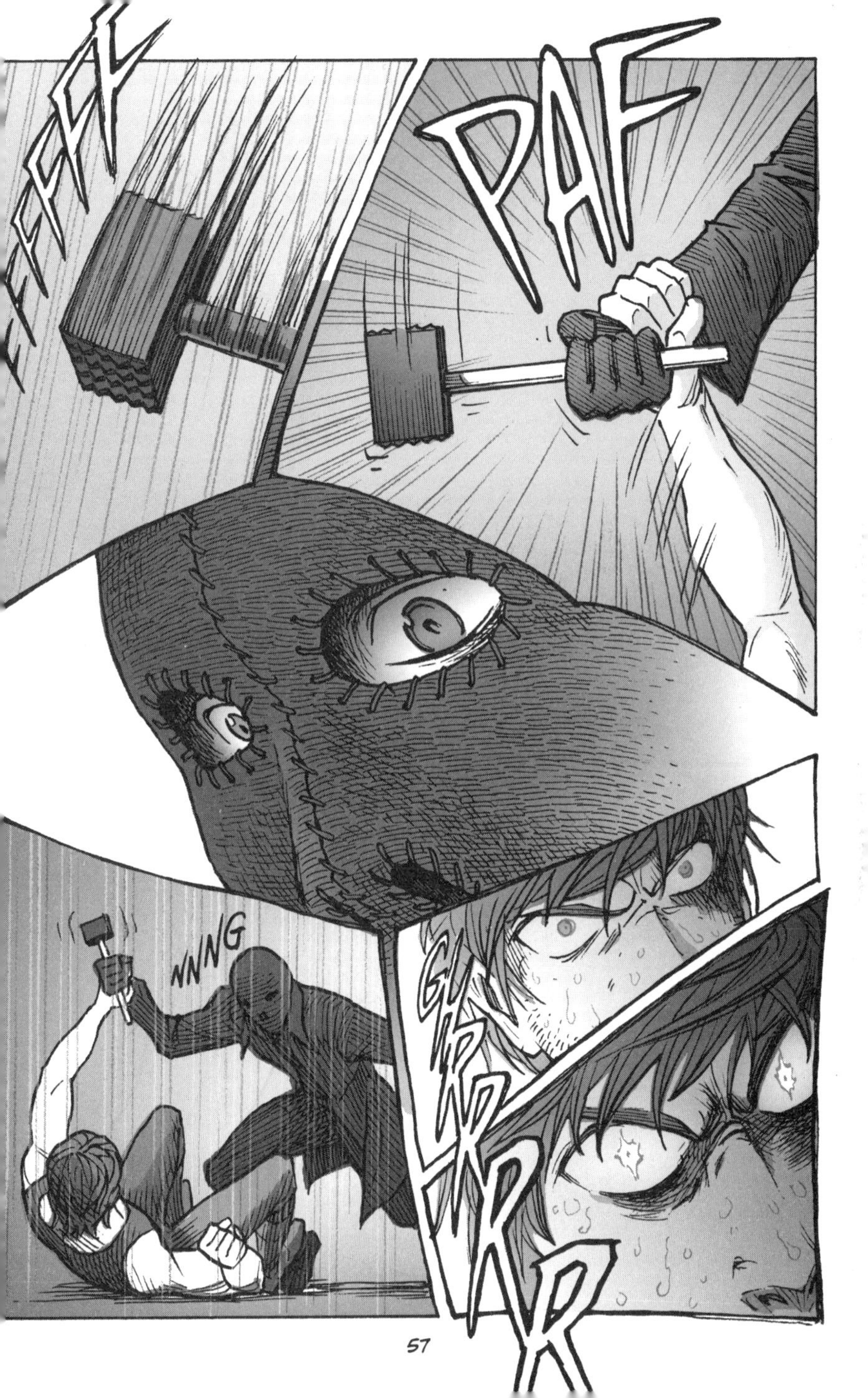
PAF
NNNG

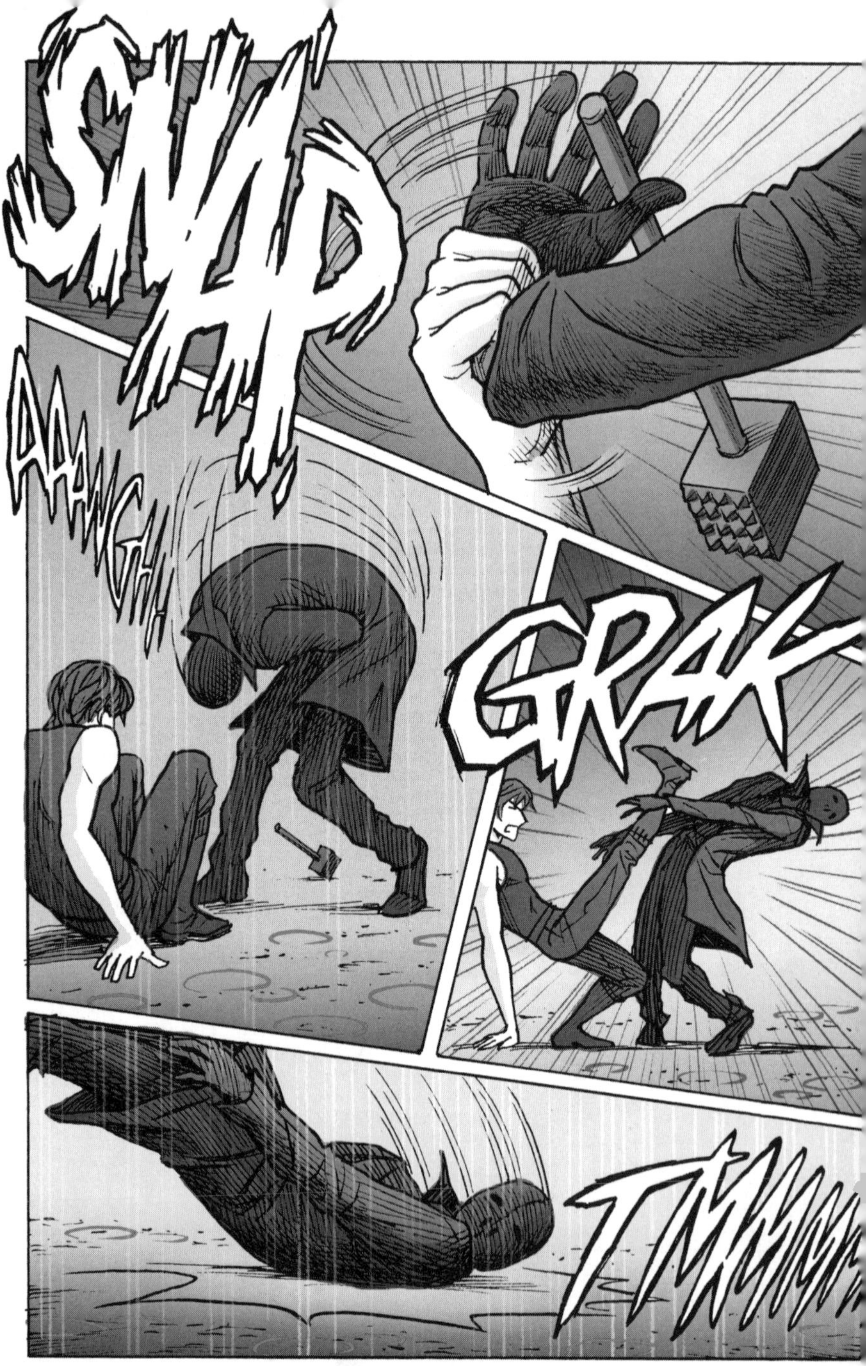
SNAP
AAAAAGTHH
GRAK
THMMM

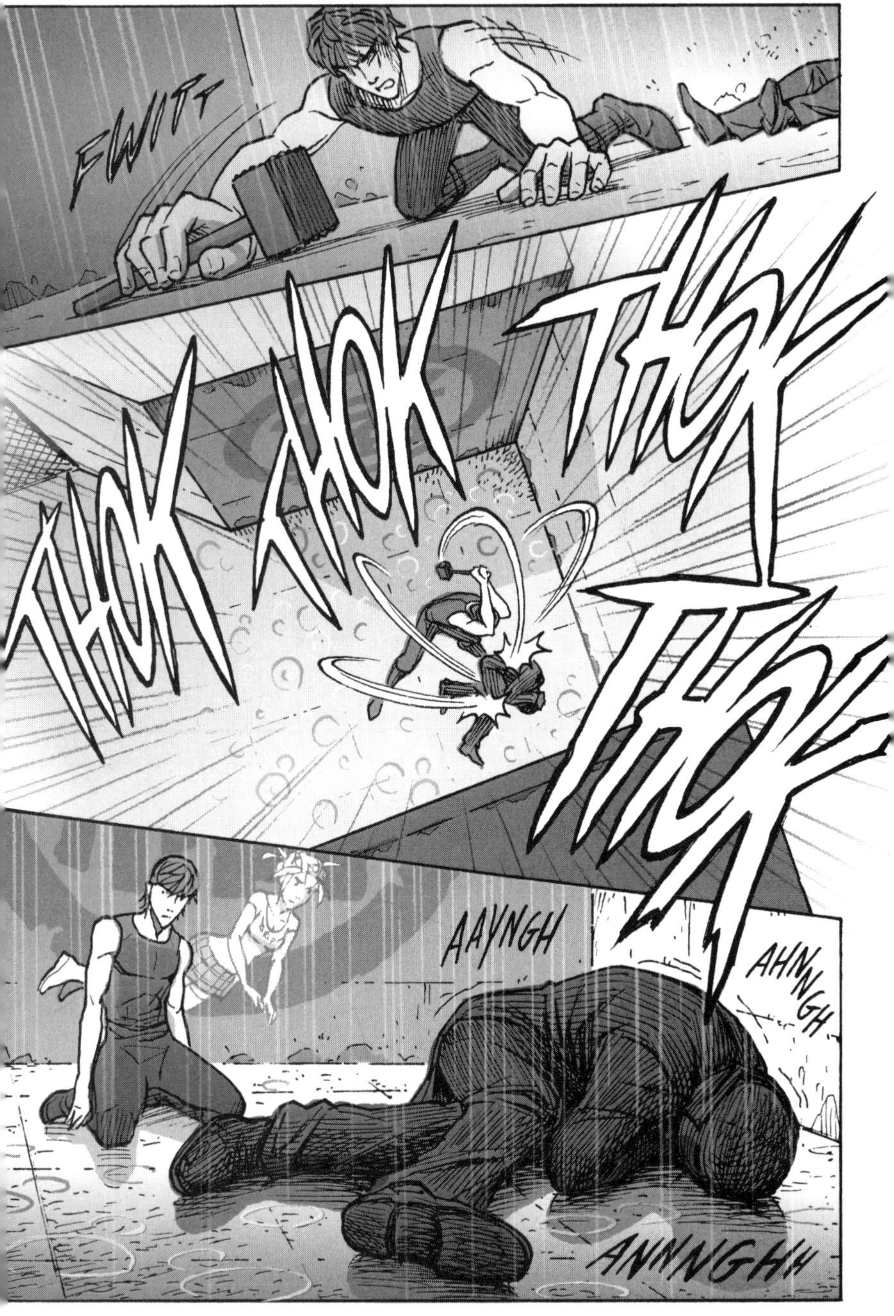
FWITT
THOK
THOK
THOK
THOK
AAYNGH
AHNNNGH
ANNNGHH

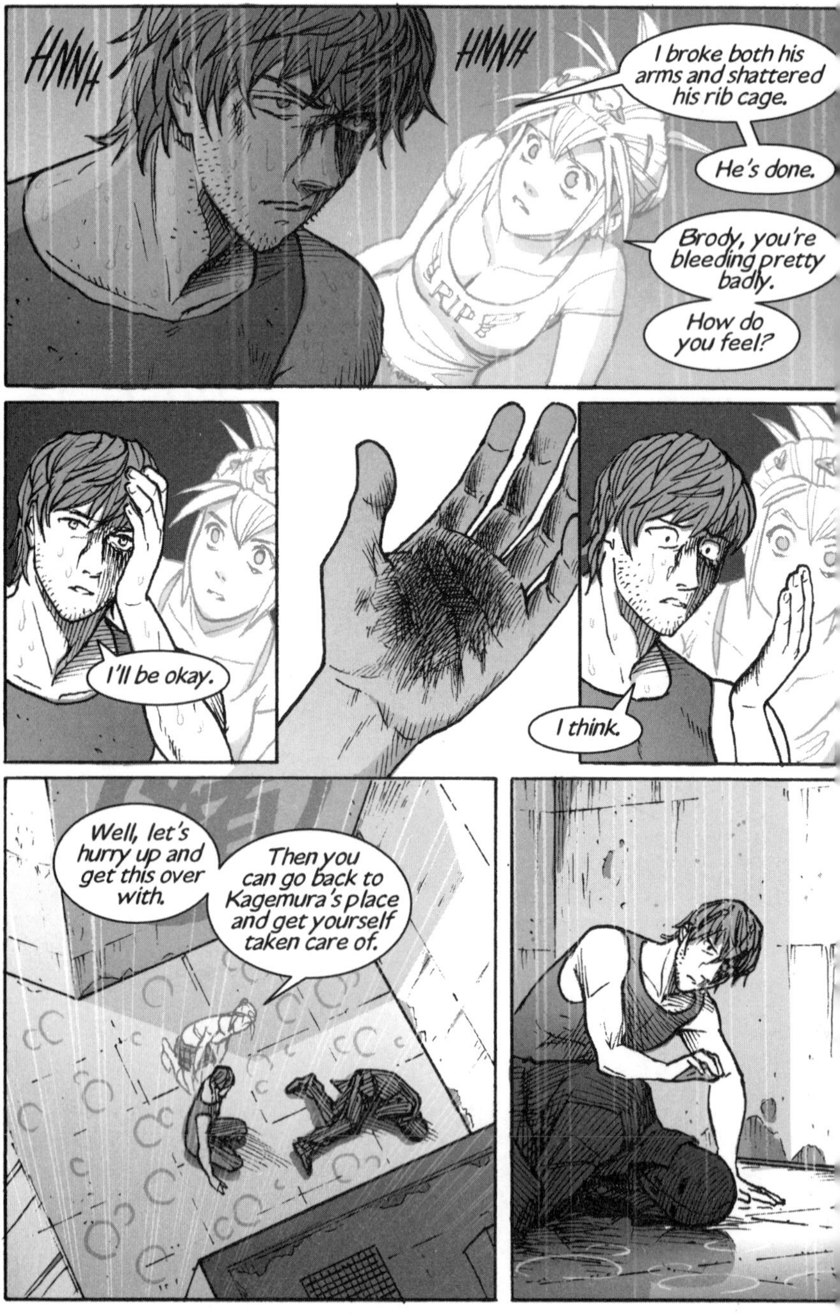
HNNH
HNNH
I broke both his arms and shattered his rib cage.
He's done.
Brody, you're bleeding pretty badly.
How do you feel?
I'll be okay.
I think.
Well, let's hurry up and get this over with.
Then you can go back to Kagemura's place and get yourself taken care of.

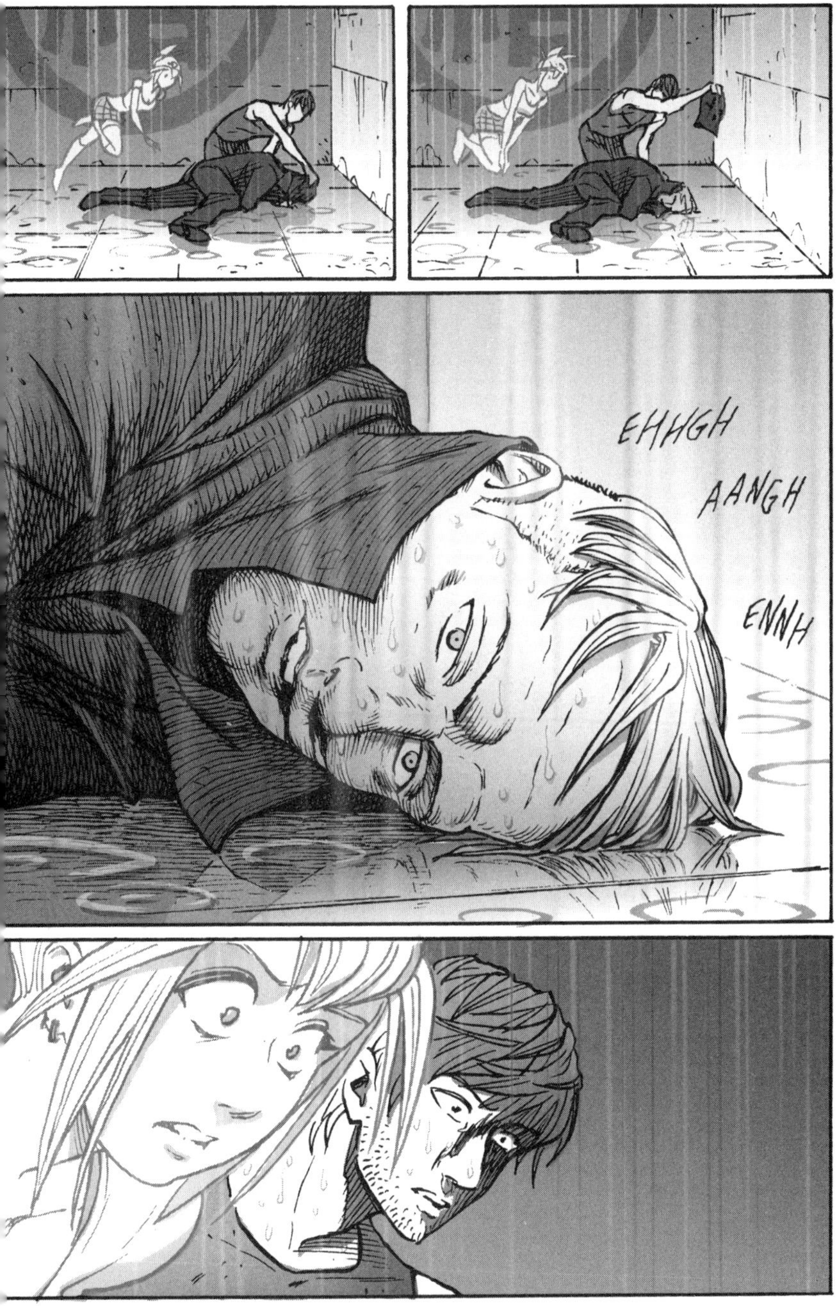
EHHGH
AANGH
ENNH

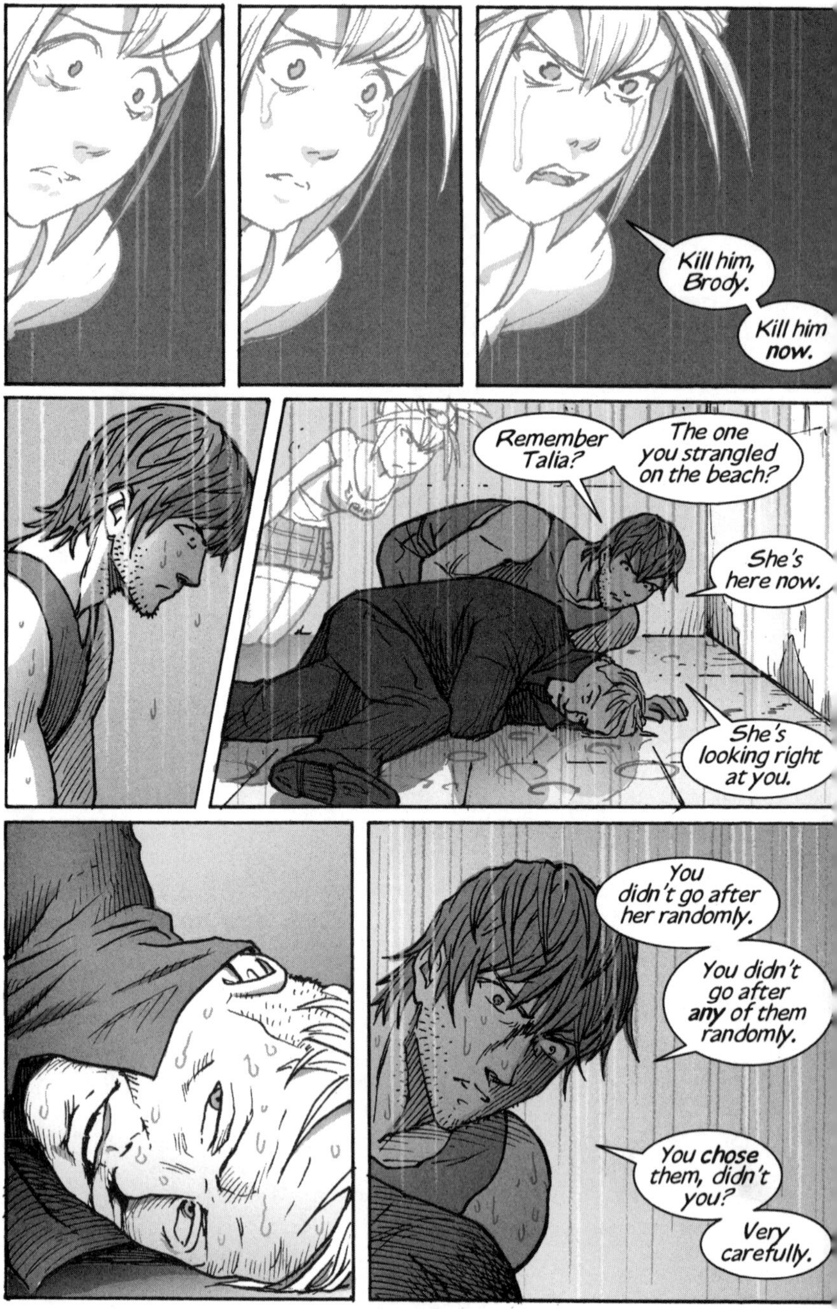
Kill him, Brody.
Kill him now.
Remember Talia?
The one you strangled on the beach?
She's here now.
She's looking right at you.
You didn't go after her randomly.
You didn't go after any of them randomly.
You chose them, didn't you?
Very carefully.

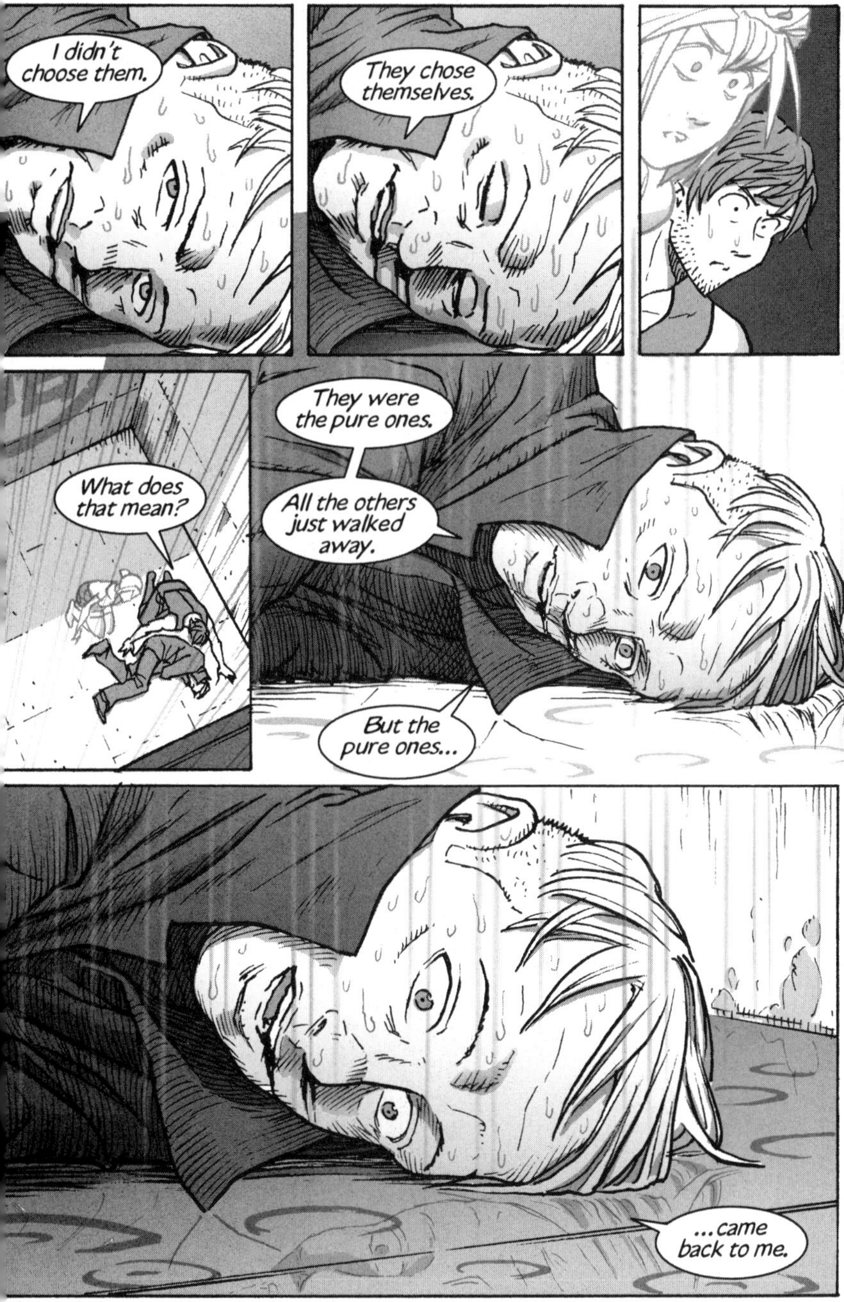
I didn't choose them.
They chose themselves.
They were the pure ones.
What does that mean?
All the others just walked away.
But the pure ones...
...came back to me.

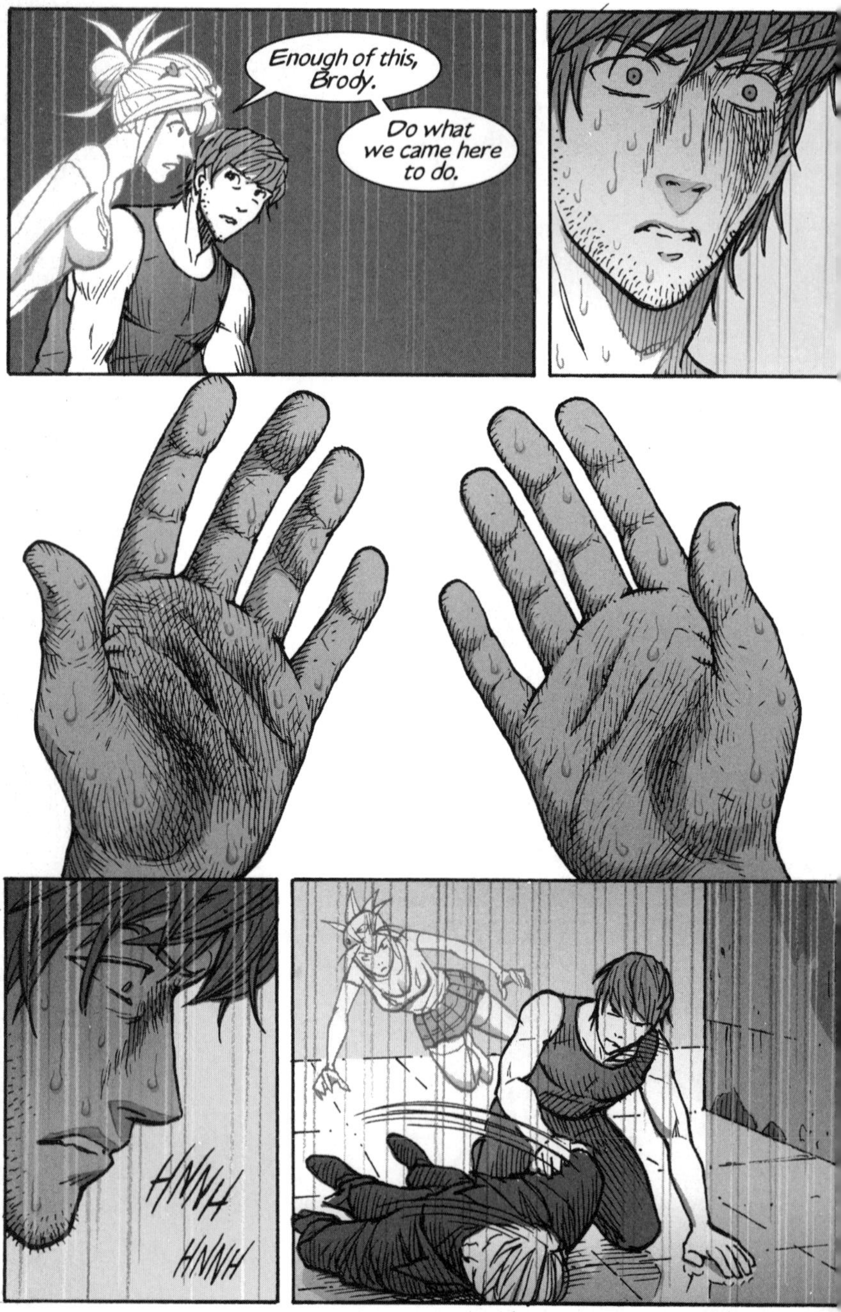
Enough of this, Brody.
Do what we came here to do.
HNNH
HNNH

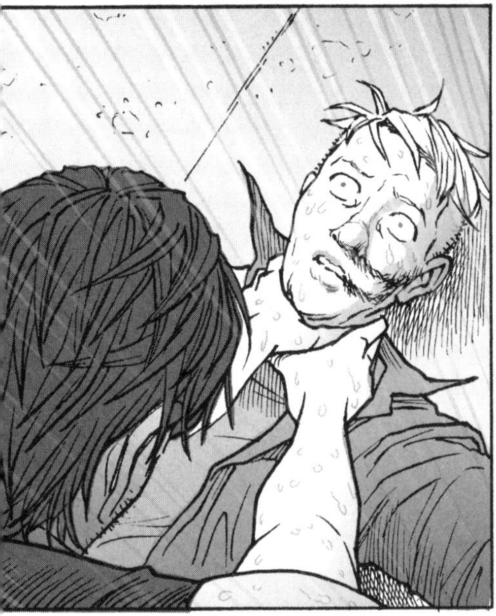

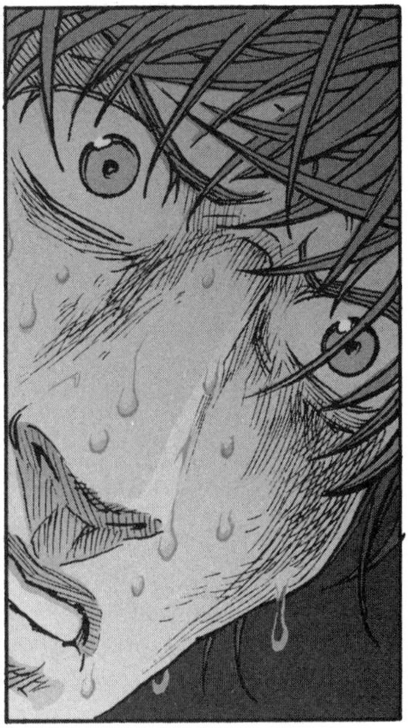

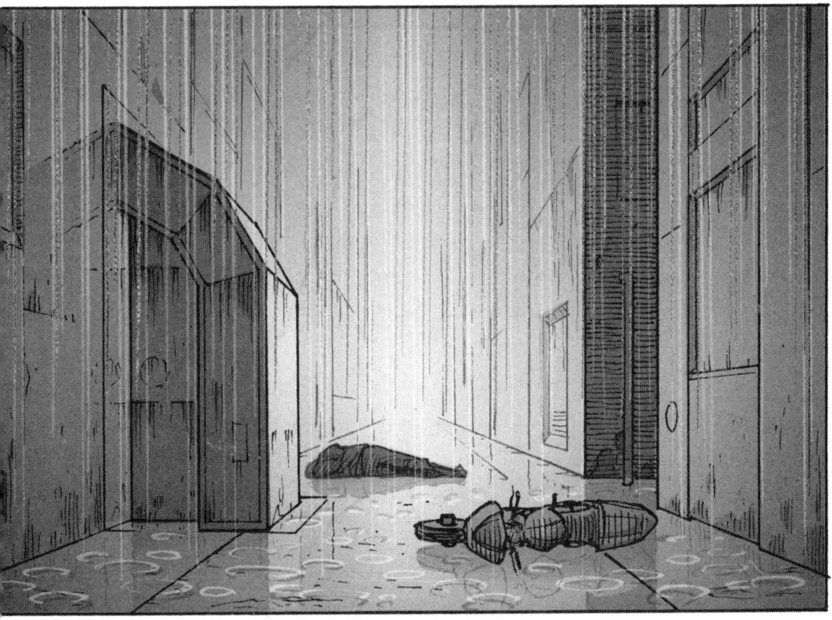

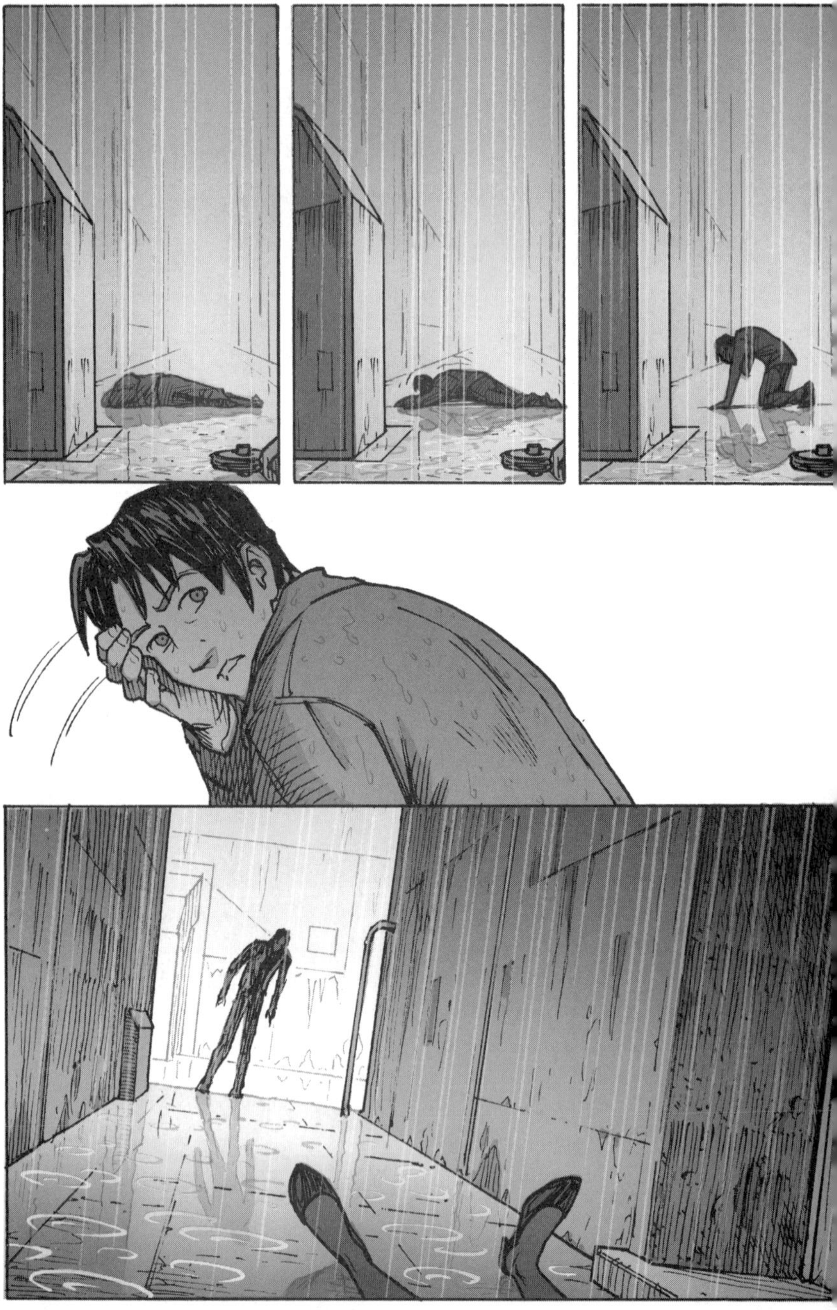

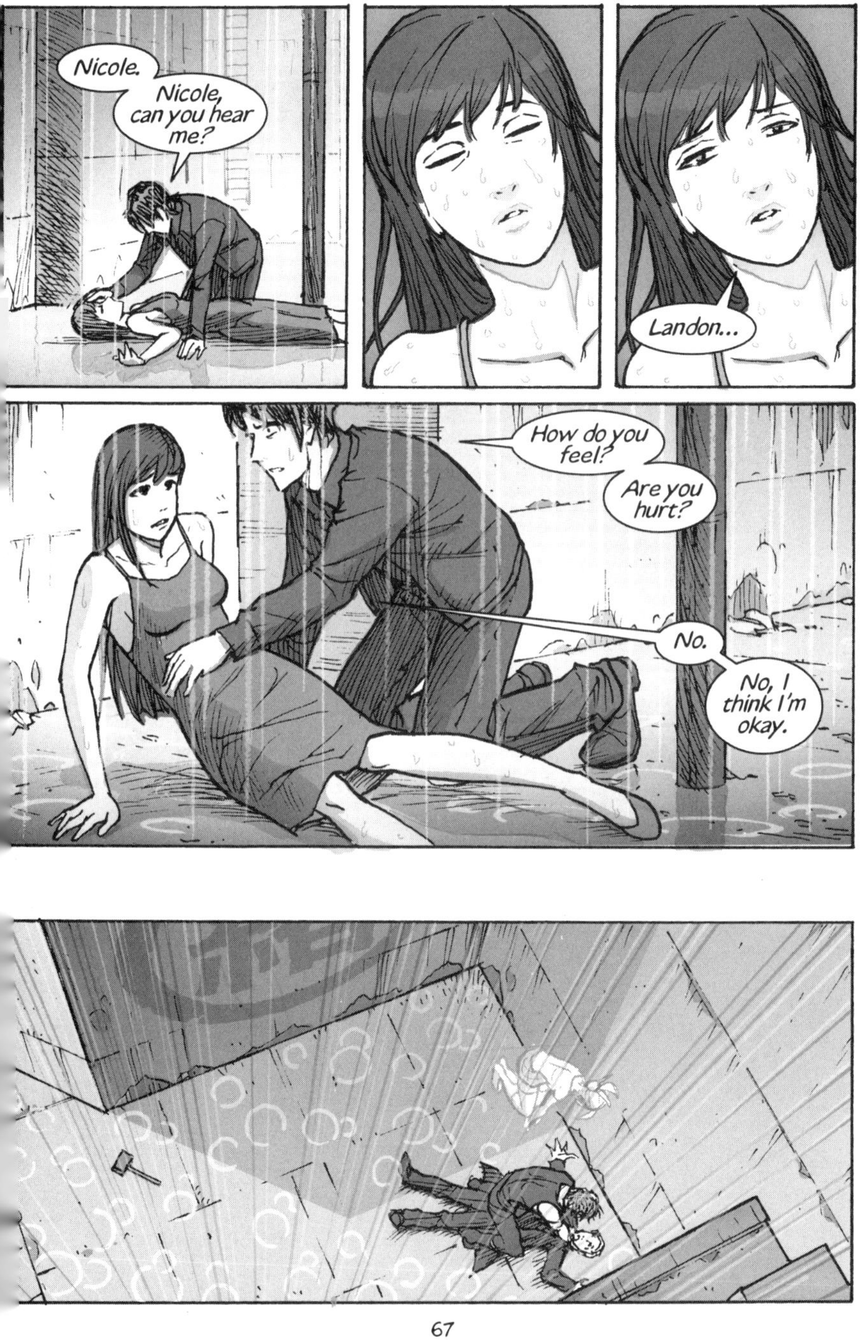
Nicole.
Nicole, can you hear me?
Landon...
How do you feel?
Are you hurt?
No.
No, I think I'm okay.

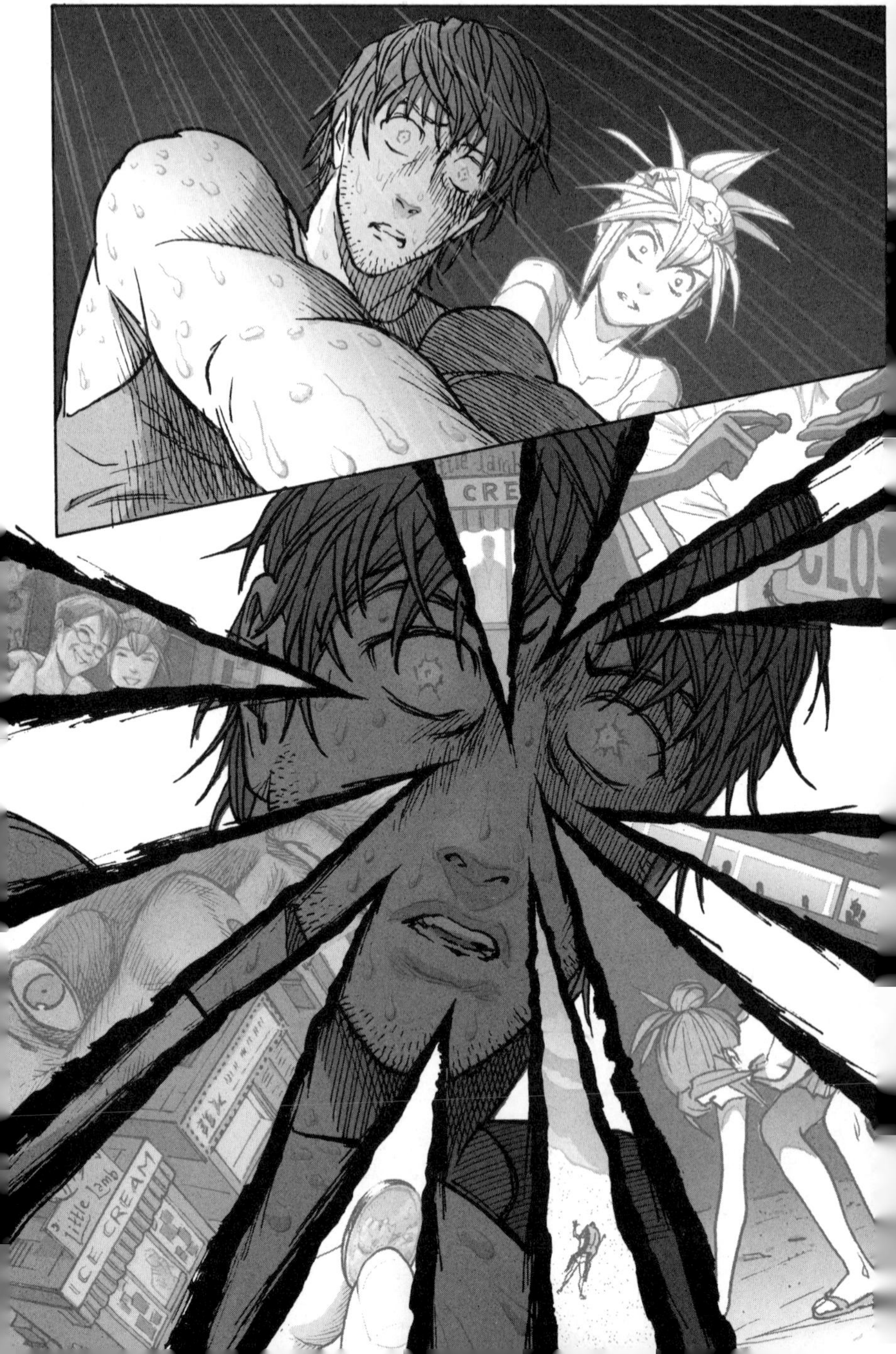
little Lamb
ICE CREAM

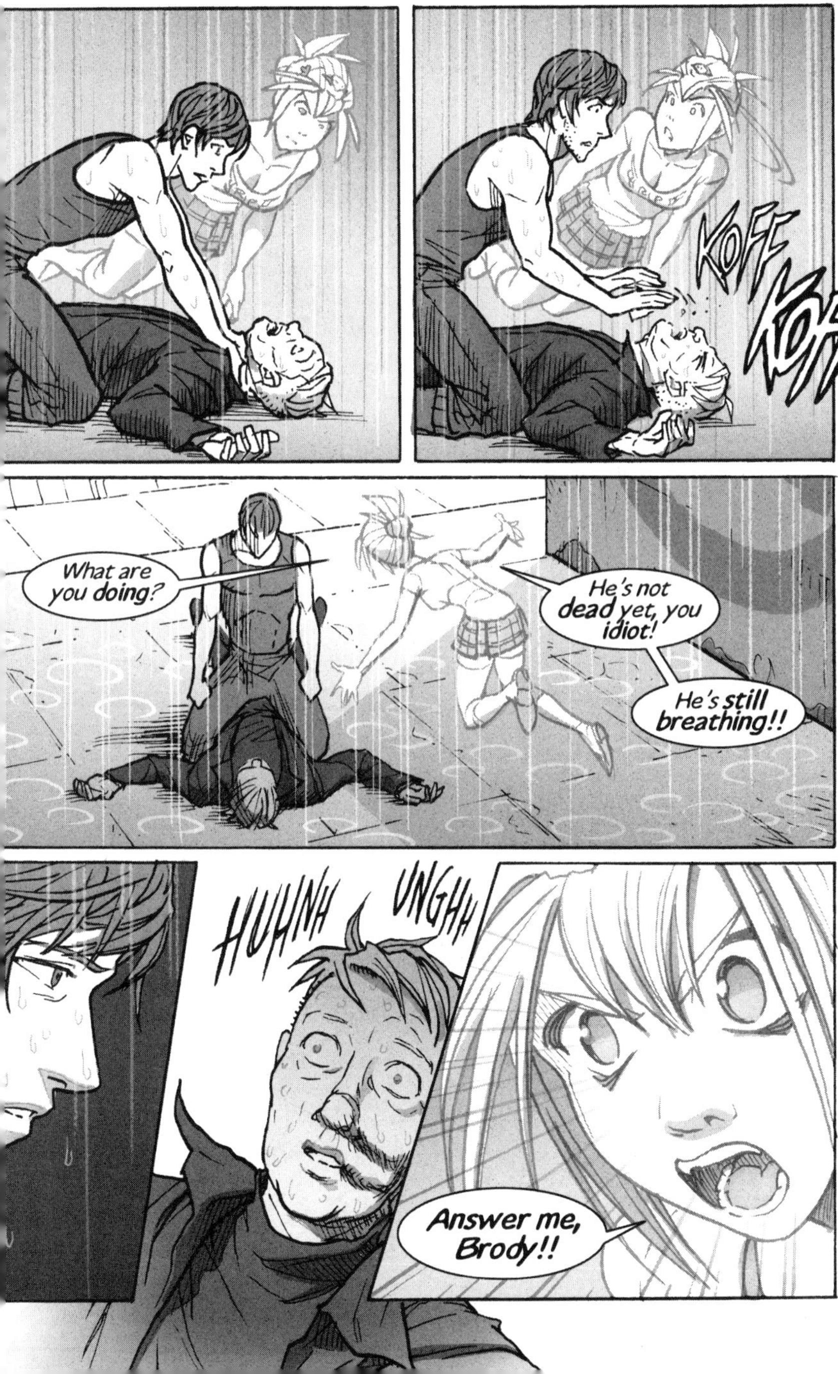
KOFF
KOFF
What are you doing?
He's not dead yet, you idiot!
He's still breathing!!
HUHNH
UNGHH
Answer me, Brody!!

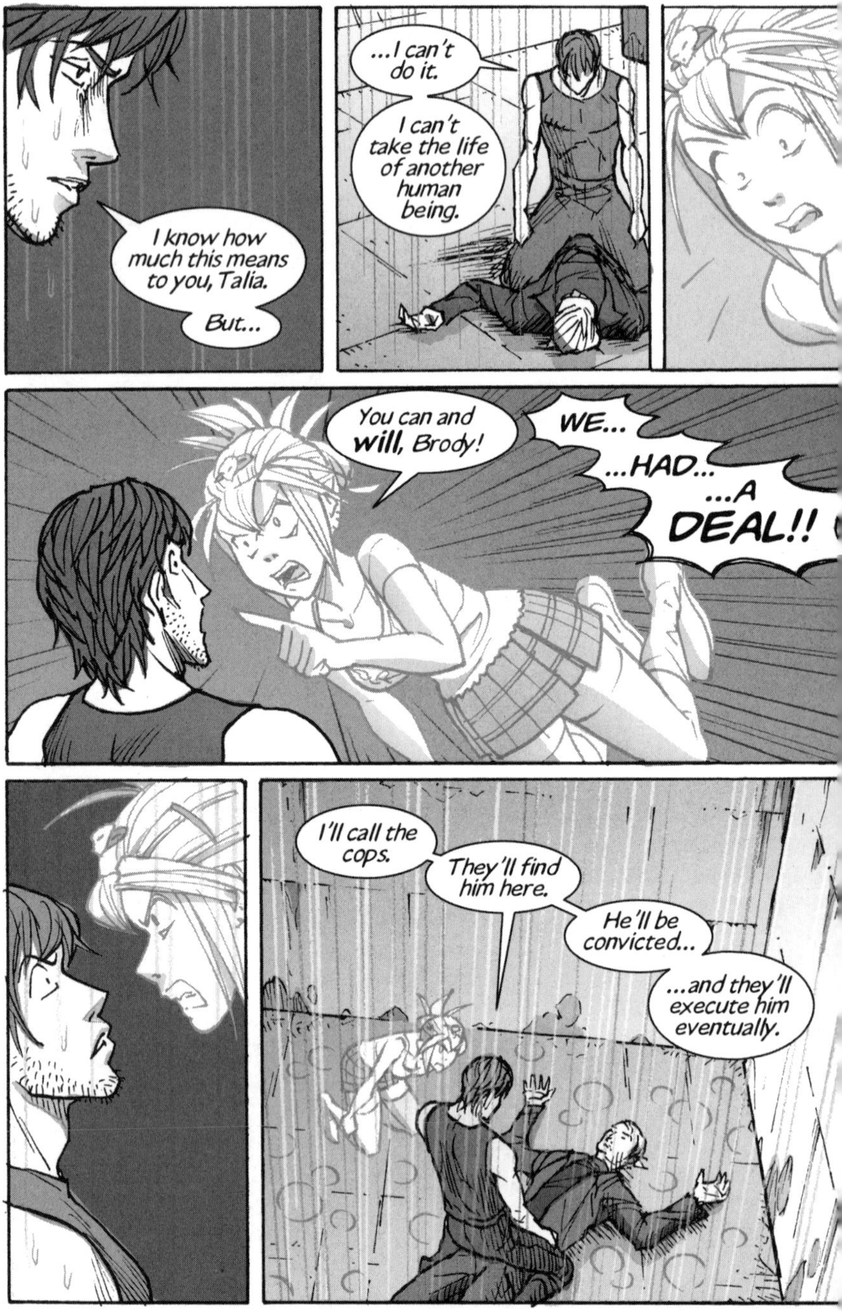
I know how much this means to you, Talia.
But...
...I can't do it.
I can't take the life of another human being.
You can and will, Brody!
WE...
...HAD...
...A DEAL!!
I'll call the cops.
They'll find him here.
He'll be convicted...
...and they'll execute him eventually.

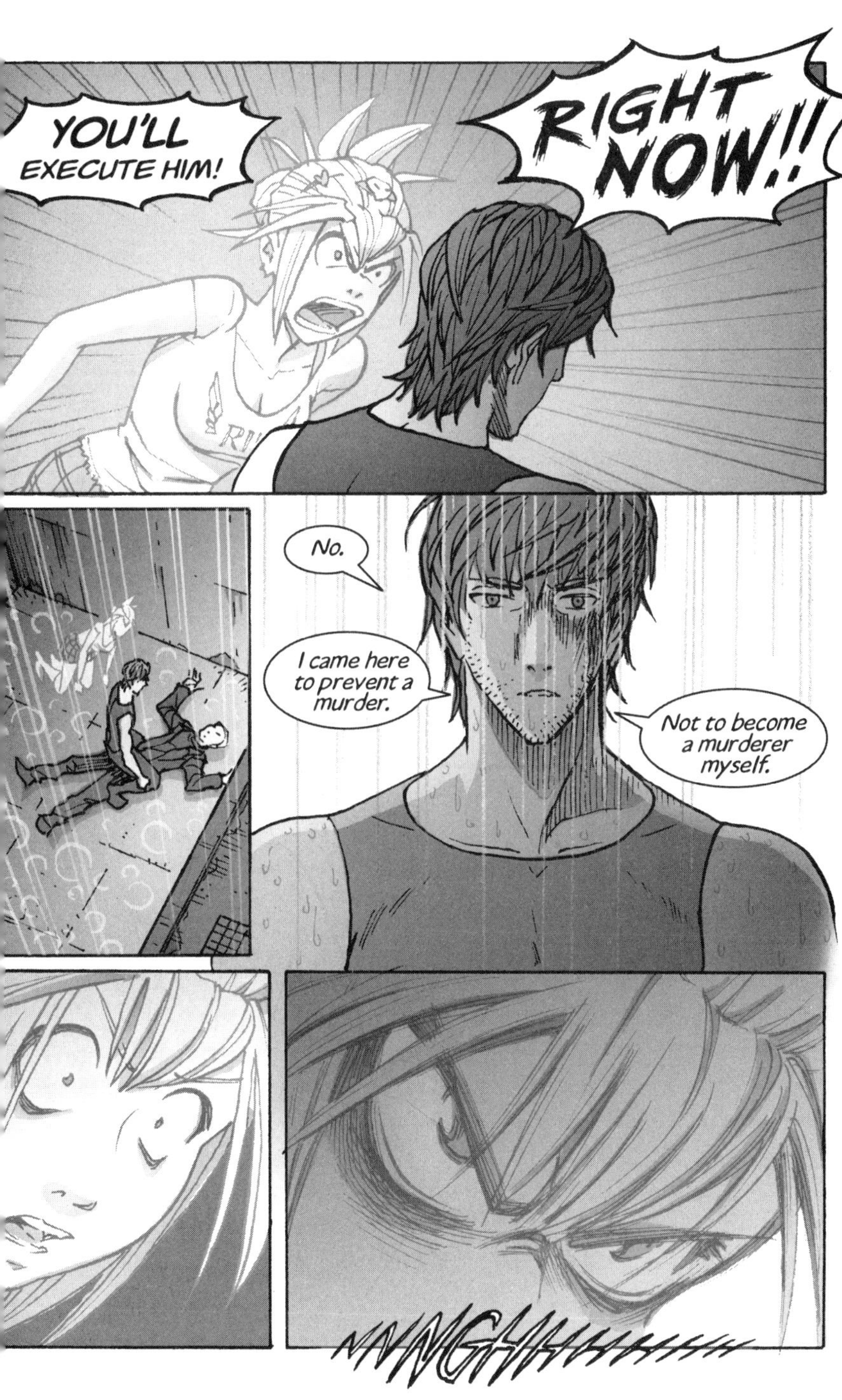
YOU'LL EXECUTE HIM!
RIGHT NOW!!
No.
I came here to prevent a murder.
Not to become a murderer myself.
NNNGHHHHHHHHH

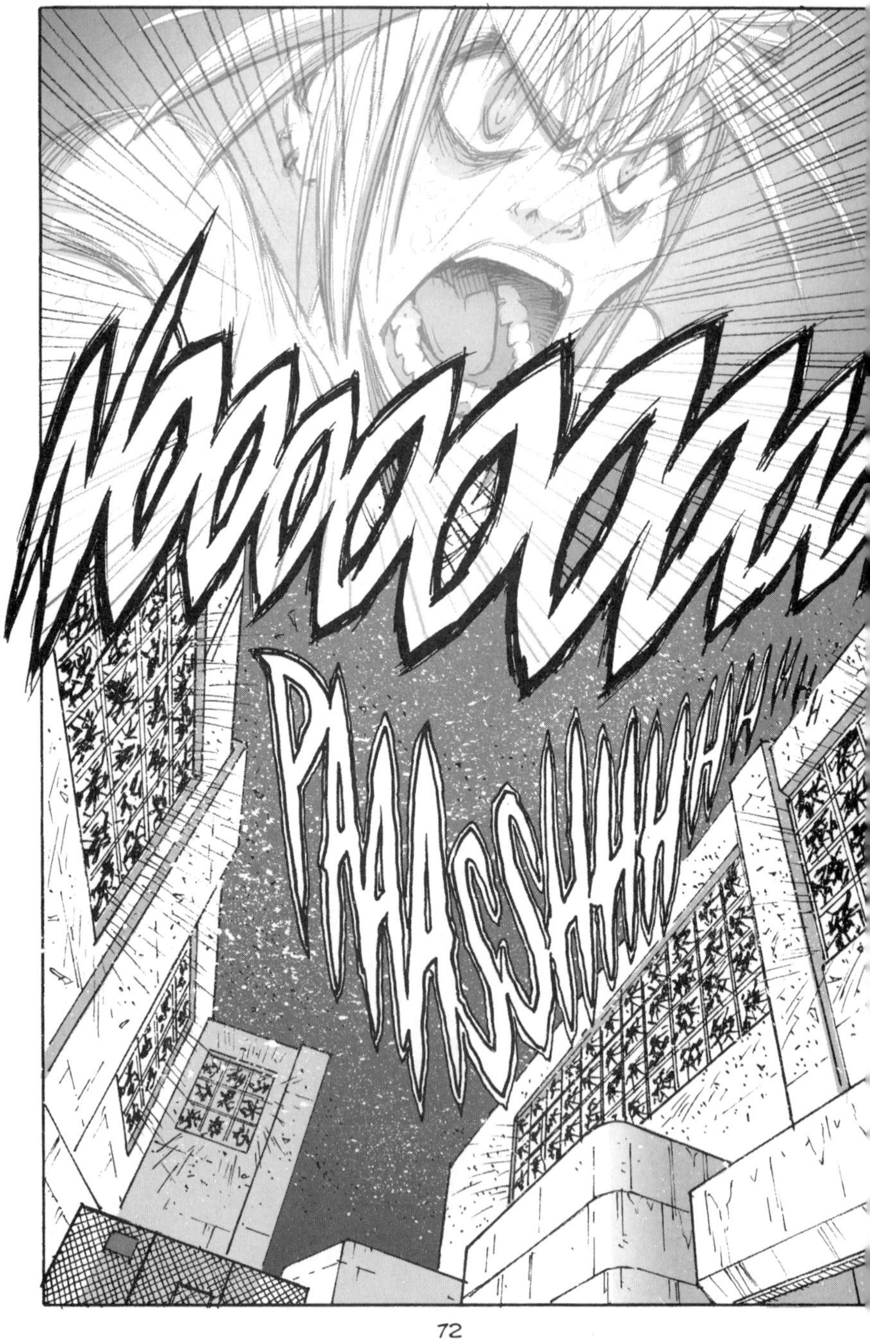
PAASHAAAH

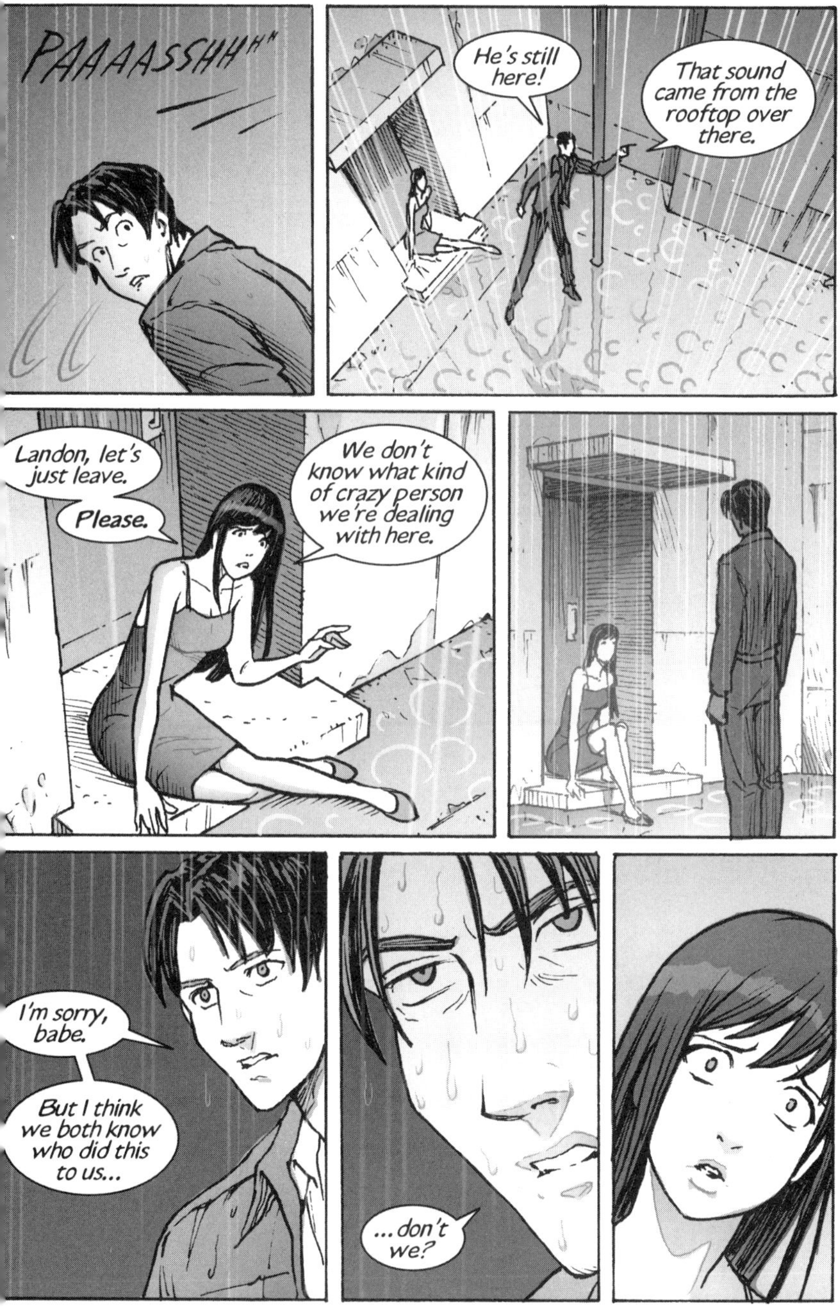
PAAAASSHH
He's still here!
That sound came from the rooftop over there.
Landon, let's just leave.
Please.
We don't know what kind of crazy person we're dealing with here.
I'm sorry, babe.
But I think we both know who did this to us...
...don't we?

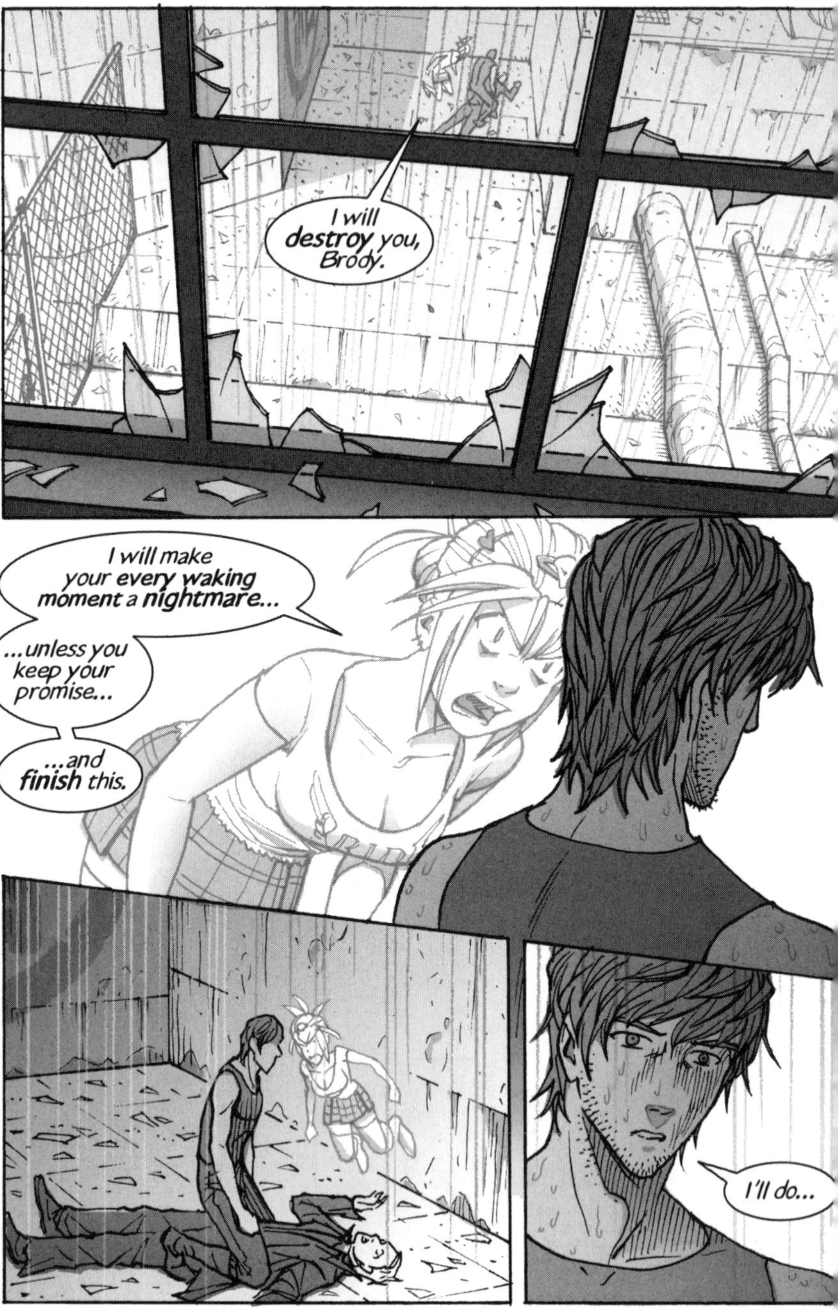
I will destroy you, Brody.
I will make your every waking moment a nightmare...
...unless you keep your promise...
...and finish this.
I'll do...

...what Kagemura trained me to do.

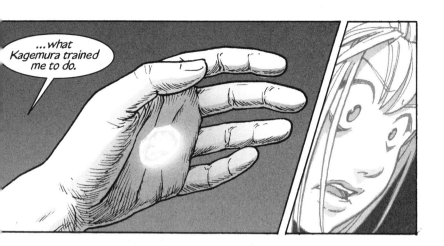

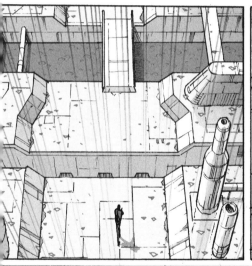

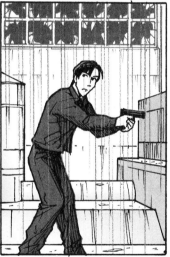

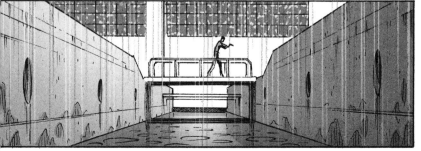

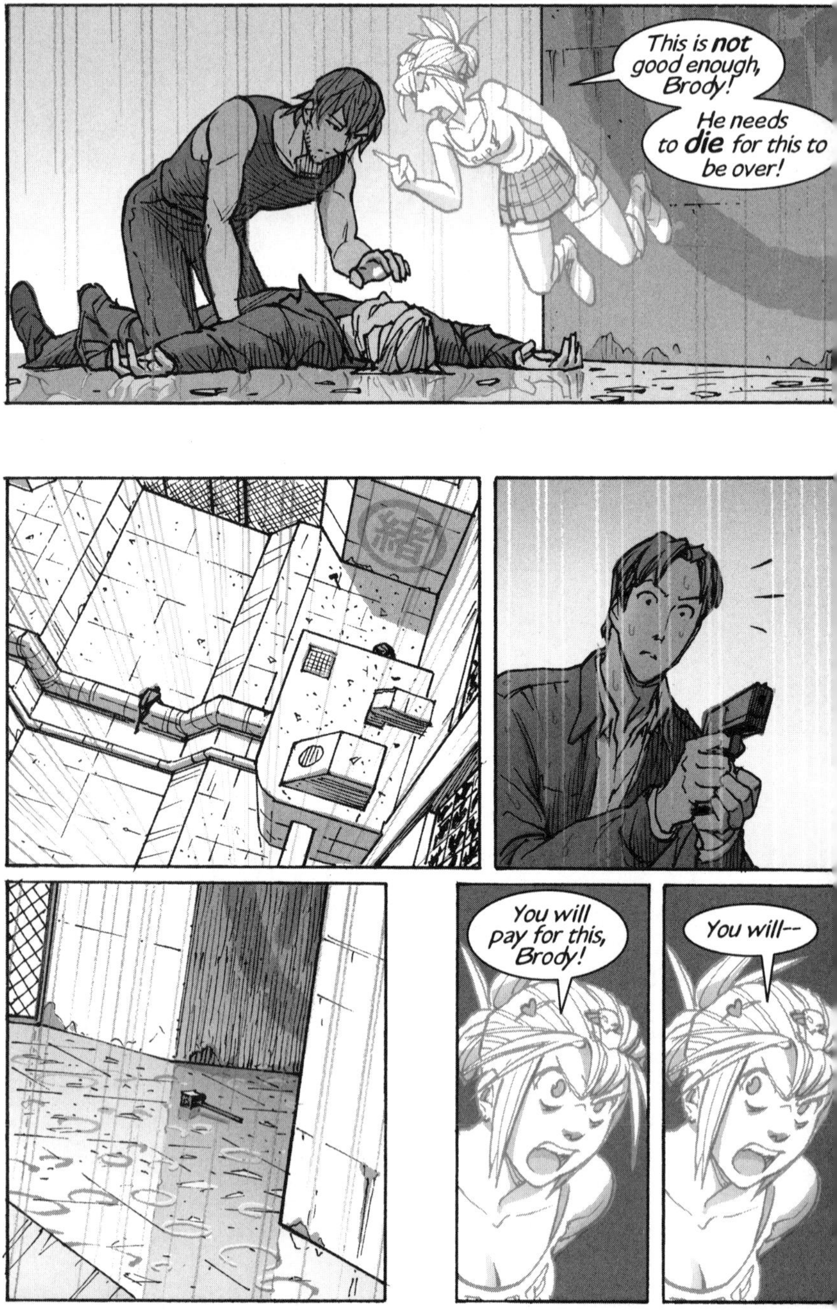
This is **not** good enough, Brody!
He needs to **die** for this to be over!
You will pay for this, Brody!
You will--

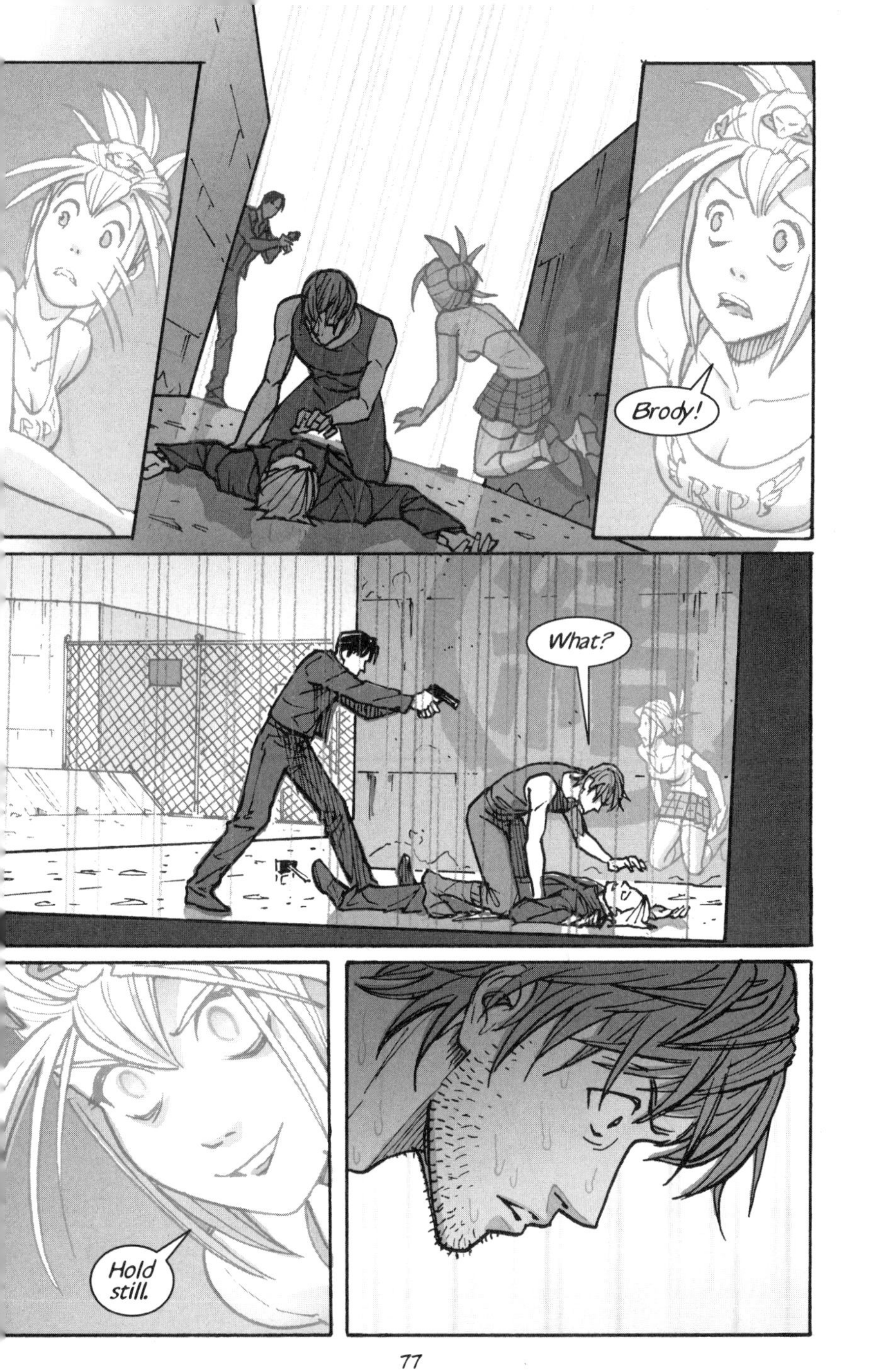
Brody!
What?
Hold still.

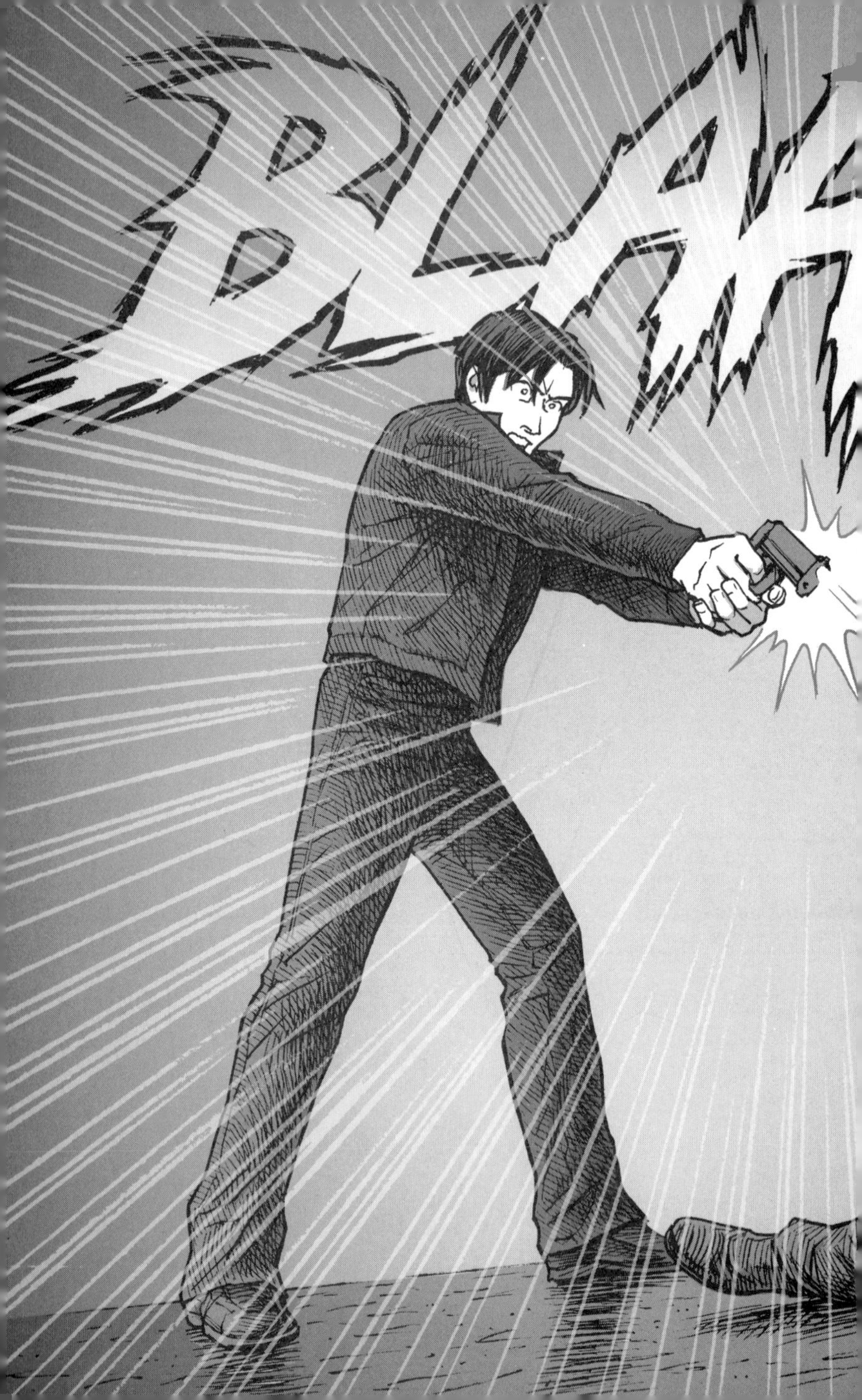

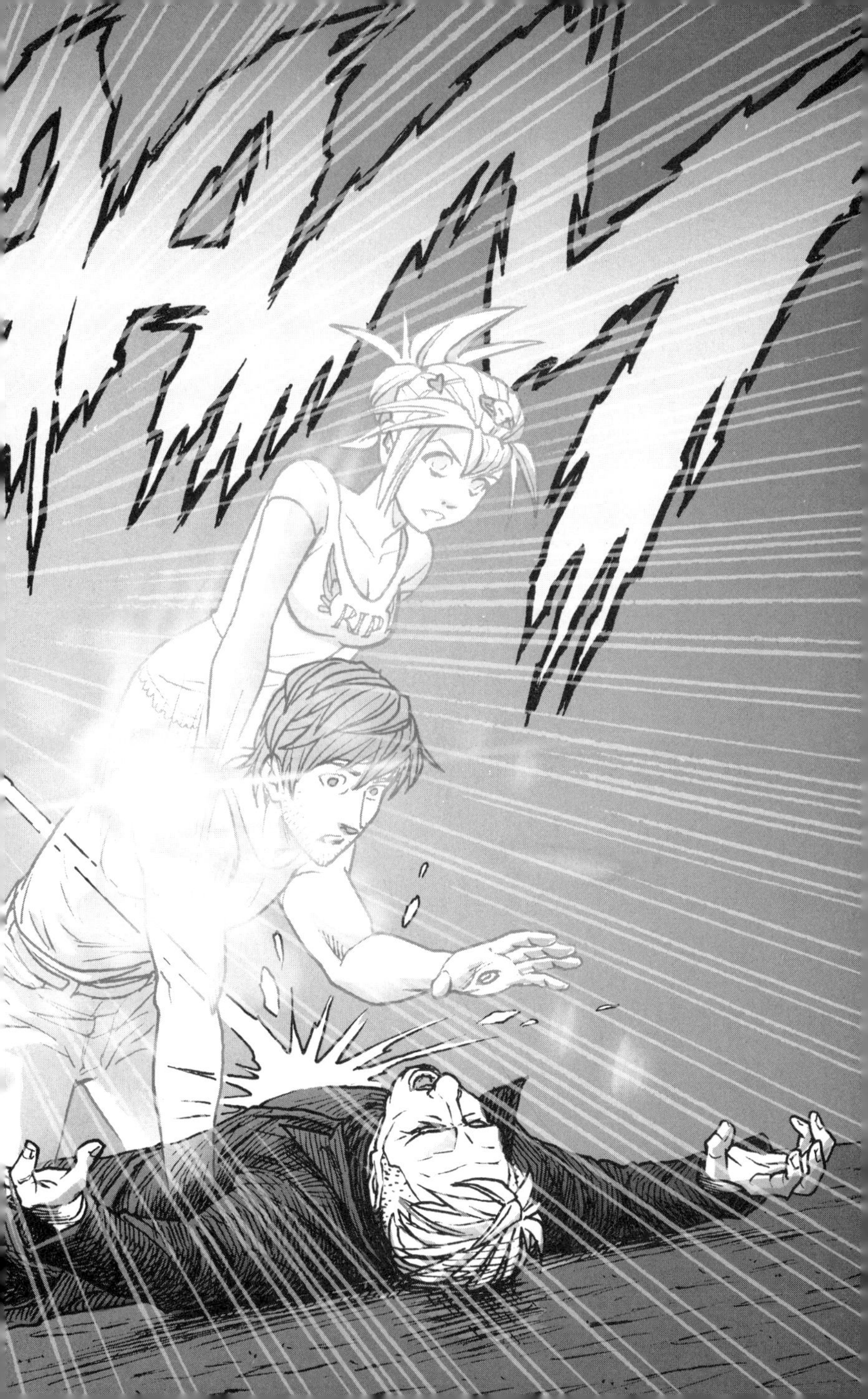
RIP

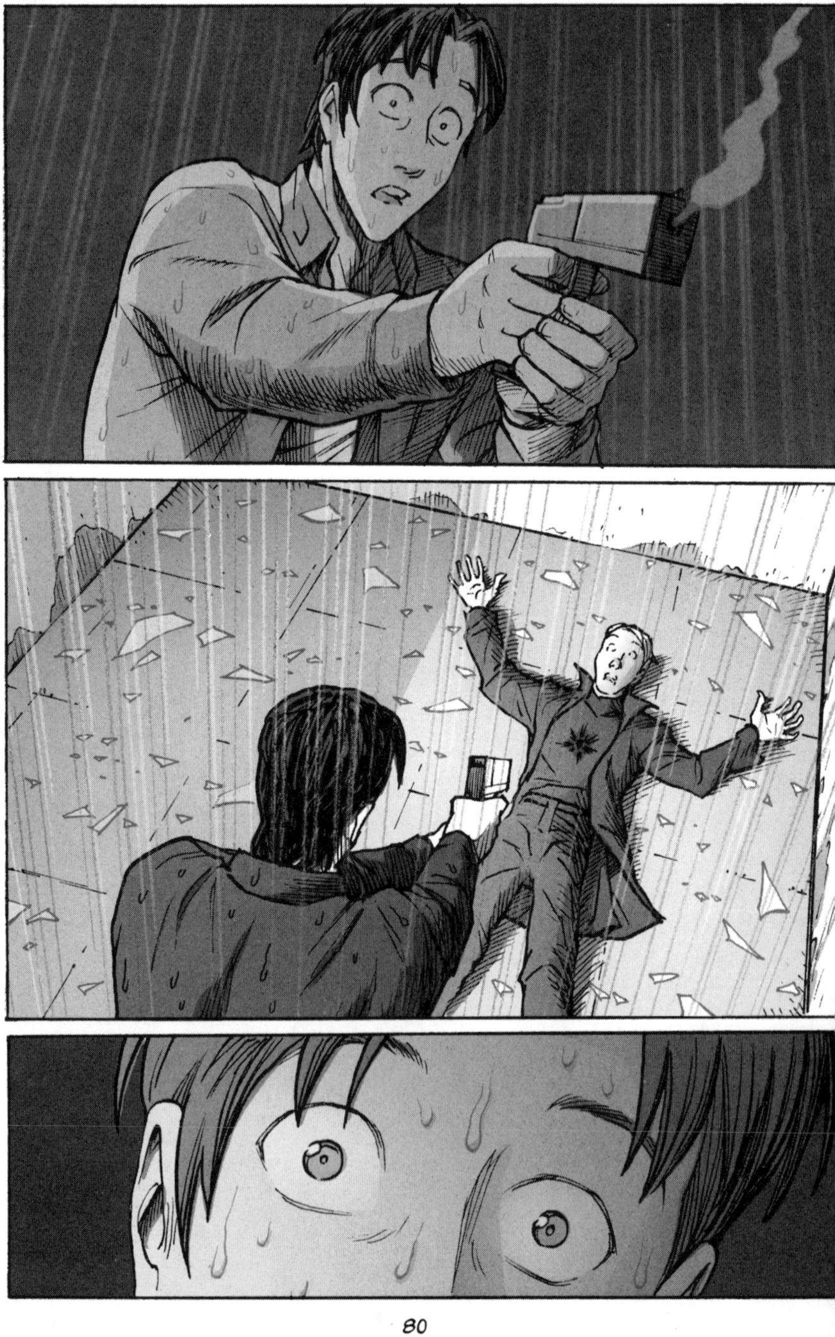

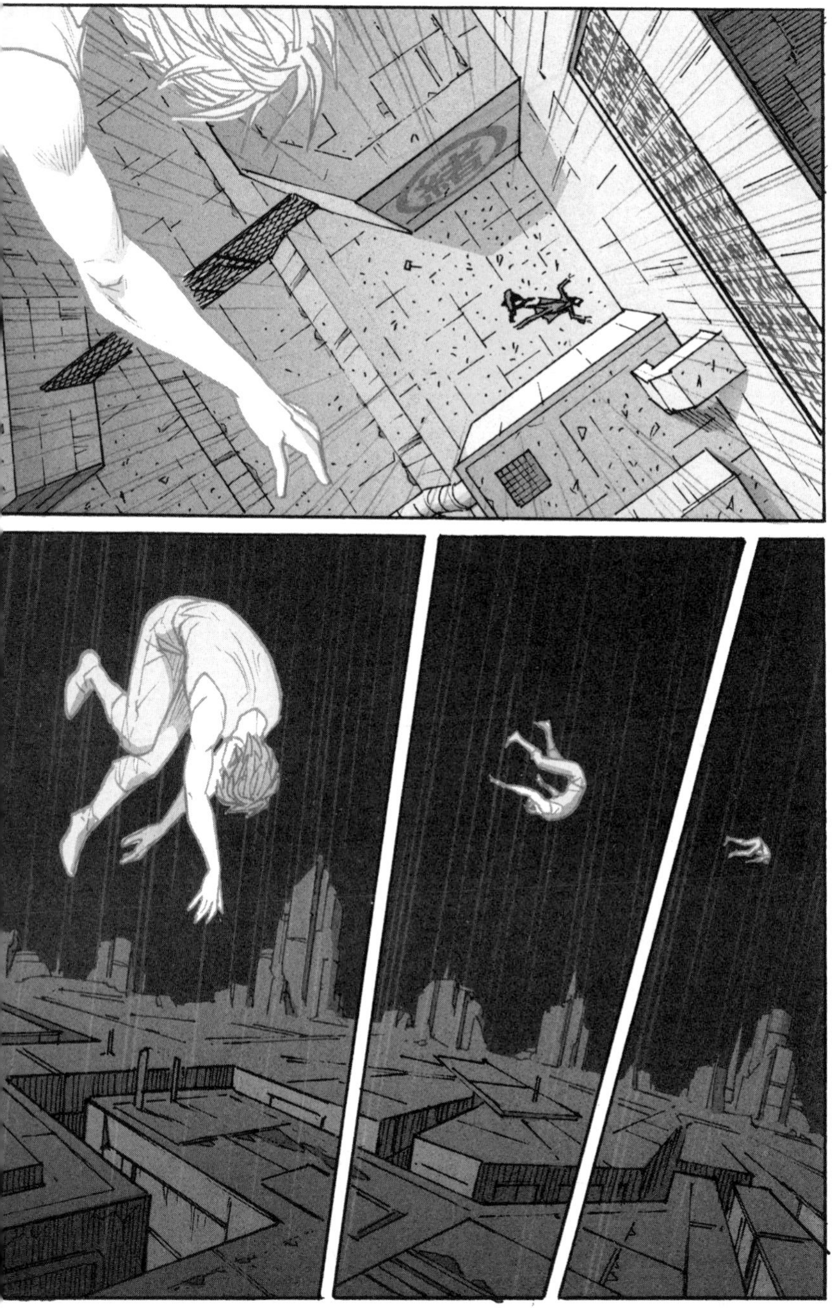

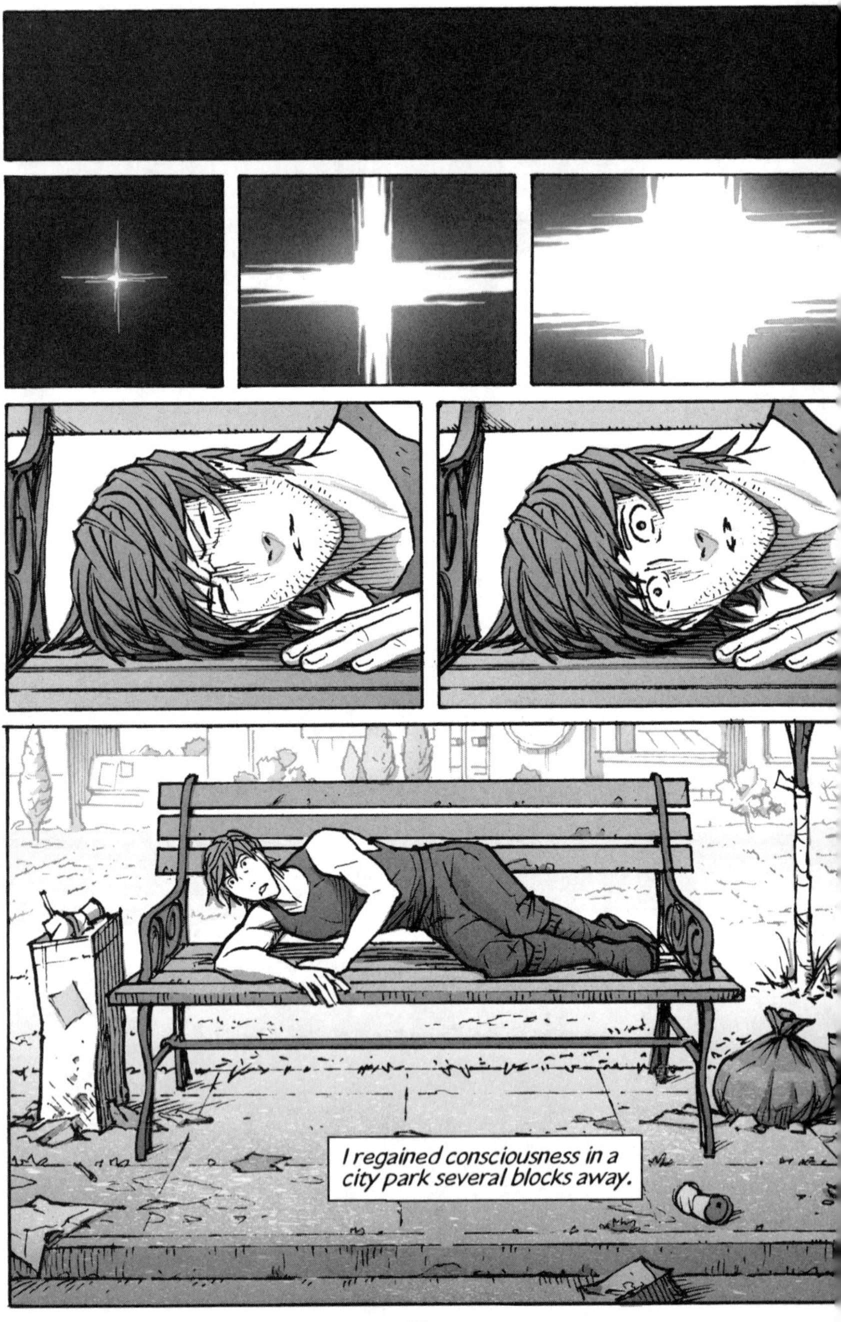
I regained consciousness in a city park several blocks away.

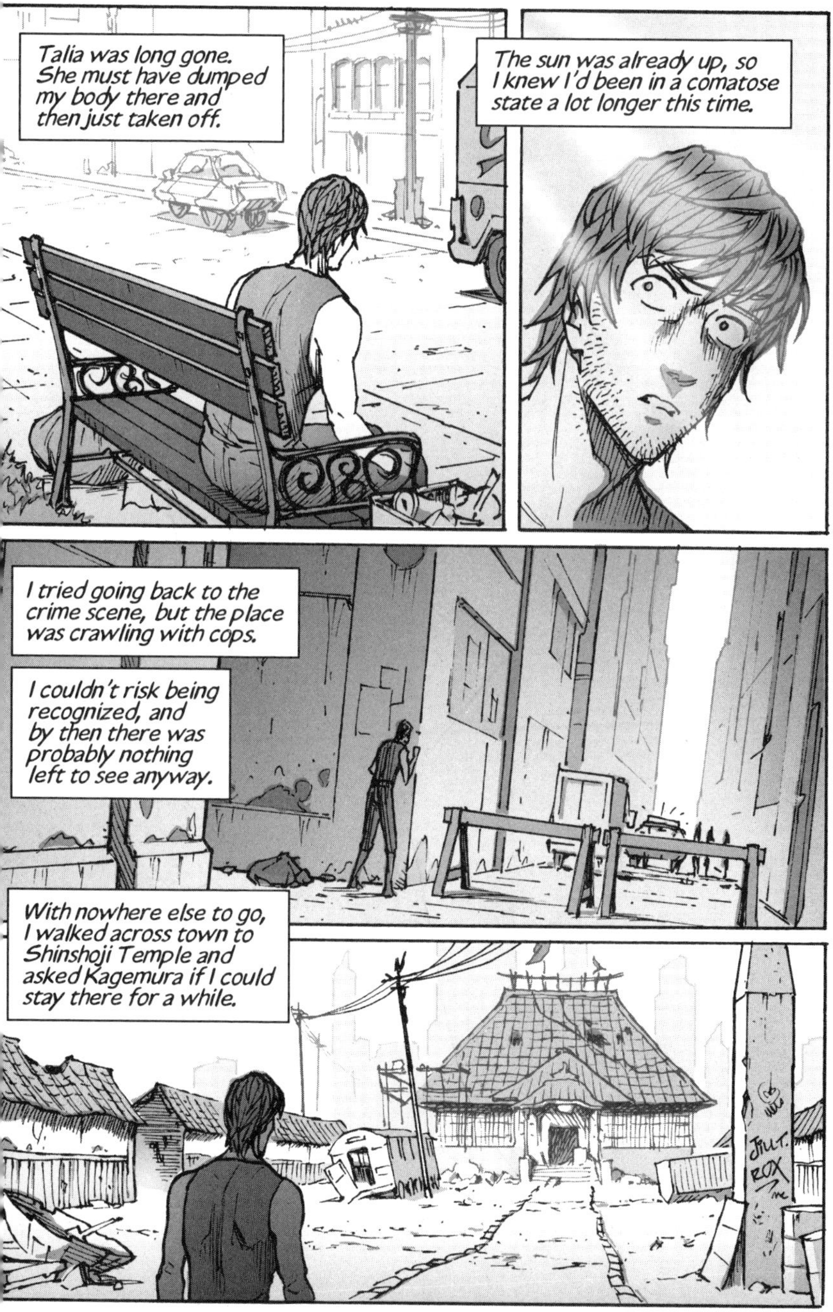
Talia was long gone. She must have dumped my body there and then just taken off.
The sun was already up, so I knew I'd been in a comatose state a lot longer this time.
I tried going back to the crime scene, but the place was crawling with cops.
I couldn't risk being recognized, and by then there was probably nothing left to see anyway.
With nowhere else to go, I walked across town to Shinshoji Temple and asked Kagemura if I could stay there for a while.

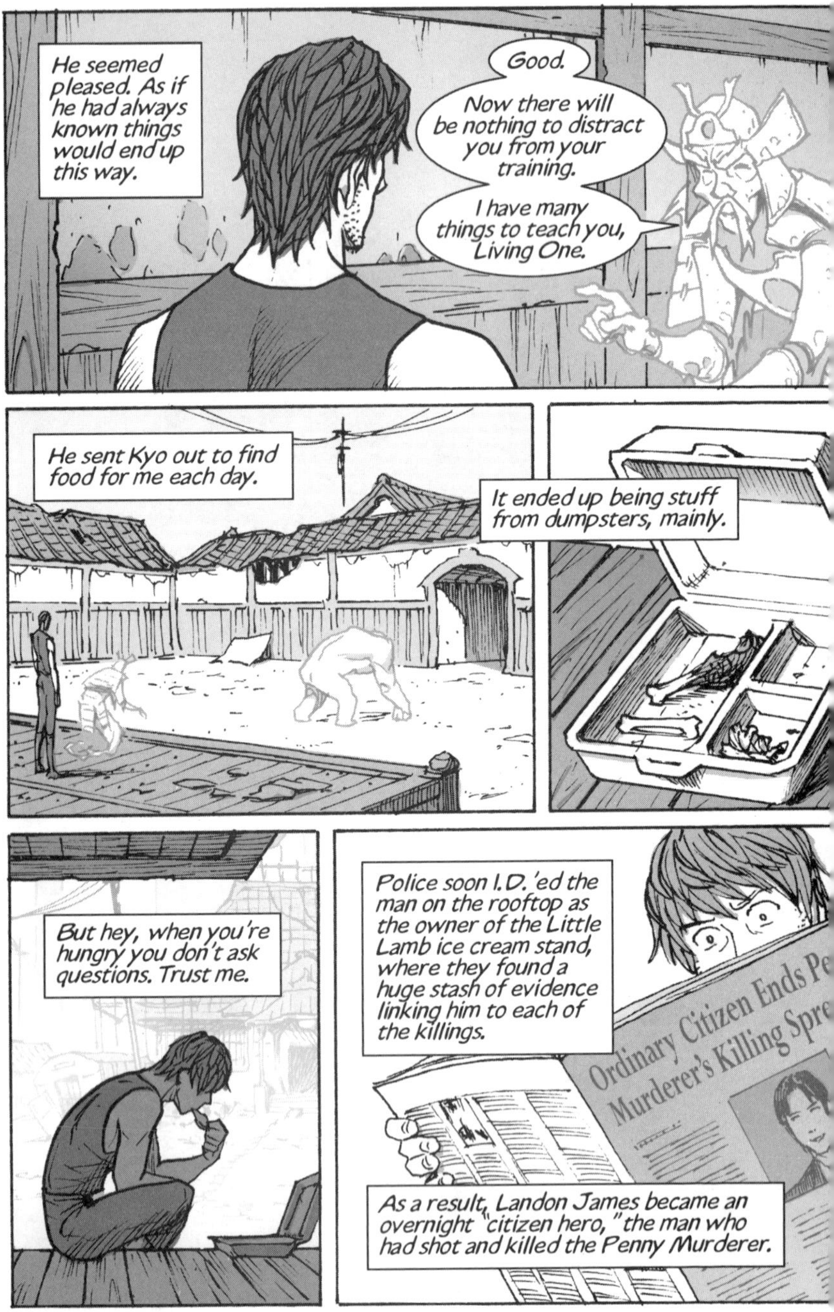
He seemed pleased. As if he had always known things would end up this way.
Good.
Now there will be nothing to distract you from your training.
I have many things to teach you, Living One.
He sent Kyo out to find food for me each day.
It ended up being stuff from dumpsters, mainly.
But hey, when you're hungry you don't ask questions. Trust me.
Police soon I.D.'ed the man on the rooftop as the owner of the Little Lamb ice cream stand, where they found a huge stash of evidence linking him to each of the killings.
Ordinary Citizen Ends Pe
Murderer's Killing Spre
As a result, Landon James became an overnight "citizen hero," the man who had shot and killed the Penny Murderer.

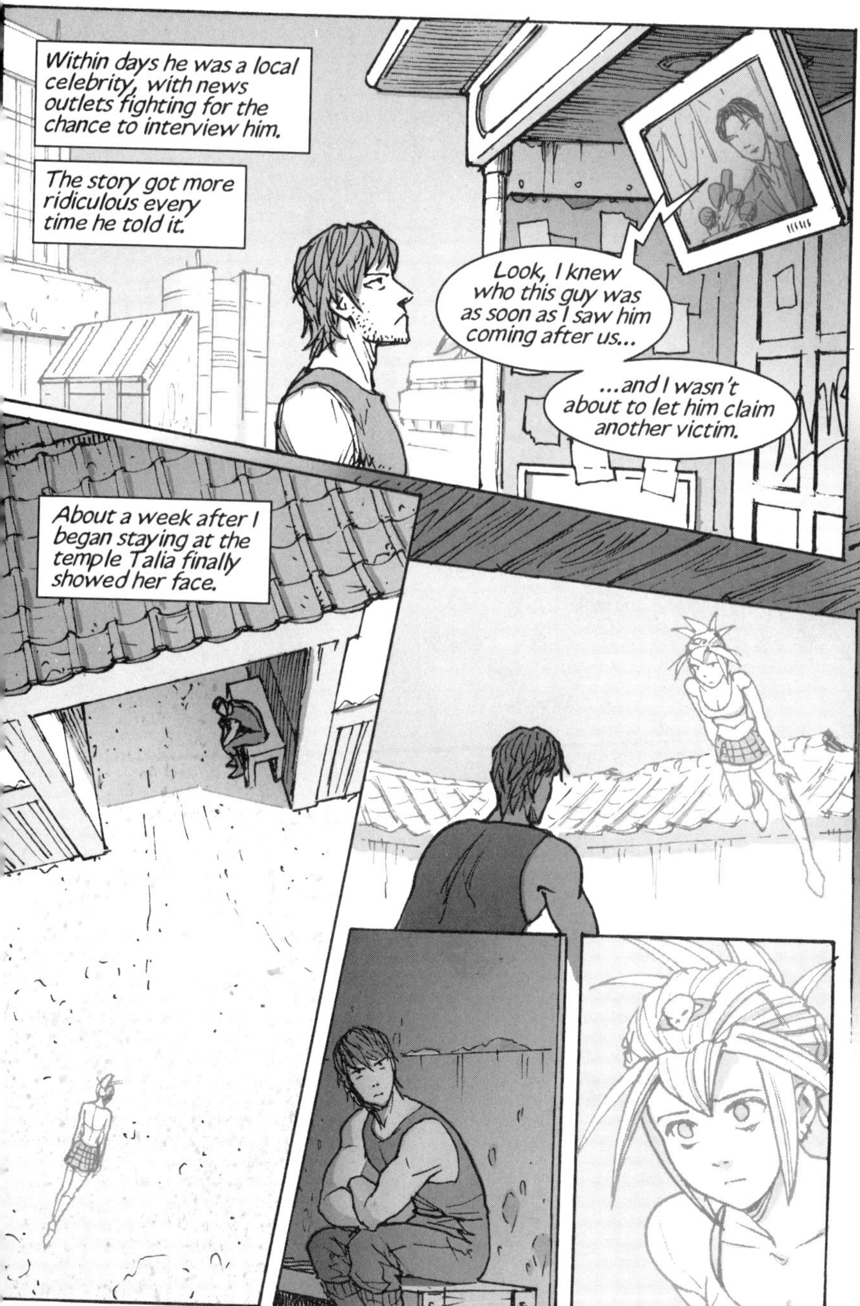
Within days he was a local celebrity, with news outlets fighting for the chance to interview him.
The story got more ridiculous every time he told it.
Look, I knew who this guy was as soon as I saw him coming after us...
...and I wasn't about to let him claim another victim.
About a week after I began staying at the temple Talia finally showed her face.

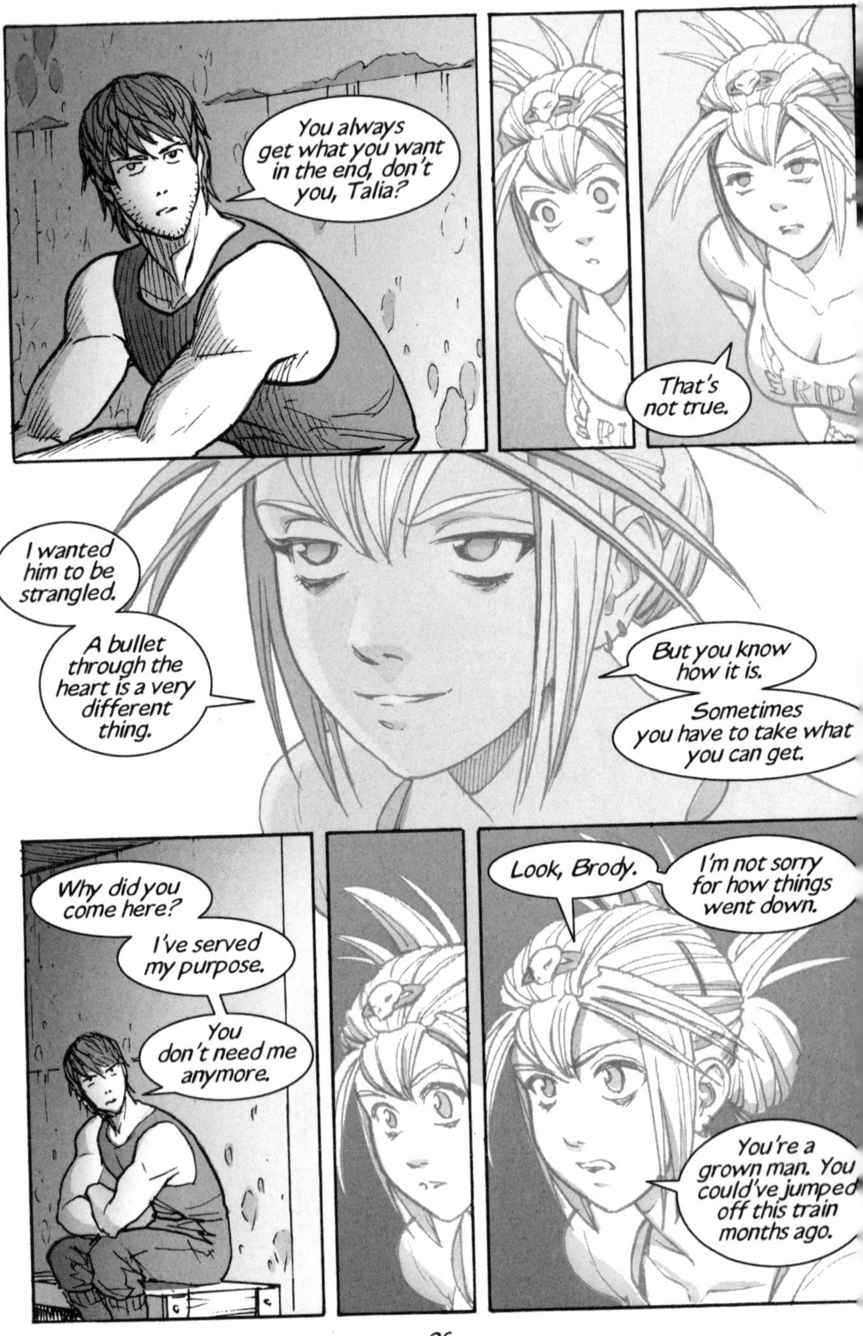
You always get what you want in the end, don't you, Talia?
That's not true.
I wanted him to be strangled.
A bullet through the heart is a very different thing.
But you know how it is.
Sometimes you have to take what you can get.
Why did you come here?
I've served my purpose.
You don't need me anymore.
Look, Brody.
I'm not sorry for how things went down.
You're a grown man. You could've jumped off this train months ago.

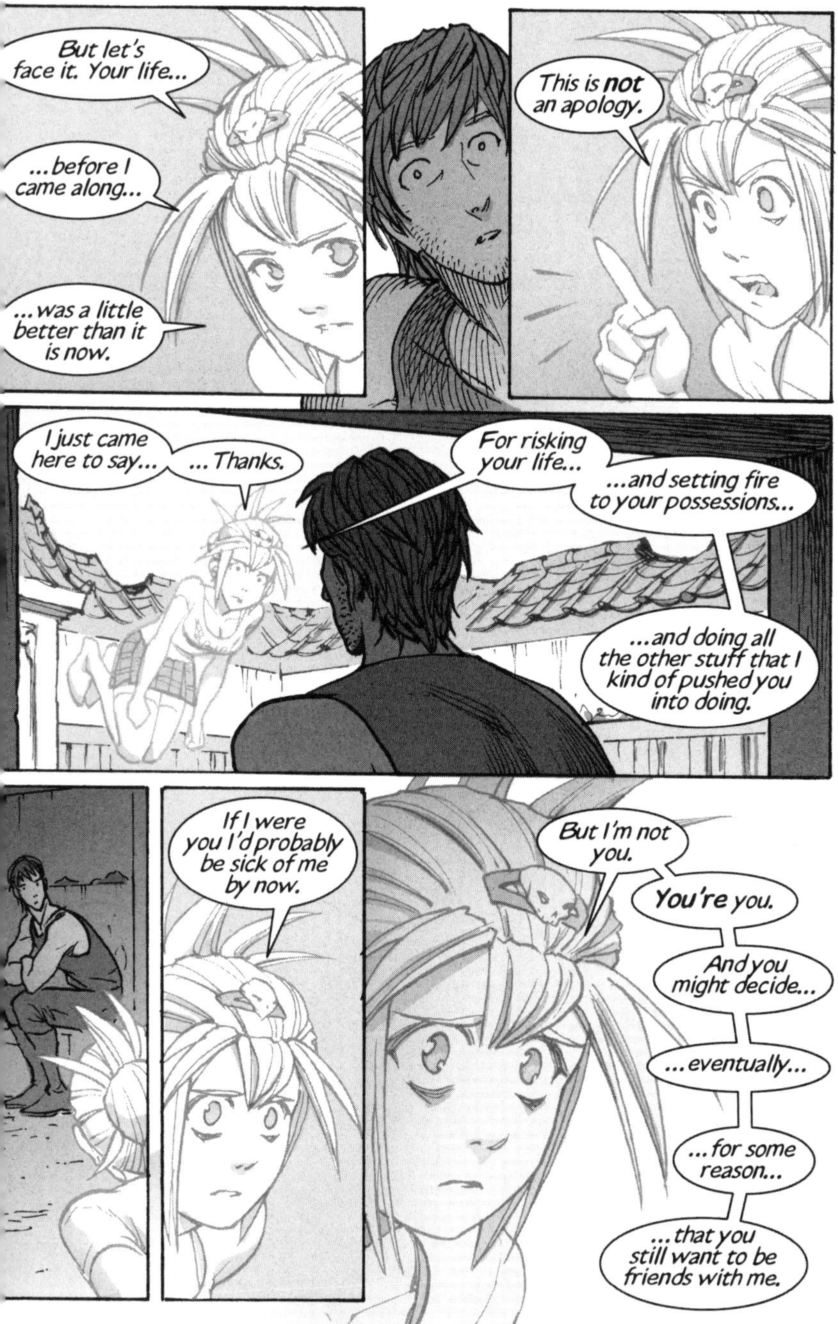
But let's face it. Your life...
...before I came along...
...was a little better than it is now.
This is **not** an apology.
I just came here to say...
...Thanks.
For risking your life...
...and setting fire to your possessions...
...and doing all the other stuff that I kind of pushed you into doing.
If I were you I'd probably be sick of me by now.
But I'm not you.
You're you.
And you might decide...
...eventually...
...for some reason...
...that you still want to be friends with me.

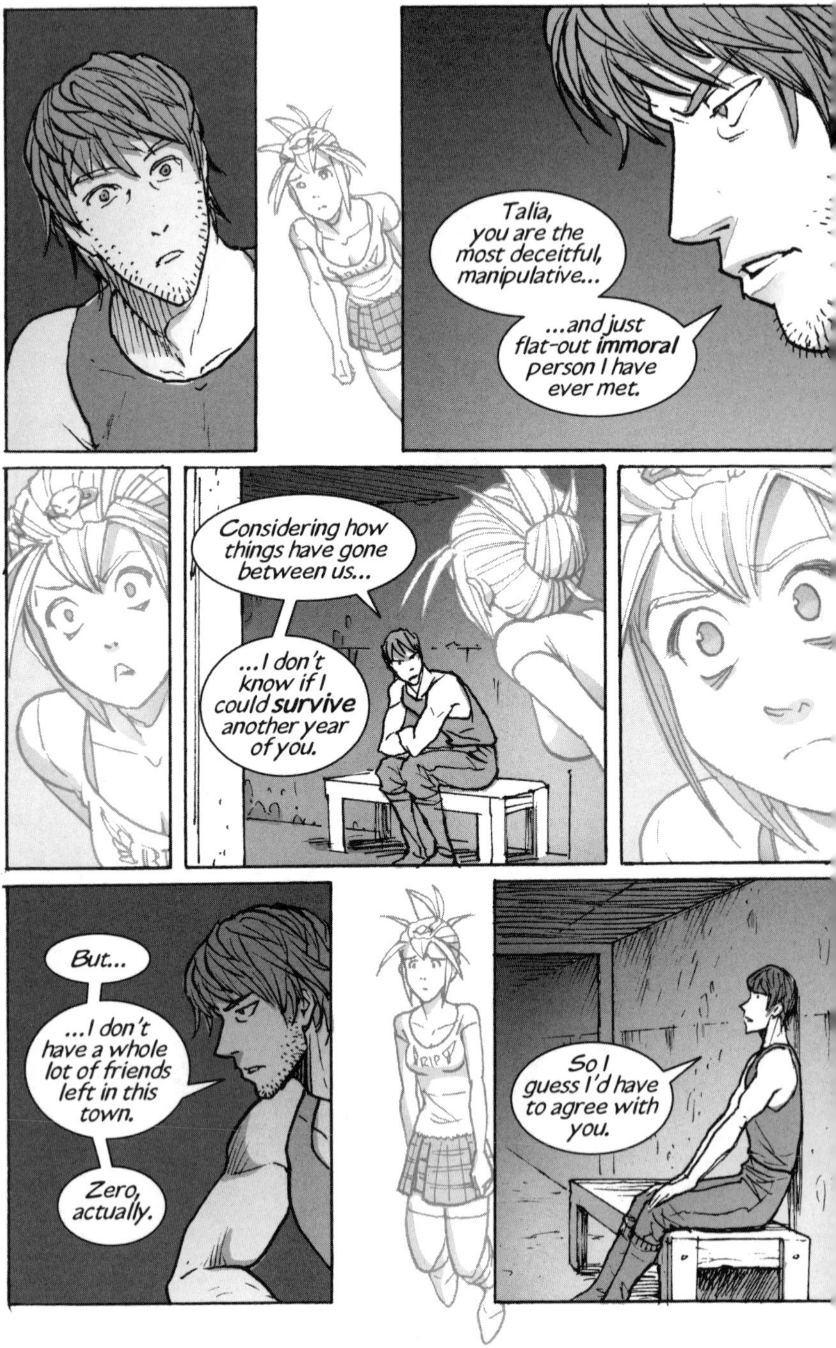
Talia, you are the most deceitful, manipulative...
...and just flat-out **immoral** person I have ever met.
Considering how things have gone between us...
...I don't know if I could **survive** another year of you.
But...
...I don't have a whole lot of friends left in this town.
Zero, actually.
So I guess I'd have to agree with you.

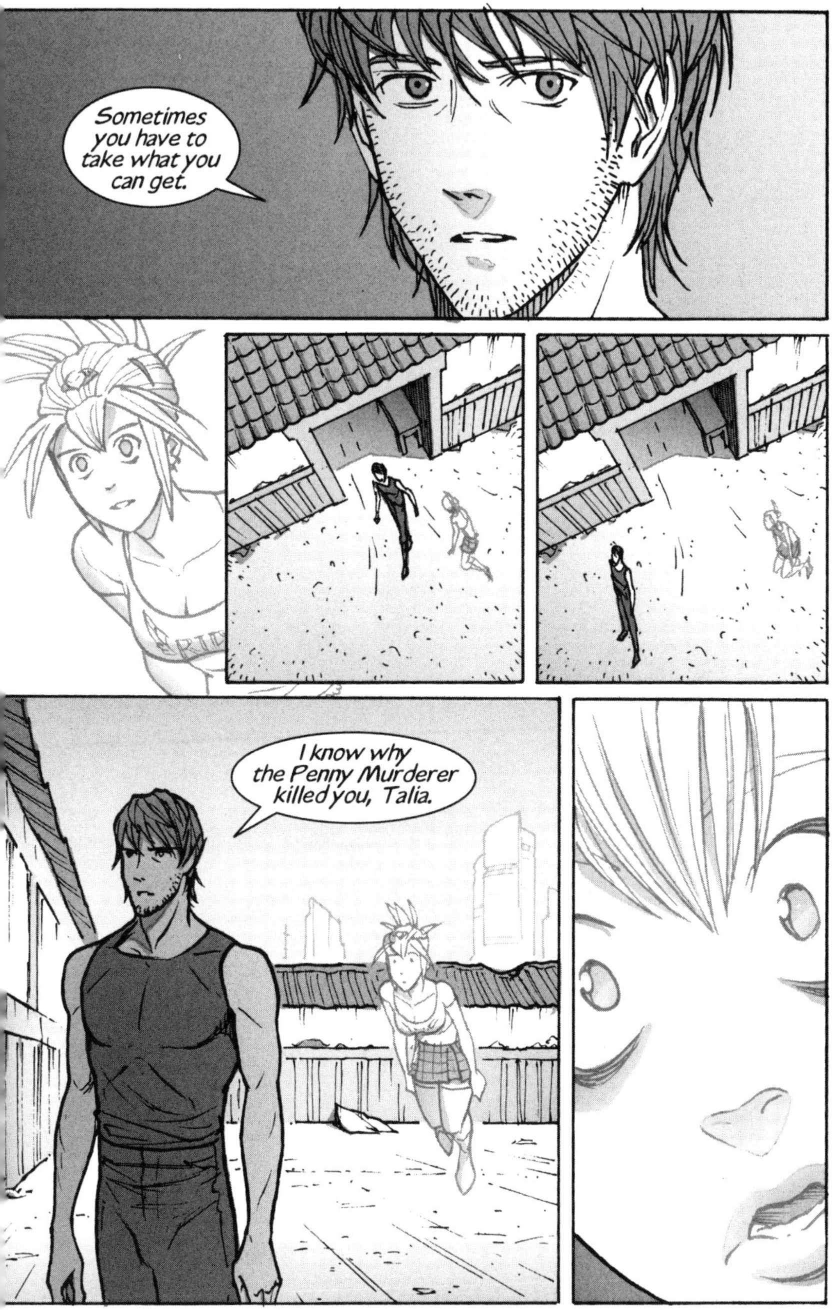
Sometimes you have to take what you can get.
I know why the Penny Murderer killed you, Talia.

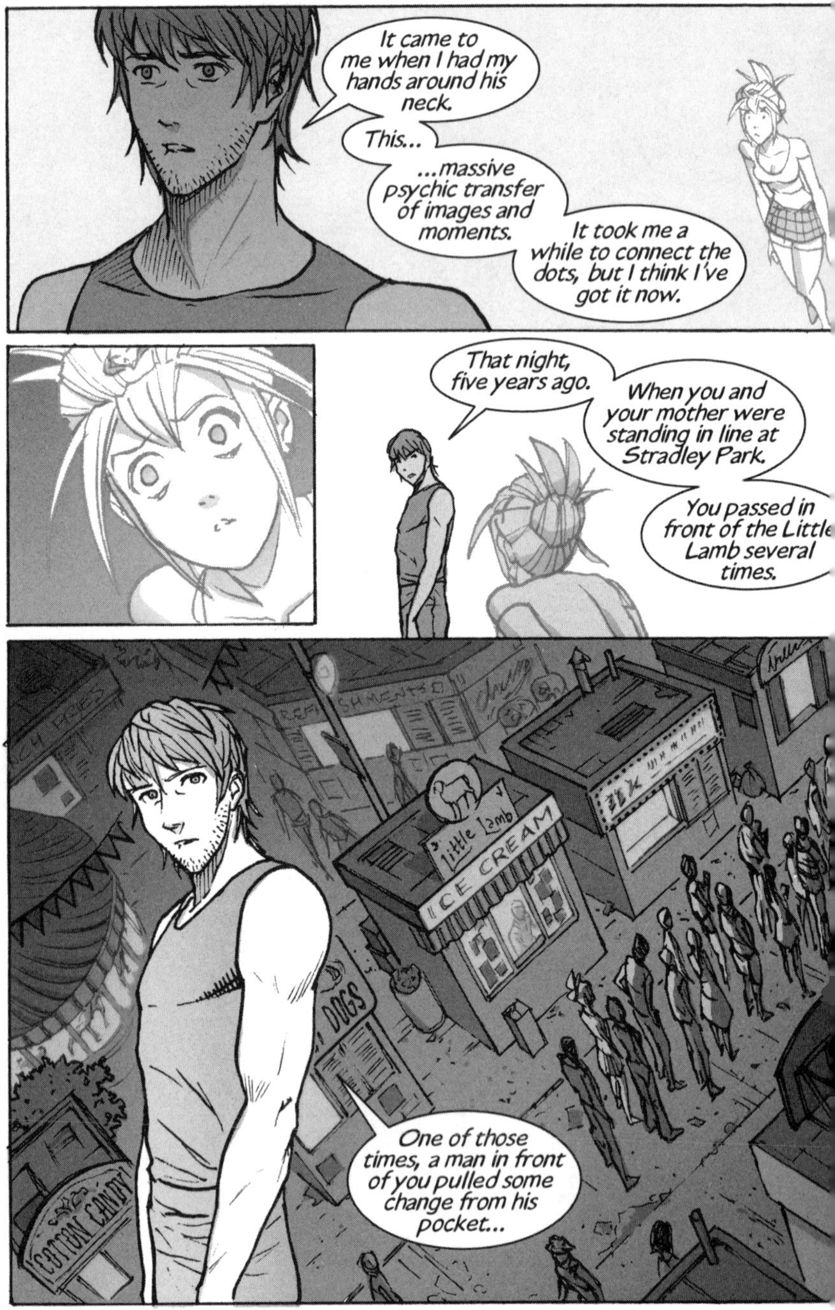

It came to me when I had my hands around his neck.
This...
...massive psychic transfer of images and moments.
It took me a while to connect the dots, but I think I've got it now.
That night, five years ago.
When you and your mother were standing in line at Stradley Park.
You passed in front of the Little Lamb several times.
Little Lamb
ICE CREAM
DOGS
COTTON CANDY
One of those times, a man in front of you pulled some change from his pocket...

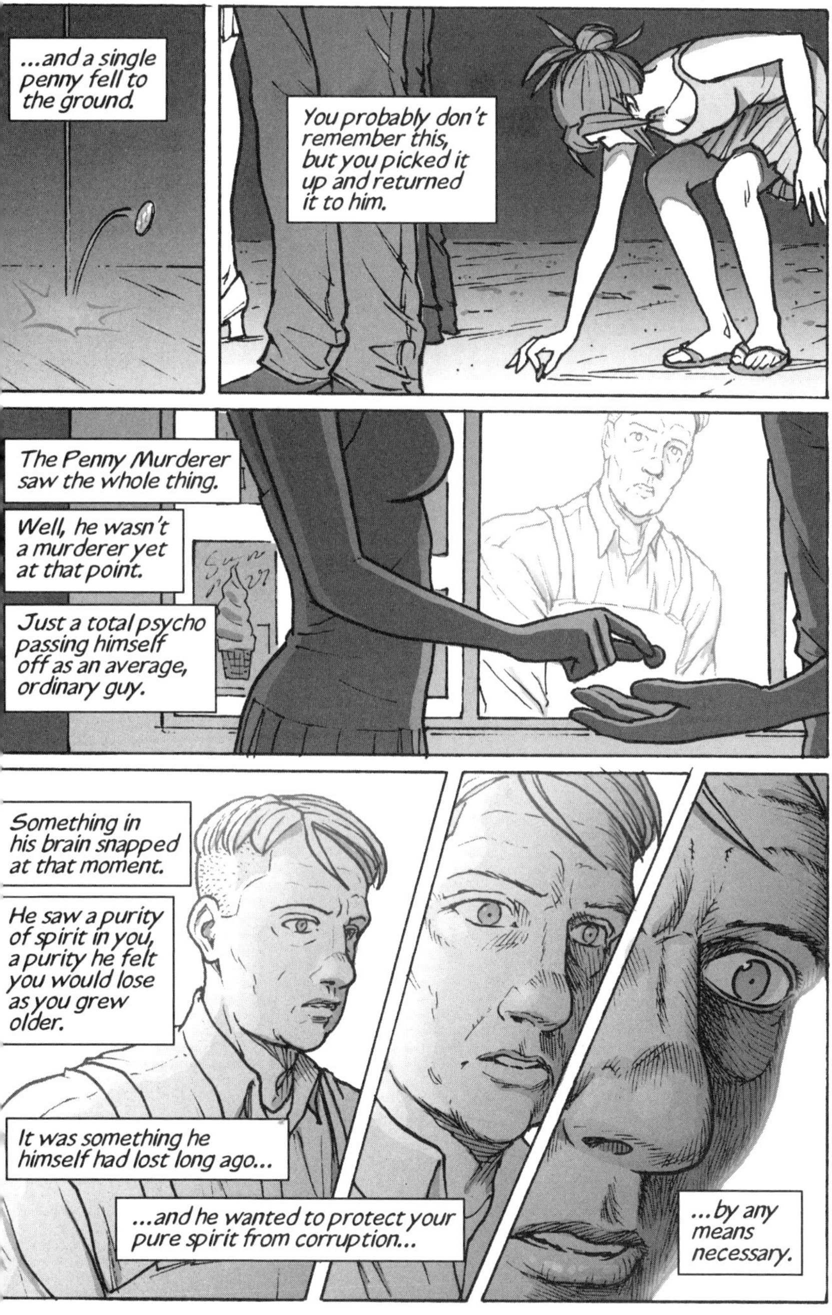
...and a single penny fell to the ground.
You probably don't remember this, but you picked it up and returned it to him.
The Penny Murderer saw the whole thing.
Well, he wasn't a murderer yet at that point.
Just a total psycho passing himself off as an average, ordinary guy.
Something in his brain snapped at that moment.
He saw a purity of spirit in you, a purity he felt you would lose as you grew older.
It was something he himself had lost long ago...
...and he wanted to protect your pure spirit from corruption...
...by any means necessary.

He closed up shop and followed you and your mother for the rest of the night.

Followed you all the way home.

A week or two later, after observing your daily routines...

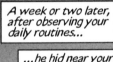

...he hid near your favorite place on the beach...

...and "saved" your purity...

...by killing you.

We were both right, Talia.

He chose you for a reason...

...but it was a reason only a lunatic could comprehend.

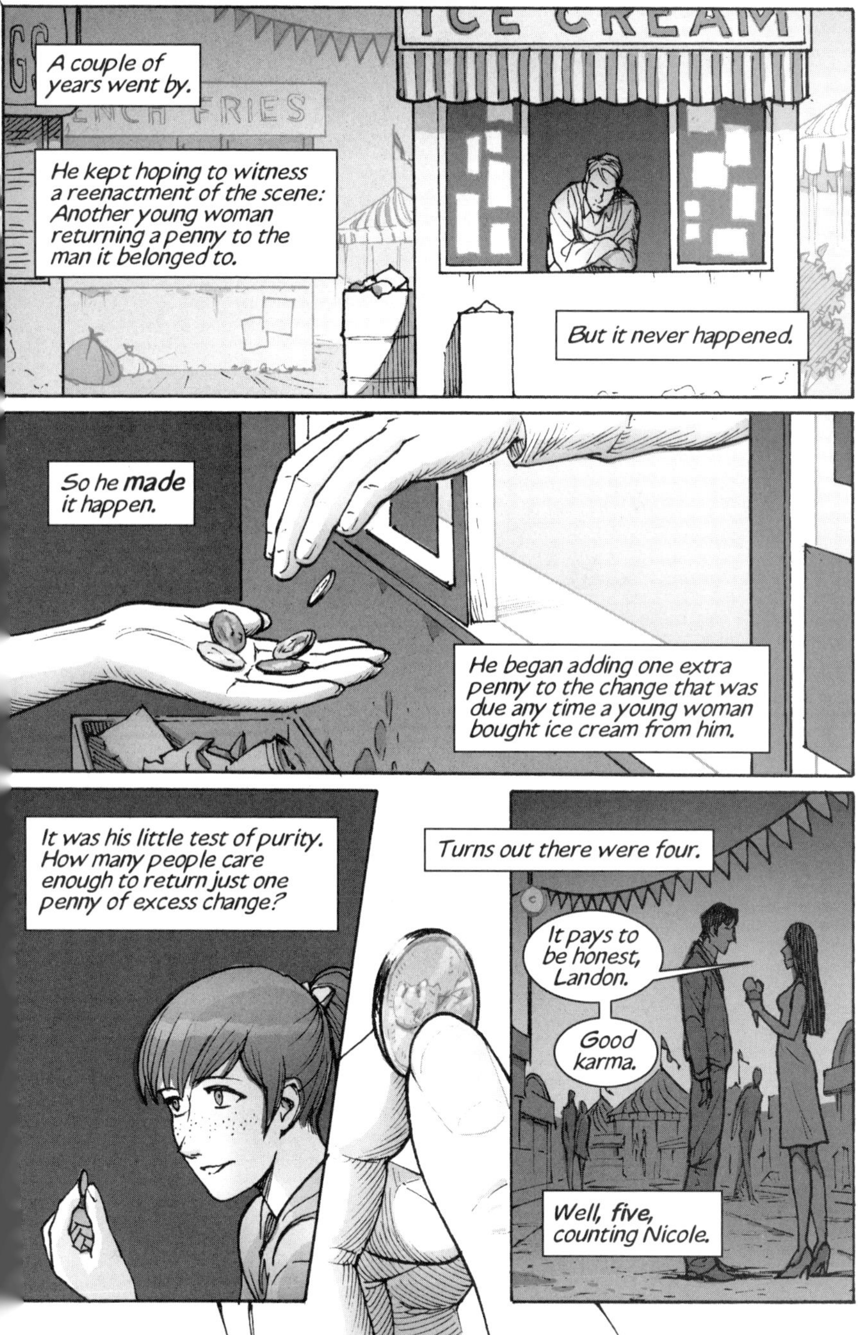
ICE CREAM
A couple of years went by.
NCH FRIES
He kept hoping to witness a reenactment of the scene: Another young woman returning a penny to the man it belonged to.
But it never happened.
So he made it happen.
He began adding one extra penny to the change that was due any time a young woman bought ice cream from him.
It was his little test of purity. How many people care enough to return just one penny of excess change?
Turns out there were four.
It pays to be honest, Landon.
Good karma.
Well, five, counting Nicole.

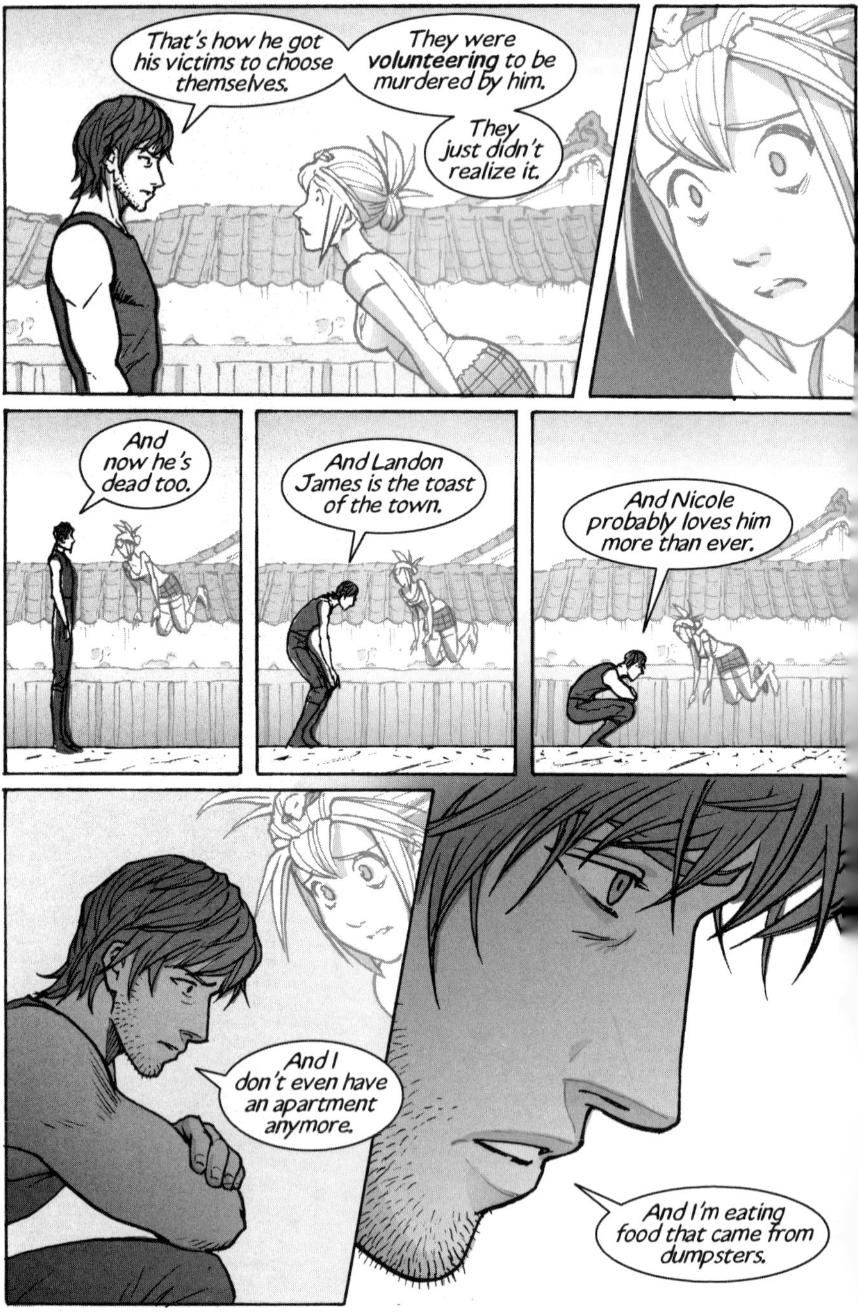
That's how he got his victims to choose themselves.
They were **volunteering** to be murdered by him.
They just didn't realize it.
And now he's dead too.
And Landon James is the toast of the town.
And Nicole probably loves him more than ever.
And I don't even have an apartment anymore.
And I'm eating food that came from dumpsters.

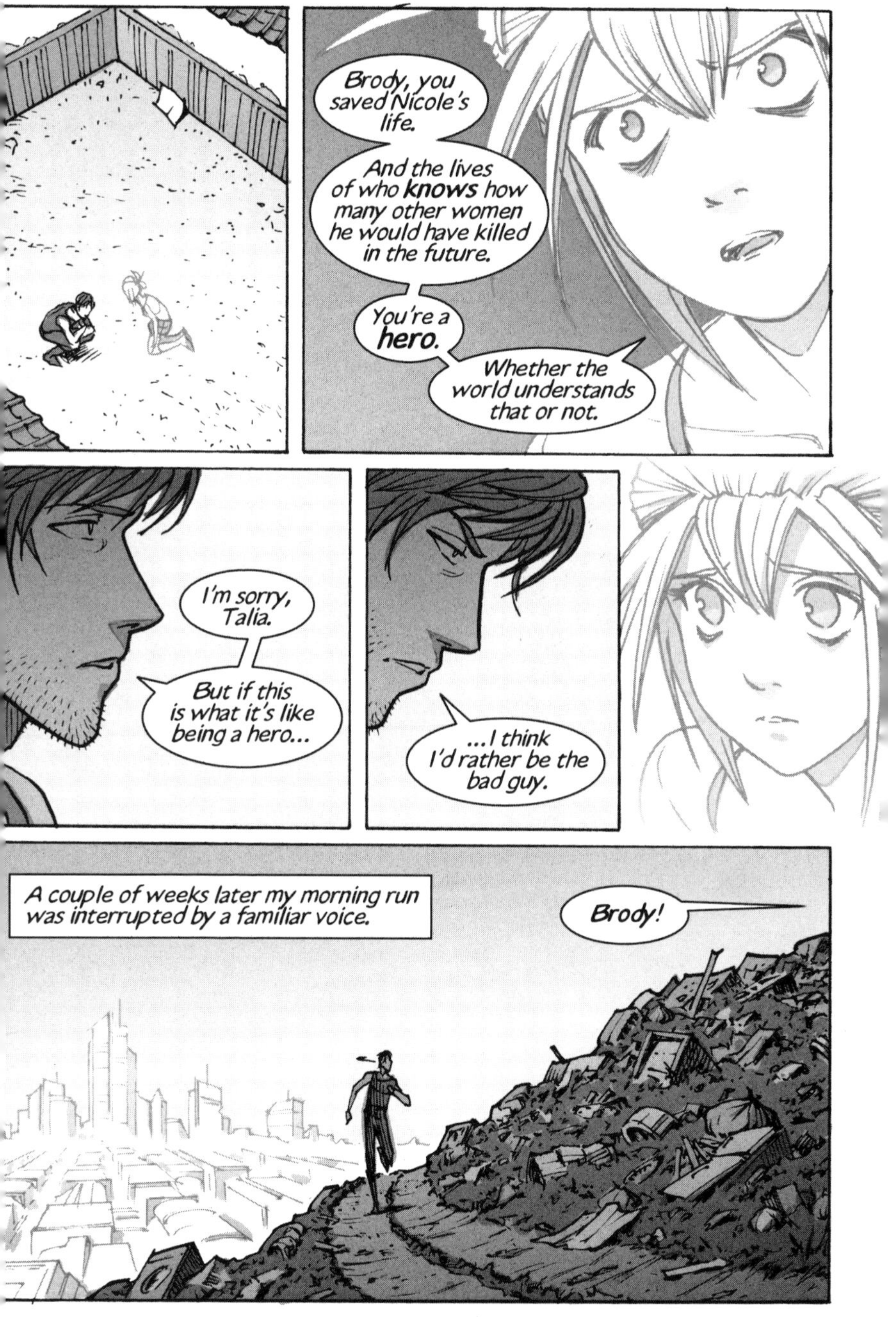

Brody, you saved Nicole's life.
And the lives of who **knows** how many other women he would have killed in the future.
You're a **hero**.
Whether the world understands that or not.
I'm sorry, Talia.
But if this is what it's like being a hero...
...I think I'd rather be the bad guy.
A couple of weeks later my morning run was interrupted by a familiar voice.
Brody!

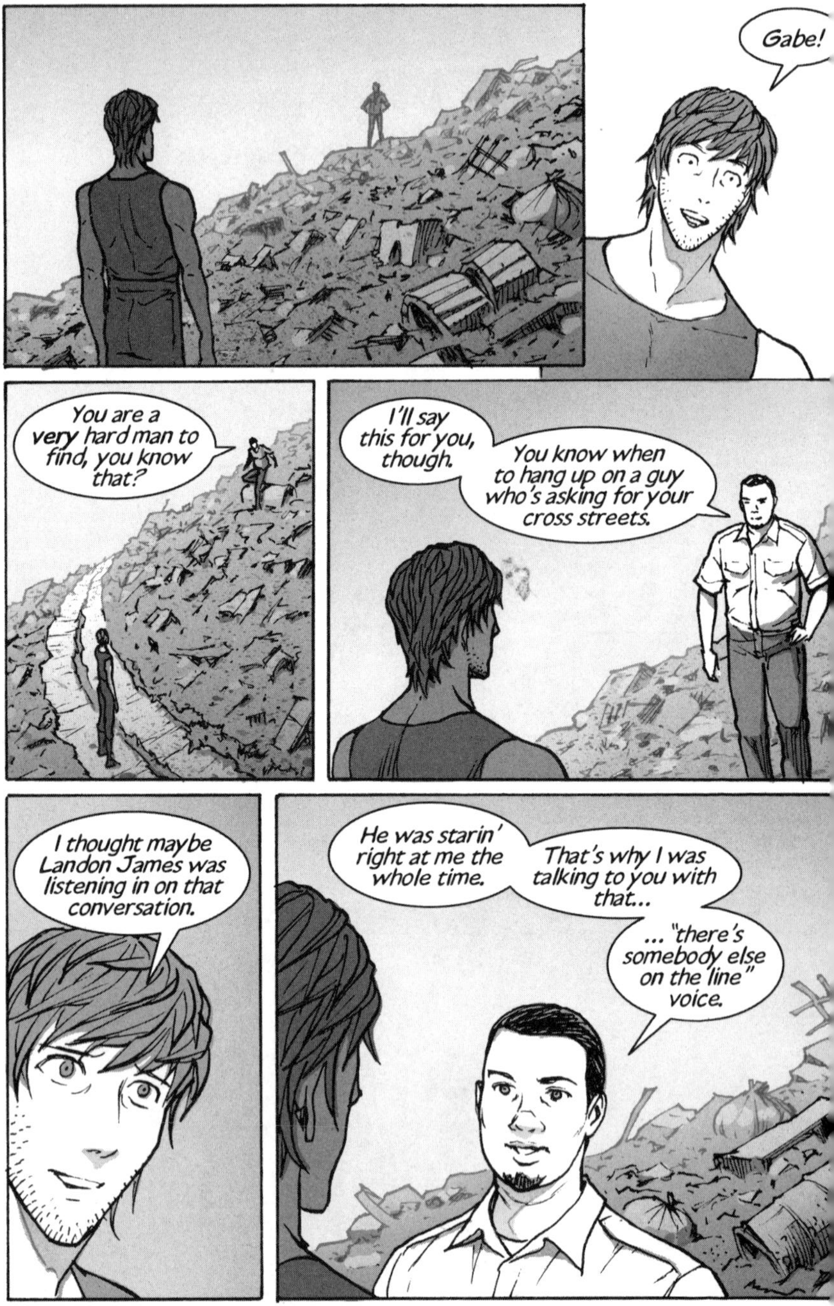
Gabe!
You are a very hard man to find, you know that?
I'll say this for you, though.
You know when to hang up on a guy who's asking for your cross streets.
I thought maybe Landon James was listening in on that conversation.
He was starin' right at me the whole time.
That's why I was talking to you with that...
... "there's somebody else on the line" voice.

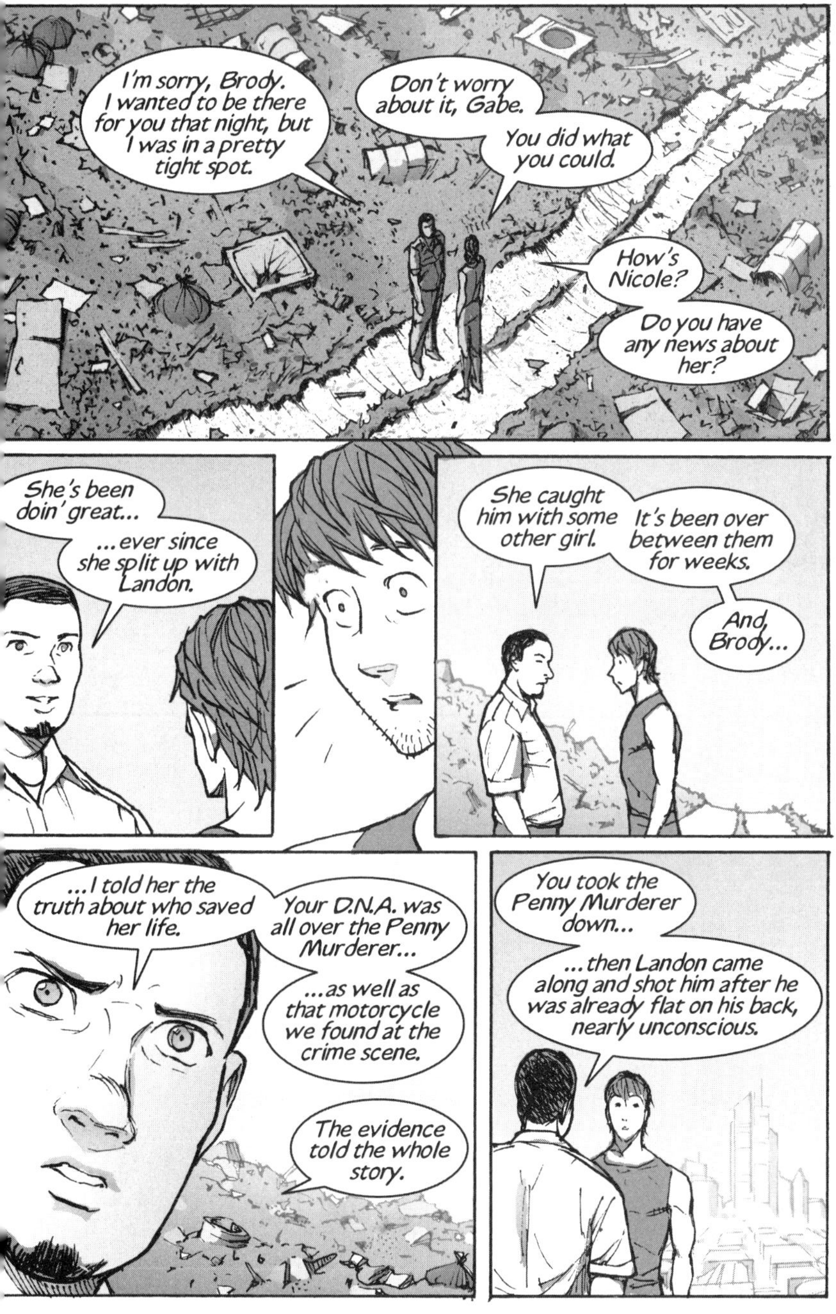
I'm sorry, Brody. I wanted to be there for you that night, but I was in a pretty tight spot.
Don't worry about it, Gabe.
You did what you could.
How's Nicole?
Do you have any news about her?
She's been doin' great...
...ever since she split up with Landon.
She caught him with some other girl.
It's been over between them for weeks.
And, Brody...
...I told her the truth about who saved her life.
Your D.N.A. was all over the Penny Murderer...
...as well as that motorcycle we found at the crime scene.
The evidence told the whole story.
You took the Penny Murderer down...
...then Landon came along and shot him after he was already flat on his back, nearly unconscious.

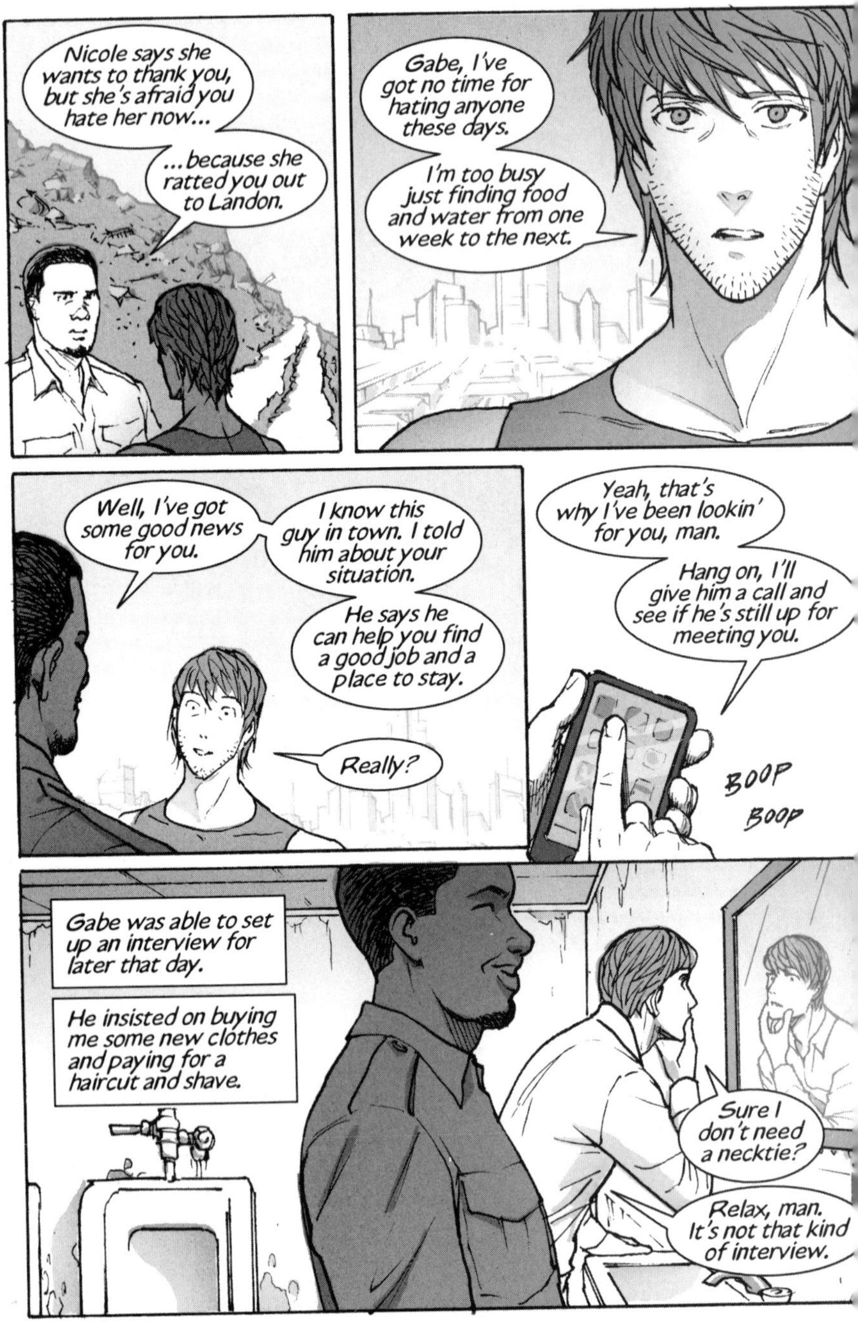
Nicole says she wants to thank you, but she's afraid you hate her now...
...because she ratted you out to Landon.
Gabe, I've got no time for hating anyone these days.
I'm too busy just finding food and water from one week to the next.
Well, I've got some good news for you.
I know this guy in town. I told him about your situation.
He says he can help you find a good job and a place to stay.
Really?
Yeah, that's why I've been lookin' for you, man.
Hang on, I'll give him a call and see if he's still up for meeting you.
BOOP
BOOP
Gabe was able to set up an interview for later that day.
He insisted on buying me some new clothes and paying for a haircut and shave.
Sure I don't need a necktie?
Relax, man. It's not that kind of interview.

Then he drove me into town and dropped me near the place I was supposed to go.

It's right up there around the corner.

Middle of the block.

Can't you come with me, Gabe? Just to make the introductions.

Trust me, Brody. You don't want me around for this.

I should have known something was up.

2673 MASON ST.

The address looked a little familiar.

KOYAMA

BOOKS · COFFEE · MUSIC

KOYAMA

KOYAMA

K'CHAK

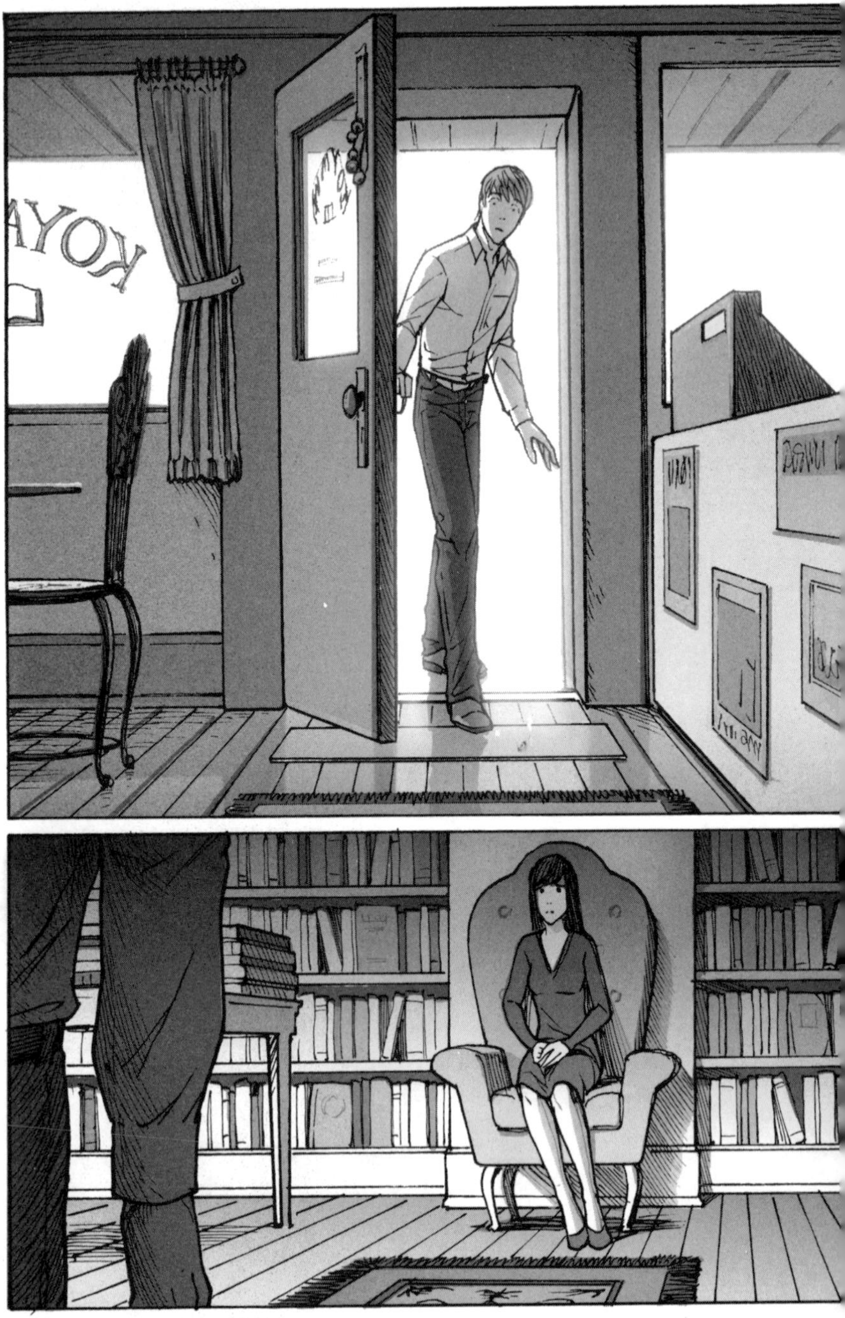

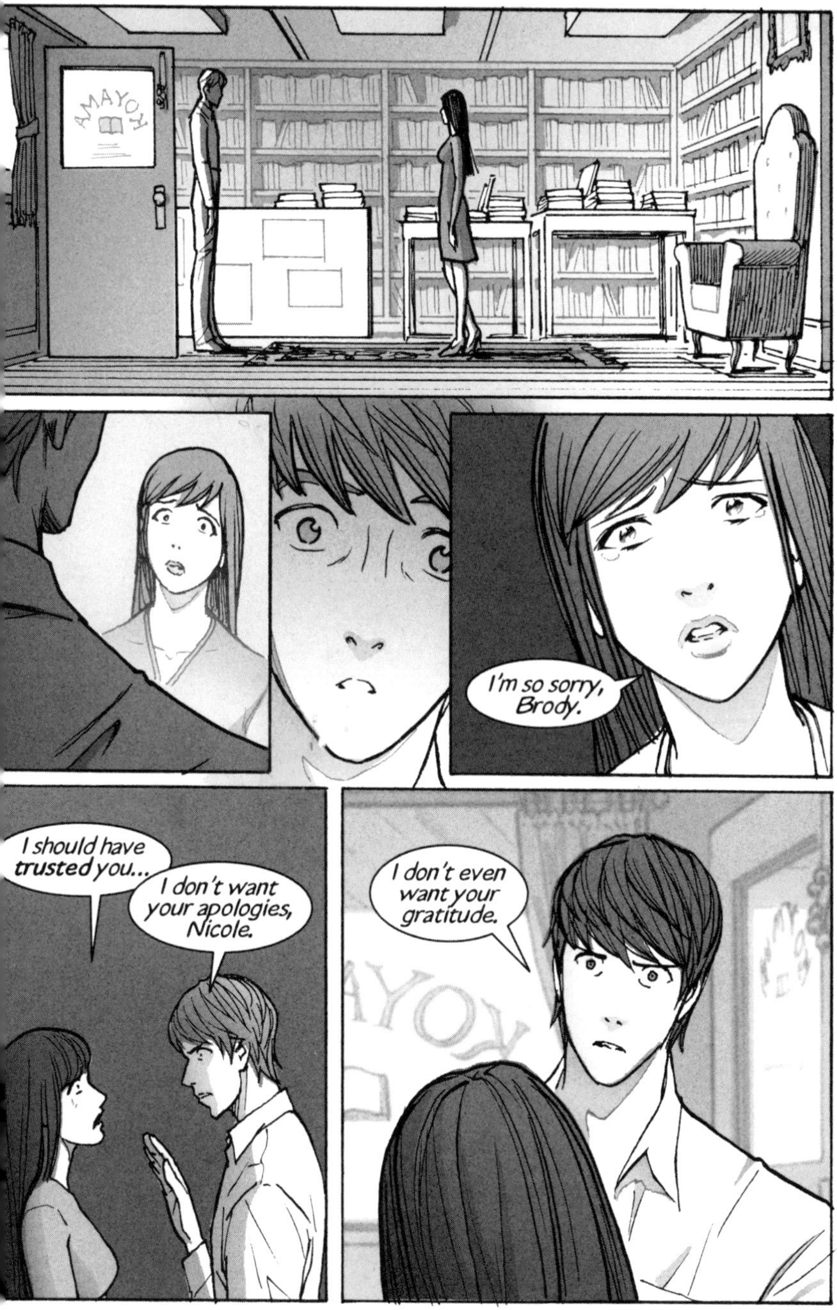
I'm so sorry, Brody.
I should have trusted you...
I don't want your apologies, Nicole.
I don't even want your gratitude.

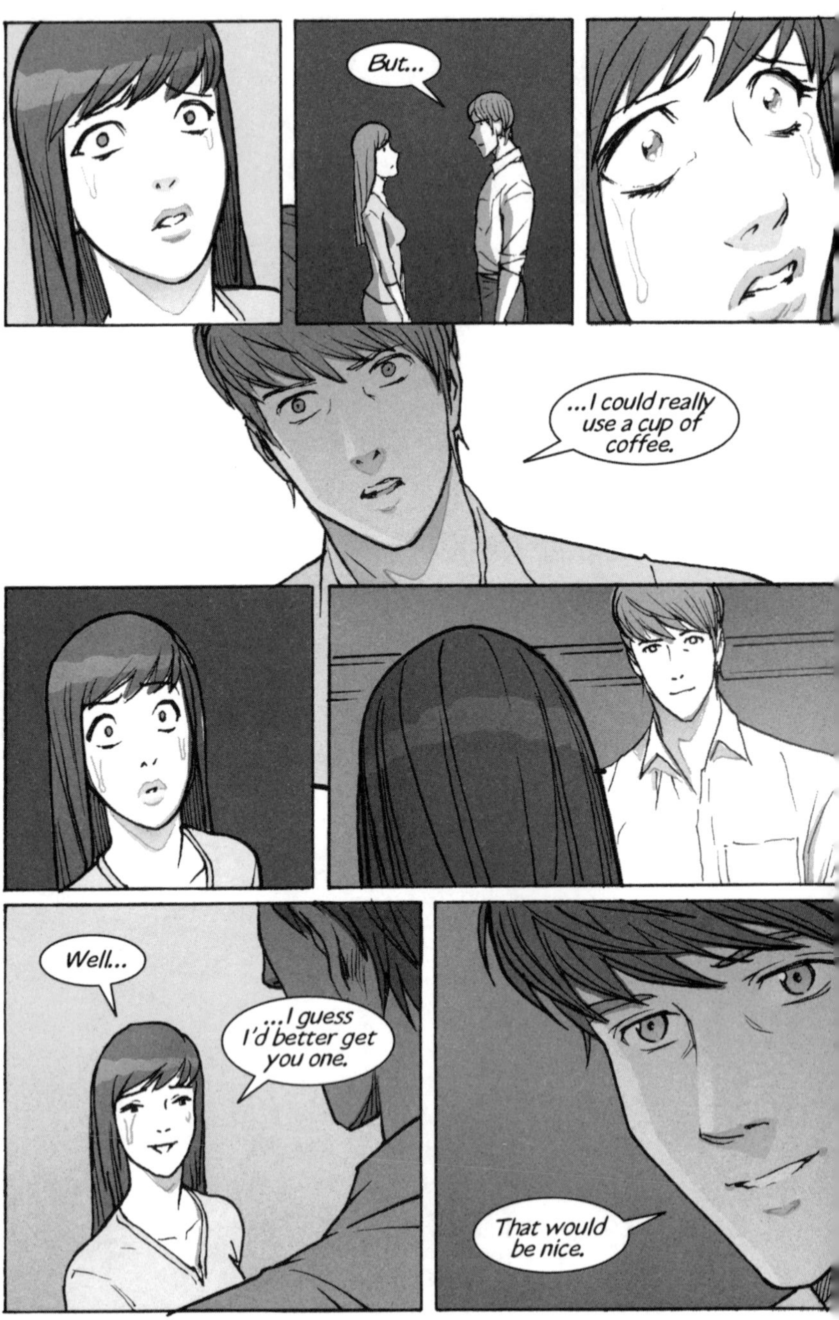
But...
...I could really use a cup of coffee.
Well...
...I guess I'd better get you one.
That would be nice.

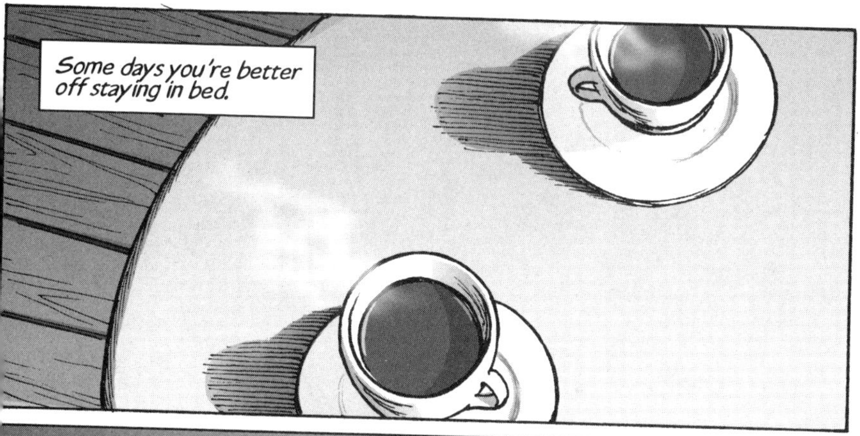
Some days you're better off staying in bed.
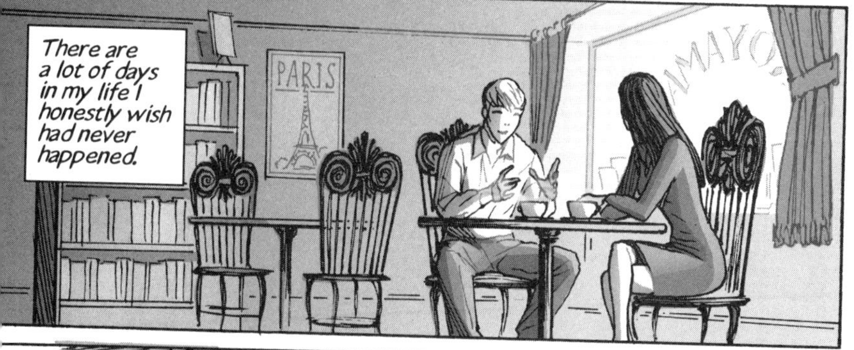
There are a lot of days in my life I honestly wish had never happened.
PARIS
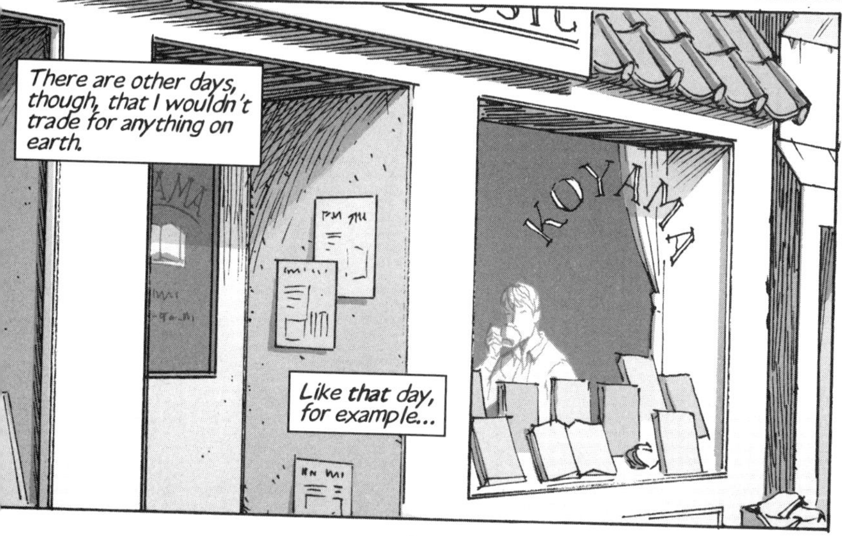
There are other days, though, that I wouldn't trade for anything on earth.
KOYAMA
Like that day, for example...

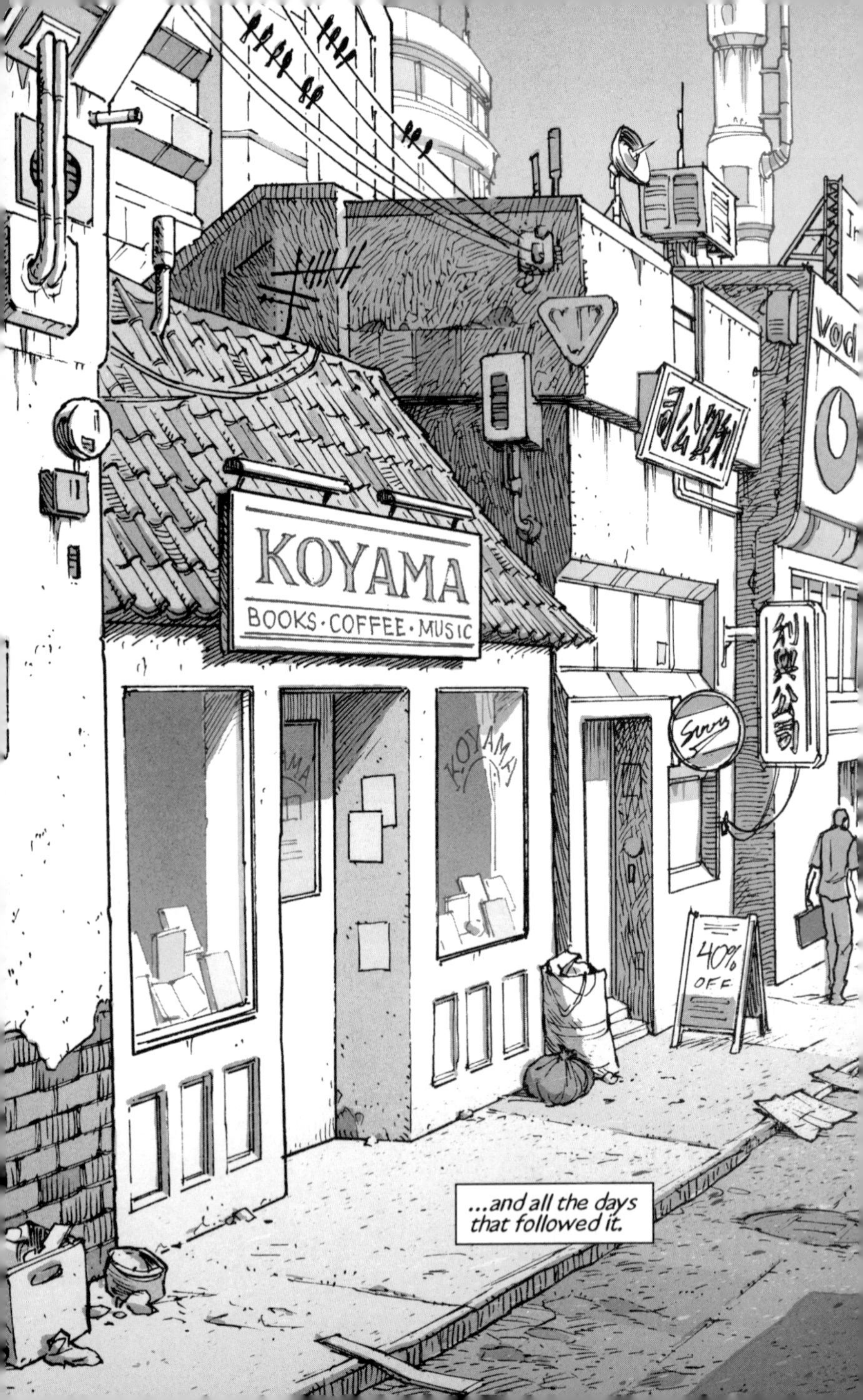
KOYAMA
BOOKS·COFFEE·MUSIC
40% OFF
...and all the days that followed it.

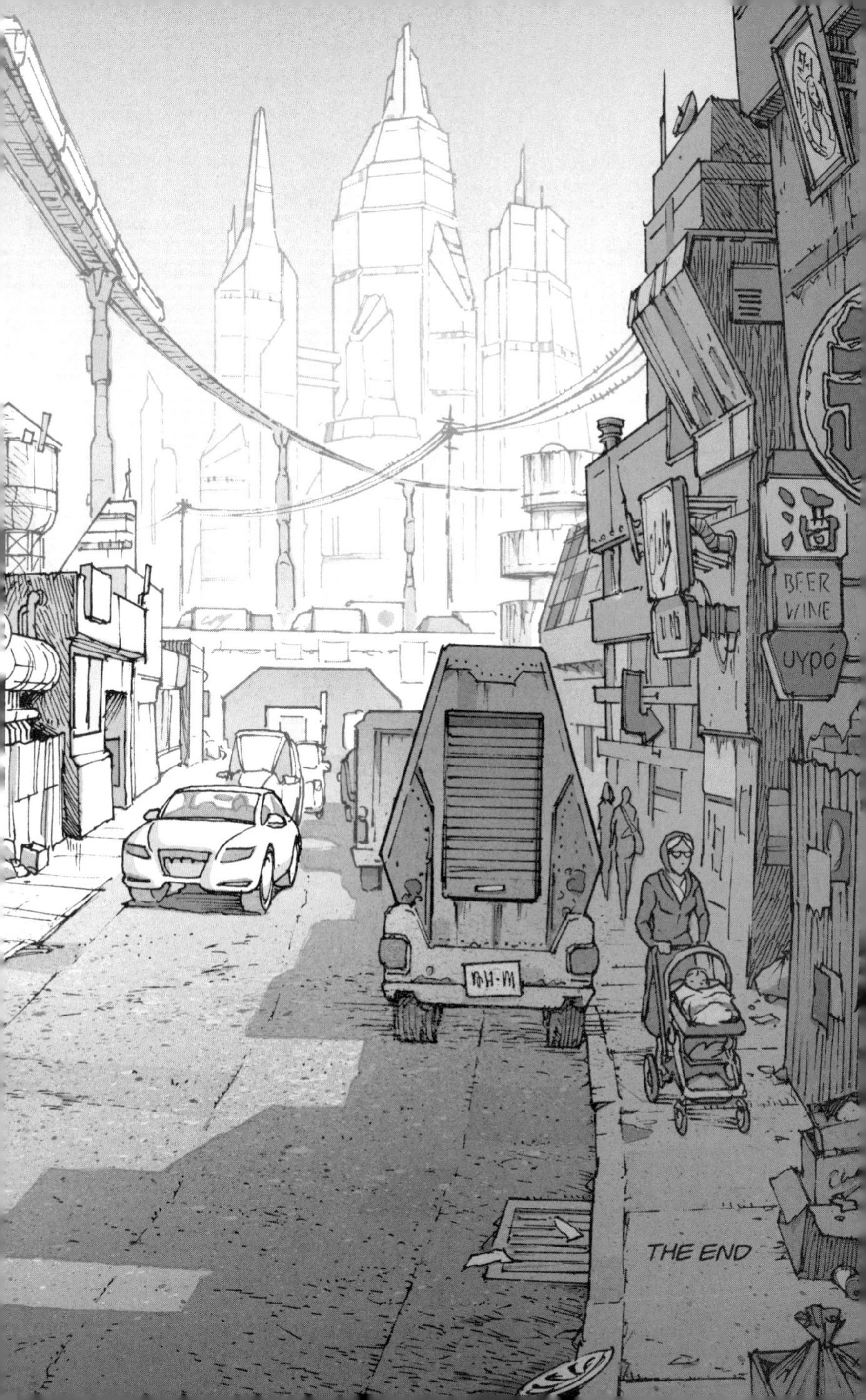
酒
BEER
WINE
UYPÓ
THE END

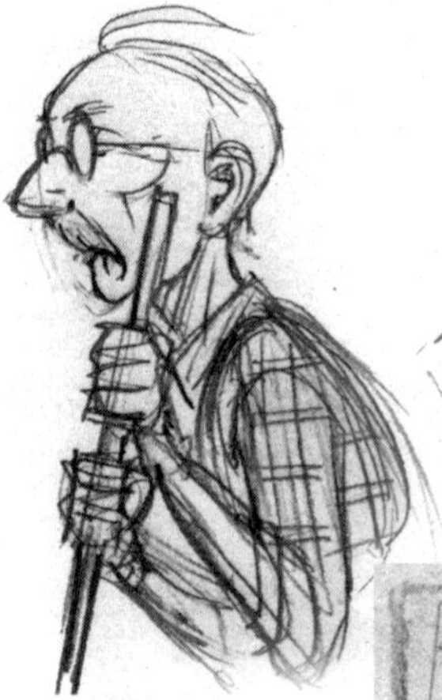

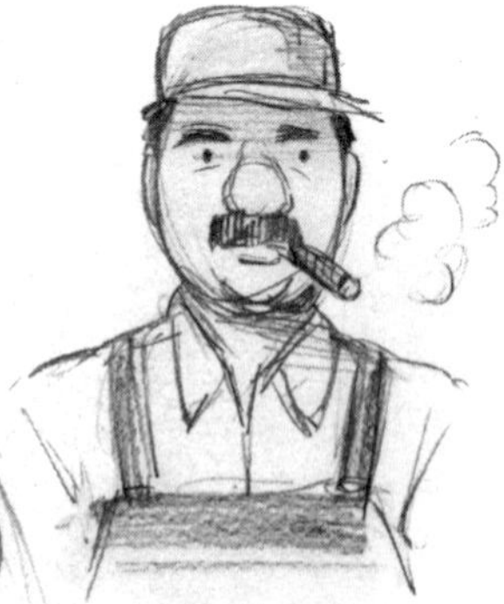

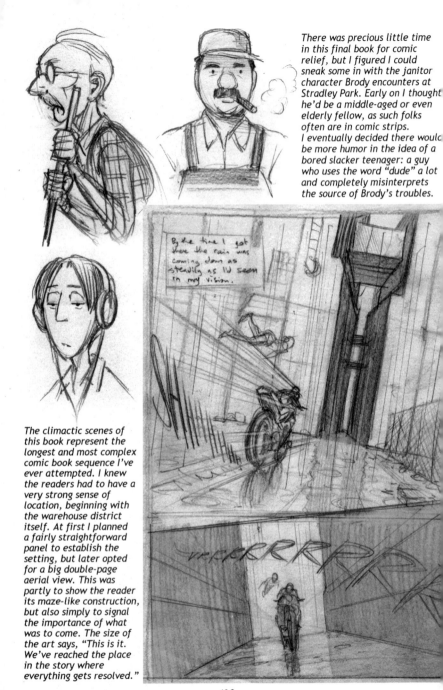

There was precious little time in this final book for comic relief, but I figured I could sneak some in with the janitor character Brody encounters at Stradley Park. Early on I thought he'd be a middle-aged or even elderly fellow, as such folks often are in comic strips. I eventually decided there would be more humor in the idea of a bored slacker teenager: a guy who uses the word "dude" a lot and completely misinterprets the source of Brody's troubles.

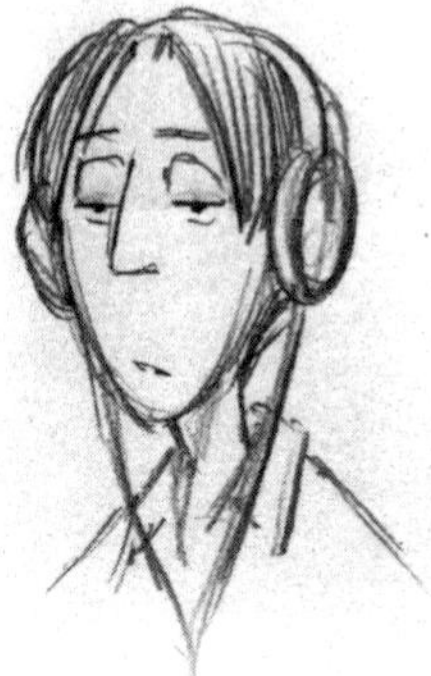

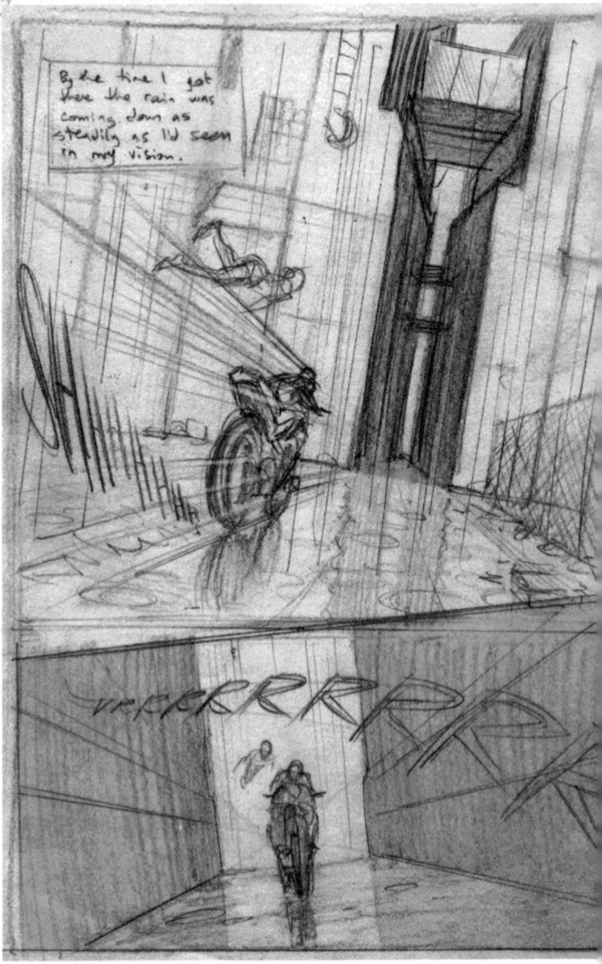
By the time I got there the rain was coming down as steadily as I'd seen in my vision.

The climactic scenes of this book represent the longest and most complex comic book sequence I've ever attempted. I knew the readers had to have a very strong sense of location, beginning with the warehouse district itself. At first I planned a fairly straightforward panel to establish the setting, but later opted for a big double-page aerial view. This was partly to show the reader its maze-like construction, but also simply to signal the importance of what was to come. The size of the art says, "This is it. We've reached the place in the story where everything gets resolved."

of the most important
›s in the whole book is
one, in which readers
given a sort of "road
" for the scenes that
about to unfold.
signed the space with
lley-like path up the
dle so that we can see
rly where the Penny
derer wants to go and
close he is to getting
e. The addition of the
l and the pipeline was
nded to give readers
e landmarks: signposts
ow close or far various
acters were from the
nlink-fence area, even
ter panels where the
e wasn't visible.

naps most crucial
l was for the reader
nderstand where Brody
in relation to Landon
ard the end of the
uence. By adding a huge
ese character to the
in the back corner I
ed to make this spot
o out" to the reader's
even before the
ificance of that location
clear. This way people
d keep their bearings
began cutting back
forth between Brody
Landon from one
nent to the next.

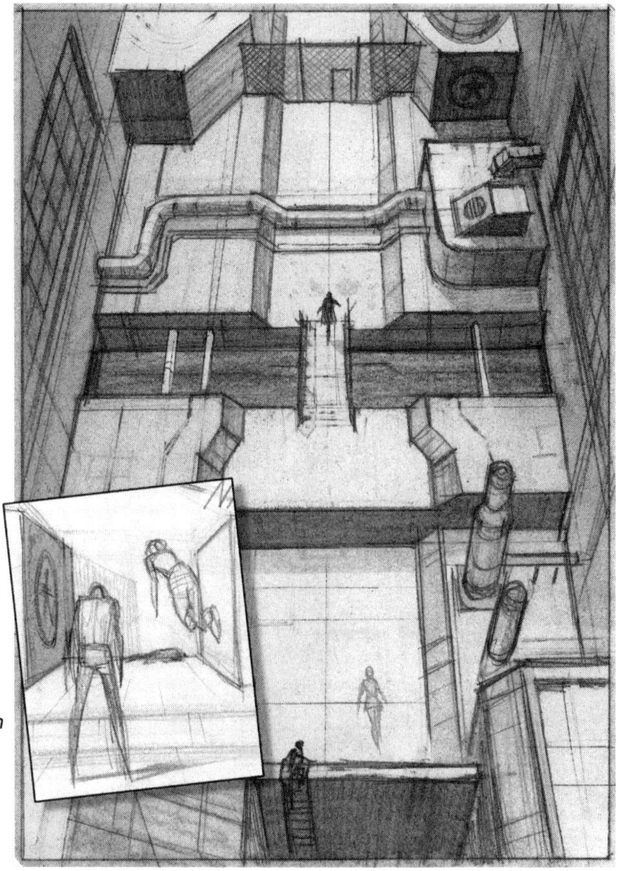

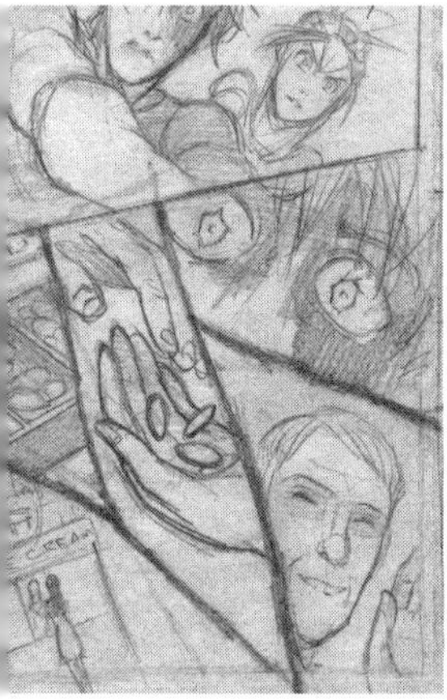

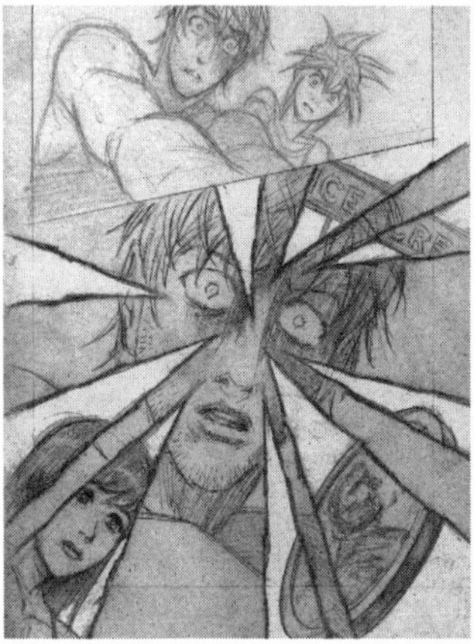

The page showing Brody's final vision went through a couple of redesigns before I found an approach that worked for me. Even after coming up with the "broken shards" method of arranging the panels I was still unsure about how many images to provide. In the end I decided it was best to squeeze in as many as possible, so as to convey the sheer quantity of information Brody received at that moment.

My original plan was to have the concluding panels of the book be reminiscent of a crane shot at the end of a movie, lifting our vantage point up into the sky as we exited Brody's world for the last time.

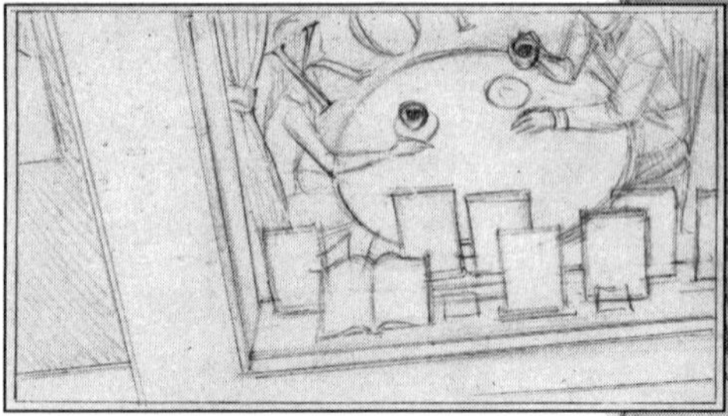

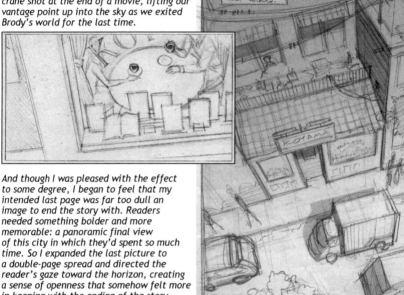

And though I was pleased with the effect to some degree, I began to feel that my intended last page was far too dull an image to end the story with. Readers needed something bolder and more memorable: a panoramic final view of this city in which they'd spent so much time. So I expanded the last picture to a double-page spread and directed the reader's gaze toward the horizon, creating a sense of openness that somehow felt more in keeping with the ending of the story.

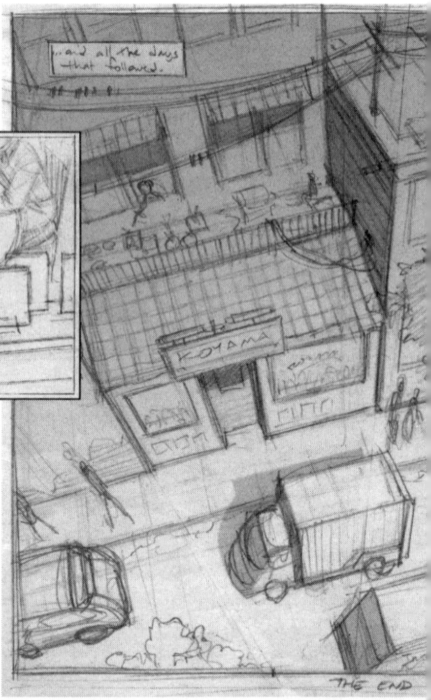
...and all the days that followed.
KOYAMA
THE END

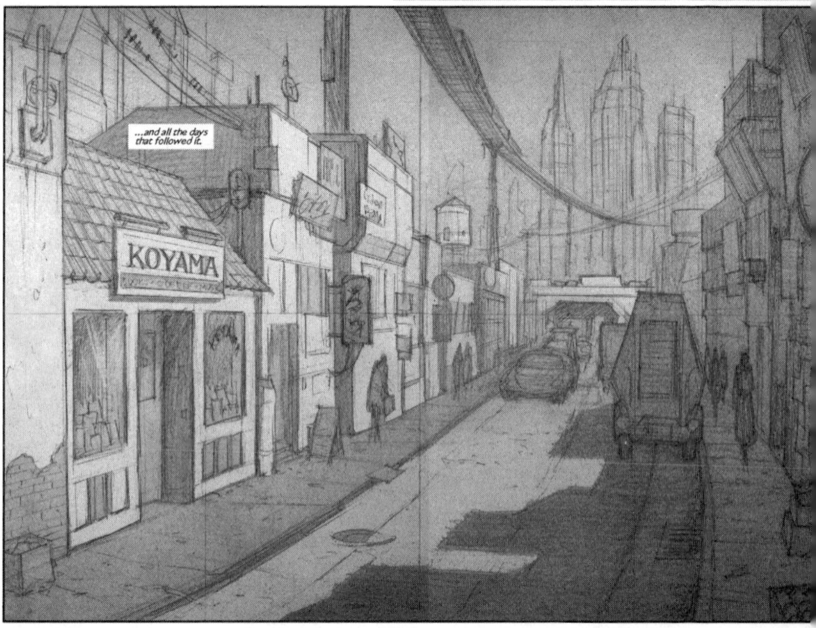
...and all the days that followed it.
KOYAMA

AFTERWORD

Without question *Brody's Ghost* holds the record for me personally as the story that took the longest to complete. When I first started preparing for it I had a two-year-old daughter; now she's eight. I have worked on it in fast-food restaurants in Japan, at public-speaking gigs everywhere from Massachusetts to California, and, of course, in my own home, page after page after page. And though not nearly as dramatic, my life during these years underwent a transformation that mirrored Brody's. When I began working on the project I was in a very low place and deeply uncertain about my future. Now, at the end, I feel very much as Brody does at the story's conclusion: That these are days I wouldn't trade for anything on Earth.

There are many people I need to thank, but three come to mind immediately as the ones without whom these books may never have seen print.

First is Jill Thompson. I dedicated book 1 to her, but really the whole series should be dedicated to her. The road to publication was pretty rocky in the early days, and at one point I was struggling to find folks willing to look at my proposal. Jill very generously put in a good word for me at Dark Horse, a company I'd long admired but had never worked with before. It is entirely thanks to her kindness that such a door was opened to me, at a time when I was seriously ready to give up on *Brody's Ghost* altogether.

Next is Dave Land, the editor at Dark Horse who felt the series was worth a shot. Due to the unusual way in which the first book was pitched, Dave actually had to put the deal together twice, resuscitating it after it had been scuttled. He could just as easily have said, "Sorry, Mark, you had your chance, but this deal is dead now and there's nothing I can do." He didn't say that, and because he didn't say that, *Brody's Ghost* was published by Dark Horse. It's as simple as that. And, of course, he provided stering advice on the first books in the series, leading me toward many interesting choices, such as the idea that the city in which the story takes place need never be named.

Finally I must thank my mother, Virginia Crilley. Even before Jill and Dave were able to help me out, my mom gave me something essential: The feeling that the story was special and worthy of publication. Over lunch one day I sat and told her the entire plot line, start to finish. I didn't have every last detail worked out at that point, but I was able to describe all the key scenes. She told me, "Mark, I think this is one of the best stories you've ever come up with." And I felt she wasn't just saying that to be supportive. She genuinely enjoyed the tale and all its twists and turns.

But lest I leave anyone out, I'd also like to thank the editors at Dark Horse who worked on the series after Dave Land: Rachel Edidin and Brendan Wright. Rachel provided terrific advice on books 3 and 4, and Brendan was there for me on the crucial final volumes, guiding me toward the best way of wrapping everything up. A last tip of the hat goes to Allyson Willsey, who helped me with the gray toning on book 5, when I needed to produce pages faster than my usual snail's pace.

But it is not enough to thank the people behind the scenes who believed in these books. I need to thank the people who bought them and read them. It was a bit of a trick getting to book 1, but I'd have never gotten to book 6 without the thousands of people who began following Brody's journey along the way. You are the ones who made it possible for me to tell this tale the way I wanted to. So thank you, friends. I'm deeply honored by your support, and I hope you had as much fun reading Brody's story as I did writing and illustrating it.

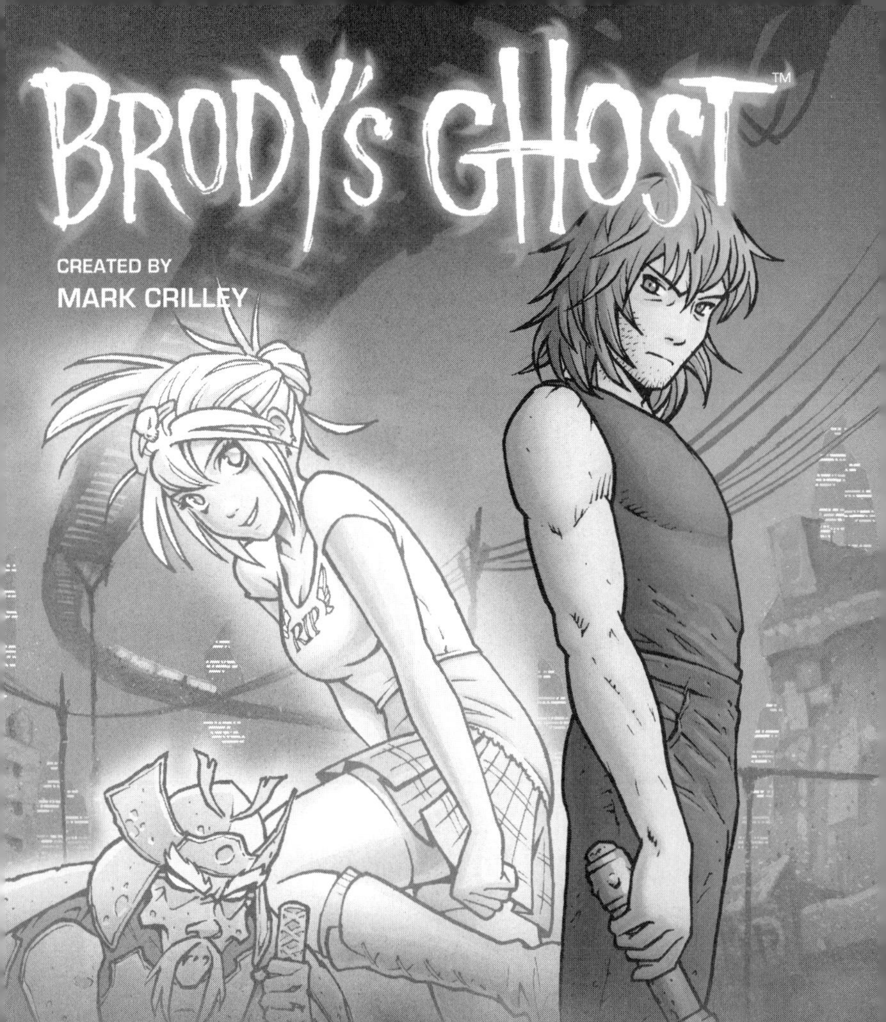

BRODY'S GHOST™

CREATED BY
MARK CRILLEY

...ly hoped it was just a hallucination. But the teenaged ghostly girl who'd come face...ace with him in the middle of a busy city street was all too real. And now she was..., telling him she needed his help in hunting down a dangerous killer, and that he must...rgo training from the spirit of a centuries-old samurai to unlock his hidden supernatural powers.

...een-time Eisner Award nominee Mark Crilley creates his most original and action-packed...to date!

BOOK 1	BOOK 2	BOOK 3	BOOK 4	BOOK 5	BOOK 6
...1-59582-521-6	978-1-59582-665-7	978-1-59582-862-0	978-1-61655-129-2	978-1-61655-460-6	978-1-61655-461-3
$6.99	$6.99	$6.99	$6.99	$7.99	$7.99

HIROAKI SAMURA

Winner of Japan's Media Arts Award, an Eisner Award, and three British Eagle Awards, Hiroaki Samura is best known as the creator of the long-running series *Blade of the Immortal*. Now Dark Horse Manga is proud to present two volumes of his other works, presented in English for the first time!

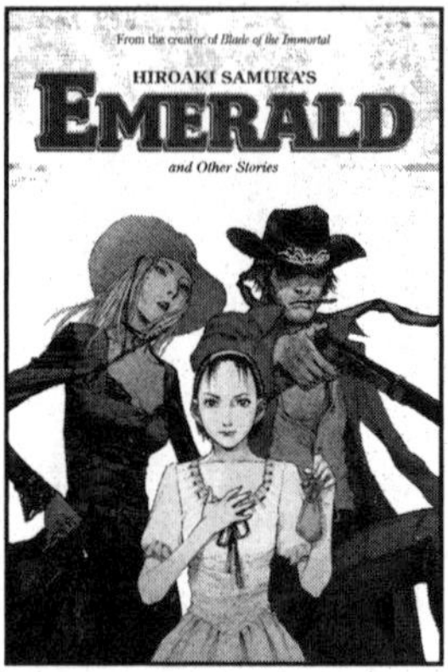
From the creator of Blade of the Immortal
HIROAKI SAMURA'S
EMERALD
and Other Stories

HIROAKI SAMURA'S EMERALD AND OTHER STORIES

A masterful storyteller bounces around genres and time periods in this unique collection! Samura tells his first explosive adventure set in the Wild West, and a series of humorous vignettes about two motor-mouthed teen girls is woven through several other riveting tales.

ISBN 978-1-61655-065-3 $12.99

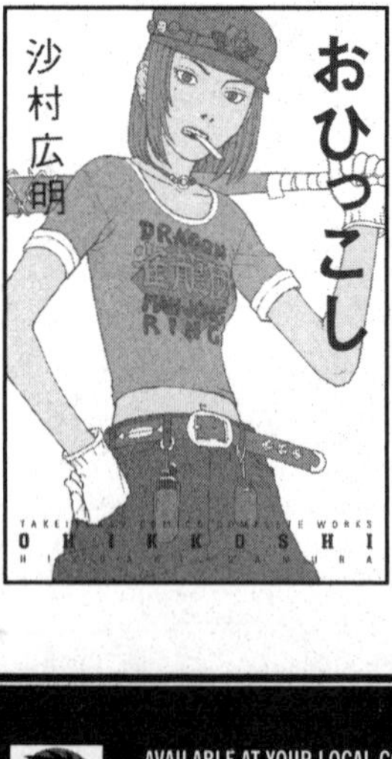
沙村広明
おひっこし

OHIKKOSHI

These stories are told with the same bold, kinetic art style and brilliantly paced storytelling that Samura's *Blade of the Immortal* epic is famous for. Featuring stories of several twenty-something art students as they fall in love, fall in lust, play in rock bands, ride motorbikes, eat, sleep (together), and try to avoid making life decisions while drunk, a genre-busting humor tale of an aspiring manga creator, and a rare, autobiographical travel piece that brings out the best in Samura's art and writing.

ISBN 978-1-59307-622-1 $12.99